MEMOIRS OF THE LIFE AND WRITINGS OF THE LATE • CLAUDIUS BUCHANAN

Publisher's Note

The book descriptions we ask booksellers to display prominently warn that this is an historic book with numerous typos or missing text; it is not indexed or illustrated.

The book was created using optical character recognition software. The software is 99 percent accurate if the book is in good condition. However, we do understand that even one percent can be an annoying number of typos! And sometimes all or part of a page may be missing from the book. Or the paper may be so discolored from age that it is difficult to read. We apologize and gratefully acknowledge Google's assistance.

After we re-typeset and design a book, the page numbers change so the old index and table of contents no longer work. Therefore, we usually remove them.

Our books sell so few copies that you would have to pay hundreds of dollars to cover the cost of proof reading and fixing the typos, missing text and index. Therefore, whenever possible, we let our customers download a free copy of the original typo-free scanned book. Simply enter the barcode number from the back cover of the paperback in the Free Book form at www.general-books.net. You may also qualify for a free trial membership in our book club to download up to four books for free. Simply enter the barcode number from the back cover onto the membership form on the same page. The book club entitles you to select from more than a million books at no additional charge. Simply enter the title or subject onto the search form to find the books.

If you have any questions, could you please be so kind as to consult our Frequently Asked Questions page at www.general-books.net/faqs.cfm? You are also welcome to contact us there.
General Books LLC™, Memphis, USA, 2012.

-ϟ- -ϟ- -ϟ- -ϟ- -ϟ- -ϟ- -ϟ- -ϟ-

MEMOIRS OF THE REV. DR. BUCHANAN. PART II. CHAP. V.

Dr. BUCHANAN was now again looking forward to his long projected journey to the south of the Peninsula. On the 12th of March 1806 he thus wrote to a friend in England.

"I proceed to Malabar in a few weeks. My de"lay has been chiefly occasioned by the difficulty of "my resigning appointments and offices here, where "there is no one to receive them. And even now, "if I get off fairly I shall wonder.

"I still continue in my purpose of going home "about the end of this year. So that I shall pos"sibly see you and your family once more."

On the 22d of March, Dr. Buchanan obtained leave of absence from the government for six months, together with renewed assurances of the countenance and assistance formerly promised; but his prepara VOL. II. B tions for his journey were again interrupted by a return of ague and fever. This attack was, however, less serious, and of shorter duration than the former; so that at the end of the month he was able to wait upon the Governor General, who kindly offered to accommodate him with one of his tents for his intended journey to the coast. During the month of April, Dr. Buchanan continued his preparations for his approaching absence; attended an examination of the Chinese class at Serampore, and made arrangements for the performance of his clerical duties. His last sermon previously to his departure was from the beautiful address in the Revelation of St. John (Chap. hi. 7—13.) to the Church at Philadelphia; which he probably considered as in some respects appropriate to that at Calcutta. Dr. Buchanan spent several of the days immediately preceding his journey with Mr. Udny, who appears to have entered with much interest into his views for the promotion of Christianity in India. The late learned and lamented Dr. Leyden had once proposed to accompany him in his tour j but this plan, though it would doubtless have proved mutually agreeable and beneficial, was finally abandoned.

The design of this extensive and laborious journey cannot be better explained than in the following quotation from the account which Dr. Buchanan afterwards published of his Researches.

" In order to obtain a distinct view of the state

» Christian Researches, Introduct. p. 7, 8.

"of Christianity and of superstition in Asia, the su"perintendants of the college had, before this period, "entered into correspondence with intelligent persons "in different countries; and from every quarter (even "from the confines of China) they received encou"ragement to proceed. But, as contradictory ac"counts were given by different writers concerning "the real state of the numerous tribes in India, both "of Christians and natives, the Author conceived the "design of devoting the last year or two of his re"sidence in the East to purposes of local examination "and enquiry.

"The principal objects of this tour were to in"vestigate the state of superstition at the most cele"brated temples of the Hindoos; to examine the "churches and libraries of the Romish, Syrian, and "Protestant Christians; to ascertain the present "state and recent history of the eastern Jews; and to "discover what persons might be fit instruments for "the promotion of learning in their respective ceun"tries, and for maintaining a future correspondence "on the subject of disseminating the Scriptures in"India."

Such were the important views with which Dr. Buchanan entered upon his intended journey; nor is it any disparagement to travels undertaken from motives either of personal curiosity, or of public utility, to assert, that the tour, which he was meditating, derived from its disinterested and sacred objects a peculiar degree of dignity and value. If our great philanthropist Howard was justly eulogized by a late celebrated statesman, for his indefatigable and selfdenying exertions in " travelling over land and sea," not to gratify his taste, or to extend his fame, but" to remember the forgotten, to attend the "neglected, and to visit the forsaken," it is not too much to say, that although the labours of that eminent person were more various and continued, it required in a man of infirm and precarious health, like Dr. Buchanan, a degree of zeal and resolution to enter upon his projected journey, which reflects upon him the highest honour. And although in each case, the love of God and of man was the prevailing motive, the object of the one was, in proportion to its extent, as much more important than the other, as enquiries into spiritual wants with a view to their relief are more weighty than those which concern temporal necessities, and as interests of eternal duration are more momentous than any which are bounded by the narrow limits of time. It must be remembered too, that with the exception of the accommodations afforded him by the kindness of the Governor General, and the hospitality of the British residing at the different stations through which he passed, Dr. Buchanan's extensive tour was undertaken exclusively at his own expense.

On the third of May, he left Calcutta on his way to the south; and on his arrival the same day at-Fulta, forty miles below that city, he wrote to Colonel Sandys as follows.

"My dear Sandys, "I am thus far on my journey to Malabar. I propose to visit Juggernaut first, and hope to be there early in June, when the grand festival of the Rutt Jattra takes place. Sir George Barlow has been so good as to lend me some of the Governor General's small tents, so that I shall travel very comfortably. My enquiries, you know, have a threefold aspect, Hindoos, Jews, and Christians. The bands of infidelity and superstition are loosening fast; and Calcutta is by no means the place it was when you were here.

"I have heard this morning that the fleet from England, which went to the Cape, is expected at Madras every day, as one of the ships is already arrived. In this fleet your friend Mr. Martyn is passenger. Mr. Jeffries has been appointed to act as my substitute in the new church in my absence; which will be about six or eight months; if indeed I should ever return; for my route is full of danger and difficulty to one infirm as I am. With some view I trust to the glory of God I have purposed; but it is He who must dispose of me and my objects as shall seem to Him best.
"I remain,
    My dear Sandys,
    Very affectionately yours,
    C, BuCtfANANv'

Dr. Buchanan, from the time of his arrival at Juggernaut, kept a regular journal of his tour, parts of which, it is well known, he afterwards published on his return to this country. He maintained also a constant correspondence during his journey with the Rev. D. Brown; and from these letters a series of extracts shall now be given, which, avoiding, for the most part, the repetition of what Dr. Buchanan himself communicated to the public, will afford a connected view of his whole tour, and contain some additional information, as well as some instructive and interesting reflections on the various scenes through which he passed in this original and enterprizing journey. It were only to be wished that these observations had been more frequent and extended. A few letters which Dr. Buchanan wrote to his friends in Europe in the course of his tour will also be inserted in their order.

The first letter to Mr. Brown, dated the 10th of May, from Fulta, informs him, that Dr. Buchanan continued in good health, and that his servants and travelling equipage were all well appointed. On the 13th he thus wrote from Contai.

"I arrived here the day before yesterday in good "health and fine spirits. My tents were first hoisted "on the backs of elephants, belonging to a Hindoo "Rajah, in my journey to the south. I ought always "to speak well of the Hindoo people.

"Mr. Mason's kindness and attention are very "remarkable; and I am in danger of being detained "in my way, like Abraham's servant, by hospitality, "before the business be done. But I see there is "much to be done by the way which I thought "not of.

"I shall leave this place to-morrow, perhaps, or "next day, and hope to arrive at Balasore on the "20th, where I propose to stay two days, and then "proceed with the pilgrims (who now cover the "roads) to Juggernaut.

"I am in haste to pass over the marshy lands of "the salt districts, lest fever should come. If it "should come here, or before I arrive at my journey's "end, and you should not see me again, I pray you "to consider it as the hand of God, giving glory to "his own cause in his own way, leading our feeble "resolves in triumph to a certain stage, and then, "calling another servant. I leave all my temporal "affairs in perfect order. I have no papers literary "or religious; so that no trouble awaits my ex"ecutors, except those in England, to whom I have "consigned the religious education of my two little "girls."

These concluding observations point out in a simple yet solemn manner the entire resignation of the writer to the Divine will, and evidently imply his preparation for every event of his journey. The spirit of calm yet devoted piety which they breathe, is at once to be admired and imitated.

In a letter on the 17th from Jellasore, where he waited for his elephant and horse, the following passage occurs.

"At Mohunpore, between Contai and this place, "I stopped a night. Juggernaut is to be found "there in miniature; having the same name and "service. The Hindoo Zemindar gave me a feast, "and presented me with a sword, a piece of fine "cloth, and ten rupees at parting. When I began "to eat, Juggernaut's bells began to ring. I asked "the reason, and was told that Juggernaut had be"gun his supper. So we ate together for near half "an hour, during which time the gongs and bells "continued a horrid clangor.

"This temple is falling into decay for want of "revenue."

On the 25th and 27th, Dr. Buchanan thus describes from Balasore his mode of travelling, and the conjectures of the natives concerning the object of his journey.

"The commanding officer here has given me a "guard of seven seapoys all the way to Cuttack, "which is seven days' march. I passed through a "jungle where tigers abound. One sprung on a "large bullock last week, but he could not carry him "off, and the bullock escaped. The hunters shewed "me their manner of shooting tigers with arrows.

"I leave this place to-morrow; and on the 4th "of June I expect to be at Cuttack. Juggernaut is "only three or four days from thence.
I find it inconvenient to have many followers. "I have therefore discharged some servants from "this place, and also a supernumerary tent. I have '' but few wants on a march as to eating and drink"ing; and I cannot be troubled with tablecloths. "I enjoy refreshing tea after my ride in the morn'' ing; for I generally ride one half of the march on "horseback, and sometimes on an elephant. I oc"casionally use my gun, at which I was formerly as "expert as any of the writers. But I feel a repug"nance in killing harmless animals which I did not "feel formerly. Tell H that during the two

"last days' march, I saw beautiful peacocks sitting "on the lofty trees by the road side, and monkies "leaping from branch to branch, holding their young "ones in their arms.

"You may direct to me to the care of the post"master at Cuttack until further notice. I am very "well known now in this country, so that all letters "will easily come to hand. Indeed there has been "a singular spirit of enquiry among the natives on "the subject of the march of a company's Padre; "and I learn from them, that I am a rich man, pro"ceeding on a pilgrimage, to worship the God of the "Christians, not far from Singhul Deep."

Dr. Buchanan's next letter is dated May 31st, from Buddruck in Orissa, from whence he began to anticipate his approach to Juggernaut, and the frightful impression of which, from the bones of pilgrims with which the road in its neighbourhood was strewed, he has painted in such striking colours in the first published extract from his Journal. The following Christian Researches, p. 19.
account of a rencontre with a Hindoo Rajah is from his letter to Mr. Brown.

"Juggernaut's temples begin to multiply as I move "on. The common huts are decorated by his hor"rid face. The Sanyasses (holy men) are now more "naked; and the talk and manners of the Byraggies "more licentious.

"The Kunka or Kannaka Rajah paid me a visit "at my tent last night. I had heard he had formerly "murdered some English sailors who were wrecked "on his coast between Balasore and Juggernaut, "and therefore resolved not to acknowledge him as "a gentleman. I accordingly desired a table to be "placed on the lawn before the tent, and one chair, "in which I sat with a book before me. The Rajah "came up with much ceremony and presented a "nuzzur. I did not rise from my seat, nor offer "him one. He was much embarrassed. I spoke to "him civilly; and presently rose up and made salam "to him as a signal to depart. The crowd of Faquirs "and Sanyasses could not understand this. After "he was gone I told them the reason, and that I "could not as a Christian Padre bow to vice, whe"ther in a Rajah or in a Priest. This seemed sorae"thing new to them; but one of them, a very old "man, said it was very proper.

"I believe I mentioned to you that it was my "purpose to move rapidly by dawk along the coast from Juggernaut to Cochin, staying a few days at "Madras. Hitherto I have suffered no inconveni"ences from beat or fatigue. I am therefore en'' couraged to try a flying course for a few weeks.

"At Jagepoor, my next stage, the names of all "the pilgrims are registered. Illustrious names for "four hundred years back are found on giving a

"small fee."

On the 6th of June Dr. Buchanan reached Cuttack, from whence he wrote the two next amusing and interesting letters.

"I arrived here yesterday after eight days' march "without seeing a white face; aboriginal Uriahs, "Burgahs, that is, Mahrattas, and Loll Jattris, being "all my society. I hear I am expected at Jugger"naut, fame having travelled before, and informed "him that a company's Padre is on a progress. No "unworthy suspicion is yet entertained, I believe; "and I am received at the Bhur or Banian tree of "each Munzil with a hurrebol by my fellow Padres "and their flocks. The scene is rather comic; but '' so it is. Notes tragic I sound not; and thus we "travel onward harmoniously together.

"I dine to day with Mr. Hartwell, register, and "to-morrow with Colonel Marley. Next day, Sun"day, is sacred; and the next to it, Monday, I dine "with the judge of the province, Mr. Ker, who has "offered me every aid in the prosecution of my "journey. On Tuesday I proceed for Juggernaut.

"The novel scenes of this place occupy my atten"tion, but I meet with nothing worthy of descrip"tion. It is just as I told you; I have not yet had "pen or pencil in my hand since I left Calcutta. I "have lived too long for natural history. What are "called manners and customs, are nearly as futile to "him who is enquiring in what state a people are in "relation to the Almighty, and to the purpose of "their creation."

"Cuttack, 8th June, 1806.

"Tigers abound in the vicinity of Juggernaut, and "kill the pilgrims. A hunting party of eight elephants "have lately proceeded from this place to kill them.

"It is supposed that eight lacks of pilgrims are "already arrived at Juggernaut.
"The Kunka Rajah, alarmed at my reception of "him, and fearing lest I should give an unfavourable "character of him at this place, followed me, and "overtook me in two marches. He requested "rnoolaquat. I explained to him the cause of my con"duct towards him. He said he repented of his for"mer sins,

and Hoped the British government would "pardon him. I told him that on condition of his "learning English *principles* I would befriend him, "if I could. He is at present under the displeasure "of our government, having defended his fort after "the conquest of the country, which cost us blood "and money. His first request was, that I would "intercede for him with the judge of the province, "that he should be permitted to visit Juggernaut, "which was formerly refused. I mentioned the cir." cumstance to Mr. Ker last night, who has given "him permission. The Rajah is now here, with an "immense Sowarree: and I suppose we shall pro"ceed together to Juggernaut.

"Much attention is paid to me by all ranks of people here, attention undeserved and unneces"sary. The tone is favourable to civilization, and "the language conciliating and decorous on all grave subjects.

"In the mean time, this world, like the wilderness "through which I am passing, has nothing interest"ing to my hopes or fears. And I have more com"fort in reading a hymn of Watts, than in contem"plating plans of improvement for India. I look to "no resting place but in a close walk with God. "To find that, is a more valuable Eugi-jxa than to find "manuscripts at Cochin.

"The commander of the troops in this province "has ordered a guard of seven seapoys for me to the "Madras frontier, Ganjam. I am glad I shall have them around me among the priests at Juggernaut.

"Tell H that there is a fort here built by a

"proud king, having the following inscription in Per"sian on the gate. 'My walls are of iron, and my "ditch is full of alligators. I shall never be taken.' "And so, because he trusted not in God, but in his "iron walls, his fort was taken by Colonel H."

Of Juggernaut % one of the principal objects of The popular orthography of this word is here adopted, as more familiar to the English reader. For an account of the Dr. Buchanan's journey, of his stupendous temple and countless worshippers, of the impure rites and ceremonies exhibited by Iris priests, and of the cruel sacrifices by which this Moloch of the East is propitiated, the public has been so fully informed by Dr. Buchanan himself, that it is unnecessary to repeat his dreadfully interesting narrative of the whole scene. His letters to Mr. Brown, though in a somewhat varied form, contain substantially the same details; and, like the extracts from his Journal, to which any who are desirous of farther information are referred, cannot be read without the deepest emotions of horror and pity, and without exciting in every benevolent and Christian mind an ardent prayer, that the time may not be far distant when these abominations shall cease, and the horrid tower of Juggernaut be replaced by the temple of the God of purity and love. A few circumstances, however, which did not appear in the Journal, shall be added from the letters to Mr. Brown, from the 14 th to the 21st of June.

"Juggernaut, 14th June, 1806. "I have lived to see Juggernaut. The scene at "Buddruck is but the vestibule. No record of "ancient or modern history can give an adequate "idea of the valley of sculls. It is the valley of origin of this idol and his worship, see the eighth volume of the Asiatic Researches.
Christian Researches, pp. 19—33.
"Hinnom. A history of Juggernaut would be 'a "roll written within and without' with blood, and "obscenity, and woe.

"I shall not enter into farther detail of the state "of superstition here. Suffice it to say, that all "you have heard is true. A short record of facts "may be committed to paper; but I have no de"sign of disclosing the philosophy of Juggernaut at "this time; and I hope that it will never be neces sary.

Such was Dr. Buchanan's intention at this period; but the time at length came when an imperious sense of duty compelled him to publish it.

"Tell H." continues Dr. Buchanan, " that the "temple of Juggernaut is so high, that men appear "on the top of it like crows; and that it is sur"rounded by a square area of great extent, in each "side of which there is a gateway larger than the "pagoda near your house."

"20th June.

"On Wednesday last, the great day of the Rutt "Jattra, Moloch was brought out of his temple "amidst the voices of thousands and tens of thou"sands of his worshippers. I was so close to him, "that his chief priest presented to me a garland "taken off Juggernaut's neck.

"When the Idol was placed on his throne, a "shout was raised, such as I can never hear again "on earth—not of melody or joyful acclamation, but a "yell of approbation. The sublimity of the scene "wrought in me strangely at times; and I had sen"tences of the Revelations and of Milton in my "mind and on my lips, which I applied perforce to "' the assembly of the first-born, and their blest "voices.'

"In Juggernaut's temple nothing is to be seen of "importance. The priests do not reside in it. They "have their wives and children without. The service "of the temple is performed by them in rotation; "and the principal abomination within is perhaps the dancing women, who twice in the day exhibit them"selves before him.

"A chief object of my journey is perhaps accom"plished by my having seen Juggernaut. For nine "days past I have been in the midst of his abomina"tions, riding about among the multitude. Nothing "has been, I believe, concealed from me. Every ques"tion is answered, and I scarcely wish to know more. "I shall continue to mix with the people two days "more, and then I'proceed to Ganjam. Mr. Hunter "is desirous that I should prolong my visit; but my "spirit of enquiry is exhausted, and my body is fa"tigued with my spirits; so that I look forward to "my journey for relief from this twofold oppression.

"I write this from the plain of sculls near the sea; "and it so happens that a scull is under my chair, "half buried in the sand."

"Juggernaut, Saturday, 21st June, 1806.
"I propose to proceed on my journey this even"ing, that I may find a place of rest for my Sabbath "to-morrow far off

from Juggernaut. My best Sab"baths are generally in the wilderness.

"The number of pilgrims here is uncertain. "Mr. Hunter has no means of probable calculation. "From the nature of the place, we perhaps did not "see more than two or three hundred thousand per"sons at the same time. But I cannot judge, any "more than I could say how many grains there are "in a handful of sand.

"Can it be that the true seed of Abraham shall "be 'as the sand upon the sea shore for multitude?' "Doubtless, it is true; and with this faith I con"clude my last line to you from Juggernaut."

Dr. Buchanan himself published his reflections on viewing the distant towers of Juggernaut from an eminence on the delightful banks of the Chilka Lake, and the design which he then conceived of some "Christian Institution," which might gradually undermine the frightful idolatry he had been contemplating, and blot out its memory for ever. This was on Sunday the 22d. On the 29th he dates from Ganjam, and thus continues his correspondence with Mr. Brown.

"I write to you from a new Presidency. I am "happy I did not die at Juggernaut (the danger was Christian Researches, p. 31. VOL. II. C

"imminent). My record is engraved in strong legi"ble characters; and it is of less importance where "I shall die; I mean in reference to my testimony "against the empire of Moloch, 'whose seat in "the whole earth is Juggernaut.' The Brahmins, "behind the Chilka Lake offered to carry me to a "Suttee in the flaming pit. Six, eight, or ten "females often accompany the Rajah; the wife in "the husband's pit, and the concubines in their own "private and separate pits.

"Juggernaut's horrors have awakened me a little, "and I have committed to paper some notices of my "route from Bengal.

"On my entrance into the Madras territory, I "have experienced great civility and attention. Here "I leave my tents, servants, and equipage, and I "proceed by dawk to Fort St. George. Mr. Cherry, "the Judge, being doubtful whether I shall not feel "inconvenience in having no servant at all, has "issued orders for a dooly to be prepared for my "steward, and has provided means of carrying him "close to my own palanquin to the extremity of "this province.

"I encounter now a new mode of travelling. "How I shall bear it I cannot tell. The chief "suffering is the want of a bed, which I have al"ready sometimes experienced. But I am anxious "to get to the capital. On the other side I shall "take my time."

"Ganjam, 1st July, 1806.

"I proceed this evening on my journey to Visa"gapatam by dawk. I dine first with Captain E. "He has been planting one lack and fifty thousand "cocoanut trees, and has made a barren land like "the garden of Eden.

"I have been among the mountains for some "days, and visited Rumbo, the famous villa on the "Chilka Lake. I *look* at what is wonderful or "great in the eyes of men.

"My residence at each of my stations is a his"tory, if it were written. New places, new cha"racters, new politics. Truth alone is the same."

"Visagapatam, 6th July, 1806.

"Before this reaches you, I shall probably be at "Madras.

"I found travelling by dawk very pleasant. It "affords me more time to stop at places of import"ance.

"The families here pay me much attention, and "have made a party for me to go out to see a cele" brated pagoda (not yet noticed by any writer, "because not seen) about sixteen miles in the in"terior among the mountains.

"I have no news for H. except that I live among "lofty mountains; from which I see ships far off "at sea, and hear the roar of the billows on the "rocky shore."

"Visagapatam, 12th July, 1806.

"The pagoda at Seemachalum is in many re"spects more interesting than Juggernaut. No "scene of nature I have yet beheld is so romantic "as the site and vicinity of this temple, which is "built on a rocky mountain. You ascend nearly a "quarter of a mile by steps of hewn stone and of "live rock. A stream of pure water issues from "the mount; and this is the sacred fountain, and "the origin of the temple. Here the idolatry of "Juggernaut is exhibited in another form; but "the substance is the same.

"I have not been able to disengage myself from "this society till the present hour. I proceed on "my journey this morning. I have passed the last "two days with Mr. C. the collector here, at his "beautiful mansion on the top of a hill, from which "we look down on the deck of the St. Fiorenzo "and the Albatross, which appear like two *little "boats* below."

"Samulcotta, 15th July, 1806.

"I intended to have passed this place without "stopping; but Colonel O'Reilly, who commands "the troops here, came to the bazar for me him"self, and prevailed on me to stay a night.

"I am in great danger of being detained fre-"quently in my future progress through these ter"ritories.

"I have this evening visited the botanic garden, "over which Dr. R. formerly presided."

From this point no letter to Mr. Brown occurs till Dr. Buchanan's arrival at Madras. In a memorandum book which remains, he notices a sail on the Godavery; and that at Ellore, where he hired bearers for Madras, he passed through a flat countiy bounded by the horizon.

On the 3d of August Dr. Buchanan thus resumes his correspondence.

"Madras, 3d August, 1806.

"I arrived here on the 31st of July, and am now "hospitably lodged in the house of Mr. H. I was "retarded in my journey by a fever, which seized "me between Rajamundry and Ongole, far off from "medical aid. It was accompanied by the same "symptoms as my former. I found a great differ"ence between this last illness in a palanquin in "a jungle, and the former, when I was surrounded "by the skilful and the good. On my arrival at "Ongole, I obtained some medicine from a native, "which was useful. I am now well again.

"Tell H. that all my way from the Chilka Lake "to Madras I did not see one scull; that the people "on the seacoast are generally without cast; that "they are humane to strangers; and that the women "used to make broths and congee for me when I "was sick of the fever. They eat pork and all "meats. The Telinga missionaries will have a fine "harvest, if they labour among them. No rain has "fallen since I left Juggernaut. The weather has "been temperate and very favourable to my journey. "I shall now, Mr. R. tells me, meet with rains in "Tanjore."

"Madras, 6th August, 1806.

"I have letters for every station to the south; and "letters from almost every station inviting me to "call. There has been so much blood shed at Vel"lore, and so many gentlemen murdered, that an "attack on *me* would not be thought strange.

"In the mean time government have *authorized* "me to proceed; and desired me to communicate "my observations on the state of the Christians in "the south. I trust, therefore, that my way is not of myself, but of Providence directing me.

"I visited yesterday the deputy Bishop at St. "Thome, and the ancient Portuguese library. Mr. "T. the Gentoo scholar, goes to see it to-morrow. "It contains, among other valuable books, the Bul"larium Magnum Romanum, or the Pope's Statutes "at large during the dark ages.

"At Tritchinopoly is another famous library, and "a Syrian church.

"Tell H. that I saw yesterday St. Thomas's bones, "preserved as a relic in a gold shrine; and that I "saw his grave, whence the Roman Catholic pil"grims carry the dust."

"Pondicherry, 13th Aug. 1806.

"I have travelled these two days with Mr. E. the "orientalist, and Mr. S. Judge of Tinavelly. Mr. "E. is extremely attentive to me, and wishes to "oblige me by every information in his power.

"It is impossible for me to conceal my name, as "was proposed. The Christians have heard of it, "and I am greeted by them as one who comes in "the name of government to do them good. I al"ready know what is to be done at the missionary "stations. Dr. R. and others informed me fully. "From every quarter there is a cry of the sheep for "a shepherd. They meet and pray under a tree, "and the Brahmins mock."

Dr. Buchanan's next letter is dated from Ziegenbalg's church in Tranquebar, August 25th. Of the visit which he paid to this spot, consecrated by the memory of the first Christian missionaries to India, and of his subsequent arrival at Tanjore, he has given an account in the work which has been already referred to This was, however, so interesting a part of his tour, that it appears desirable to give a sketch of it from his correspondence, together with a few particulars, which were either wholly omitted, or but partially detailed in his Journal.

"I have just visited the tomb of Ziegenbalg, "which is on the side of the altar in the church

» Christian Researches, p. 65—81.

"he built. It was consecrated on the 2d of October "1718, and he died on the 23d of February 1719. "I heard divine service performed in the Tamul "tongue, and about two hundred natives sung the "hundredth Psalm. During the sermon some of "them wrote on an olla or palmyra leaf. The "missionary told me that the catechists sometimes "take down a whole sermon in this manner, and "repeat it to the children in the evening.

"I also visited Ziegenbalg's dwelling-house, built "by himself, and not altered since his time. I in"spected the records of baptism commencing in "May 1706. Mr. C. a missionary here, told me "they had some thoughts of celebrating the hun"dredth anniversary this year, but they had no "money.

"I then visited the library in which Ziegenbalg "first preached; and afterwards a small chapel on "the sea-shore, in which he sometimes exhorted. "The library is extensive and valuable, but in a "perishing state. Here I found the Hindostanee "Psalter; and I am informed that at Tanjore I shall "find a Hindostanee Grammar, published about "sixty years ago.

"The Jesuits at Pondicherry have a fine collec"tion of ancient Indian history. They very politely "gave me all the books I wanted, and letters of in"traduction to their brethren in the south. They "also furnished me with a late statement of their "churches in India; and Padre B. requested leave "to correspond with me in Latin.

"Dr. John is at Tanjore, where I expect to see "him and Mr. Kolhoff in two or three days.

"The most pious man I have yet found is Mr. S. "a young missionary lately arrived. He assured me "that there are some real Christians among the "Hindoo converts. At Cuddalore I passed a night "with Mr. H. At that place the Cadet Company "(one hundred and twenty strong) is now esta"blished on account of the salubrity of the situ"ation.

"At the celebrated pagoda of Chillumbrum near "Porto Novo, I was admitted (I know not why) "into the interior, while the priests made Pooja. I "never had such a clear revelation of this idolatry "before. The dancing girls were present. The "Judge of the place, Mr. R. had introduced me to "the Brahmins the evening before in the outer "court. During the ceremony two immense bells "were rung and drums were beat. My heart began "to palpitate a little, from ft&r I believe; and I "hastily retired. This is a remarkable scene. I "could easily pass a month at every stage. This is "more illustrious than classic ground. For here "Ziegenbalg and Grundler preached the Gospel to "men, whose descendants I have conversed with, "and who can justly appreciate the heavenly gift. "The Danish Governor here invited the missionaries "to meet me. Tanjore is the grand theatre of the "Gospel in late years, and to that place I proceed "this afternoon; but I shall stay one day at Corn"beconum, where the oriental E. is Judge. He is "very anxious to see some pages of a Portuguese "book which I procured from the Jesuits at Pondi"cherry. It is about three hundred years old. He "is a great admirer of the genius of Xavier, and "thinks that a Protestant missionary of such powers "might convert Hindostan."

"Combeconum, near Tanjore, Aug. 27, 1806. "In the midst of some horrible looking blood-red "idols, I shall write a few lines. Mr. E. is not yet "arrived here, having supposed that I should have "staid longer at Tranquebar; which I should have "done, had I not been afraid of a number of enter"tainments. These are sometimes useful, for the "best information I generally obtain is from the "chief people. They were all much surprised at the "interest I took in the ancient mission of Ziegenbalg. "The missionaries themselves were ignorant of "many subjects of my enquiry; and were a good "deal ashamed, I believe, at my notice of the former "glory of the mission compared with its present "state. I have reason to believe that the three "London missionaries, Desgranges, Cran, and Mr. "Palm, are three holy men; and it appears as if " Mrs. P. is a help meet in the Gospel. She learns the "the glory had now departed from Germany, and "was given to England. So Mr. S. speaks. He is "a promising young man; and as his society gives "him only three hundred rupees a year, I gave him "a half year's salary to buy some clothes and books. "Though he has been but two years in India, he "pronounced a very good sermon in the Tamul "tongue, which the native catechist told me was "perfectly intelligible to all the congregation.

"It is a pleasant thing to see an assembly of "natives listening most earnestly to a sermon. "Every one of them can read the Bible; and Lu"ther's first Psalter (the German Gesang Buch) is "very familiar with them. They sing a great va"riety of tunes with much propriety."

"Tanjore, 1st Sept. 1806.

"This is the grand scene of all. This is the "garden of the Gospel.

"Some days before my arrival here, the Resident, "Major Blackburne, wrote to me, inviting me to "reside at his house. This was unexpected, for as "yet I had no communication with Tanjore. On "my arrival there, I first waited on Mr. Kolhoff, "and he shewed me two rooms, which he had pre"pared for my reception. He told me that the "Rajah (Serfogee) was impatient to see me, and "had directed the Resident to let him know when I

"language faster than her husband, and devotes herself to the "real object of the mission. Mr. P. is at Jaffnapatam."

"came. I asked how the Rajah came to know me. "He said that the Resident had a copy of my Me"moir, and of Mr. Mitchell's Essay.

"Mr. Kolhoff is first in piety, in ardour, in meek"ness, and in knowledge of the Tamul; for he has "been brought up chiefly in India. His counte"nance is more expressive' of amiable qualities of "mind than that of any man I ever saw. Major "Blackburne admires him much."

"Tanjore, 2(1 Sept. 1805. "On my arrival here on Friday last, the 29th of "August, great numbers of Christians came to visit "me; and Mr. Kolhoff introduced some particularly "to me, as being truly godly and intelligent men. "He gave me also an account of many triumphant "deaths lately, both of men and women, young and "old.

"As I went to the Resident's house I passed "through a long street inhabited by Christians only. "They stood in rows as we passed, and bowed affec"tionately to their pastor, the young women combing forward with lively confidence, and soliciting "his benediction. The infants also form themselves "in little rows, and waiting his approach make the "customary salutation, ' God be praised.'

"When we arrived at the Resident's, he told me "that the Rajah had appointed next day (Saturday) "at noon to receive me. I proceeded accordingly "to the palace, accompanied by the Resident: the "Rajah arose on our entrance, and taking me by "the hand led me to a seat on his right. He spoke "English very well, and intimated that he knew me "very well. After some conversation, he carried "me up to his splendid apartments, which are or"namented with the portraits of the Tanjore kings. "All around there is a display of gold, silver, and "mirrors, English paintings, libraries, musical in"struments, orreries, portfolios of oriental drawings, "and many curiosities in art and nature. Finding "that I wished to hear the music of the *vina,* he "ordered up the chief musician. He has a band of "twenty performers, of whom twelve play on the "vina, and one on the harp. The whole black "band can read English music. In the evening his "Highness sent the band to Major B. where I dined. "Six vinas and six singers played ' God save the "King,' in Tamul words, applied to the Maha Rajah. "They played also a variety of English overtures "and Indian airs, the master of the band sitting by "and keeping time.

"My visit to the Rajah was very long. Our "chief conversation related to Mr. Swartz. When "I first mentioned his name, his Highness led me "up to the picture of the reverend apostle. He "then shewed me the design for the groupe for the "marble monument, now executing by Mr. Bacon a Described by Sir William Jones in the third volume of the Asiatic Researches.

"in England. It represents the Rajah coming to "the bed of the dying Swartz, and taking him affec"tionately by the hand, while a number of boys are "weeping at his feet.

"When I was about to depart, the Rajah pre"sented me, to my great surprise, with a picture "of himself, a miniature about six inches in length, "elegantly set in a gold and silver frame, and "glazed. We then went down stairs and resumed "our seats. I took this opportunity (having pre"viously acquainted the Resident with my purpose, "who communicated it to the Rajah) of thanking "his Highness, in the name of the Society at home, "and of all Mr. Swartz's friends in India, for the "remarkable kindness shewn by the Rajah to that "worthy man, and to his successors, and for the "munificent support granted lately by the Rajah to "the body of Christians in his dominions.

"To this he replied in suitable terms, declaring "it to be his purpose to befriend the Christians *for "ever.* He then called for pawn; and immediately "afterwards a servant came up with four pieces of "gold cloth of different kinds, which the Rajah "taking into his hands presented to me. He then "put a chaplet of flowers round my neck, (this is "the usual etiquette,) and a bracelet of flowers on "my arms, and leading me and the Resident, one "in each hand, to the steps of the hall, he bowed "and retired.

"The Rajah has lately erected a college for "Hindoos, Mohammedans, and Christians. Fifty "Christian boys are admitted, and taught, by "schoolmasters provided by the missionaries. The "expense of this institution is (according to the "account of the Resident) about five lacks of ru"pees. But this includes the expense of buildings. "It is also a charitable asylum for the aged, and a "choultry for travellers, there being an apartment "for every denomination. His Highness wished "me to visit his college. It is about fifteen miles "from Tanjore. He is now constructing a brass "orrery to represent the Tychonic system; which "he wishes to believe rather than the Copernican, "as it is the system of the Brahmins. He is still "a heathen; but Dr. John says he is a Cornelius. "The Brahmins fear him for his learning, and "dread the result.

"Last Sunday (the 30th August) was a great day "among the Christians at Tanjore. It being ru"moured that a friend of Mr. Swartz was arrived, "the Christians flocked together from all quarters. "Divine service was performed three times. In the "morning we all proceeded to Mr. Swartz's church "in the fort. It is a large commodious building, "not inferior to your Calcutta church. Mr. Kolhoff "read prayers in English, and I preached. When "I came to the mention of the faithful ministers "whom God had sent to his people in this place, "there was a general commotion, and Mr. Kolhoff's "tears flowed fast, which not a little affected his "flock. Having understood that the missionaries "seldom prayed for the reigning prince of the "country, I thought it expedient to say, (in enume"rating the themes of gratitude of the church "here,) 'and it is their bounden duty to pray "for the long life, peace, and prosperity of the "present most excellent Prince, who hath mani"fested by many munificent acts his regard for "their happiness and welfare.'

"At eleven o'clock the Tamul congregation as"sembled, filling the whole church, and Dr. John "preached a powerful and eloquent sermon in the "Tamul language.

"In the vestry all the native teachers and preach"ers came to make their speeches to me; and "among others the celebrated Sattianaden, the "Hindoo preacher. He is now stricken in years "and infirm. His black hair is grown grey. He "is rather stout, and has a placid look, which is "rendered more pleasing by his wrinkles and age. "He said to me, alluding to some part of my ser"mon, ' This news from a far country is refreshing "to our souls.'

"We dined at Mr. Kolhoff's at one o'clock, and "at five we went to the small church out of the "fort, in which Mr. Swartz first preached, and "where now his body lies. It is close by the "schools and Mr. K's house and mission garden. "Here Mr. Horst preached in the Portuguese "tongue from these words, ' Ye who were once afar "off,' &e. This was a solemn service. The organ "was drowned by the human voices, which sung a "tune of Luther's in a noble manner. I was sitting "with my feet on the granite stone which covers "Swartz's grave. Upon the stone is an English "epitaph in verse, written by the present Rajah. "In the evening Mr. K. catechized (or superin"tended the exercise) in the schools; and the "sermon of the morning was read over by one of "the short-hand writers, and every boy's olla was "examined to see how much he had written.

"Having expressed a wish to hear Sattianaden "preach, it was intimated to the people, and "they were desired to assemble at the little "church next morning (Monday) at nine o'clock. "Accordingly a great number came together, and "the venerable minister delivered a sermon full of "fire. His natural eloquence and various intona"tion were truly calculated to command attention. "Both Mr. Kolhoff and Dr. John were affected by "the discourse. It had reference to the former "darkness in India, the light of Ziegenbalg and "Swartz, the present endeavour to spread the Gos"pel, and lastly the light of heaven. He addressed "the young generation chiefly, and they responded Referring to an interesting custom, which Dr. Buchanan has fully detailed in his Christian Researches, p. 71. VOL. II. D

"as usual to many of his sentences. He made "great use of the Bible; but in quoting a passage "he called upon a lower minister to read it with a "distinct voice, to which he himself listened as to "a record, and then proceeded to expound. His "prayer for the Church of England at the end was "full of fervour; and the psalm which concluded "the service was sung with an ardent devotion.

"I went up to Sattianaden in the presence of "the people, and addressed him in a few words, "hoping he would be faithful unto death, like his "old master Swartz. The women and aged men "crowded round and shed tears. The whole mul"titude came after the sermon to Mr. Kolhoff's "house and garden. The catechists and aged "Christians came into the Verandahs, and while "Mr. Kolhoff and myself were engaged up stairs, Dr. John addressed them in an affectionate and "impressive manner.

"Mr. Kolhoff had been praying that there might "be an outpouring of the Spirit in these days at "Tanjore, and circumstances made him believe "that it was approaching. His success is indeed "great. The congregation is doubled since Mr. "Swartz's death.

"Not wishing to leave this people without some "mark of my regard, I have given Mr. Kolhoff fifty "pounds sterling as a 'donation to the native cate"chists of the Protestant mission,' to be distributed "according to Mr. K's pleasure.

'The Resident requested that I would dine with "him on Monday evening, and invited all the mis"sionaries to meet me. "Mr. Kolhoff has presented me with a gold and "agate snuff-box, which belonged to the late Rev. "Mr. Swartz; and the mission here has given me "from the library a Hebrew Psalter, which he con"stantly used: and also his Greek Testament. "You shall have the latter if you like.

"I proceed to-morrow to Tritchinopoly to Mr. "Pohle, an aged missionary, and a good Hebrew "and Syriac scholar.

I procured here a beautiful "gilt Syriac Testament, and some tracts in Syriac, "translated from the German by Mr. Swartz. "There is in the library a copy of Schultz's Hin"dostanee Grammar, published at Halle, in 1745. "Nor is that the first; for Schultz mentions one "printed some years before by the Dutch ambas"sador at Agra, Johannes Josua Ketelaer; and "edited by David Millius at Utrecht.

"I am now going to inspect Mr. Swartz's cor"respondenee, which fills two boxes. He kept the letters of his friends, and destroyed his own. I "could stay a month at Tanjore, but I must be "gone. No fear of Vellore Brahmins or Mussul"mans in this land. The Christians form a firm "phalanx around me. But if I should not be per"mitted to proceed farther, I may be thankful that "something is done here., 'Tell H. that I have seen many wonderful "things of late, but that I cease to wonder at any "thing; and that I should be glad to have her, or "some other little girl like Augusta, along with "me, that I might enjoy the pleasure of seeing her "*astonished* now and then.

"The interesting scenes of the Christian missions "have lately obliterated from my mind the poor "Syrians and Jews, although I am just on their "borders; and being on the borders, I can get no "information. about them from any European. "Every body refers me to Colonel Macaulay.

"Mr. Pohl6 told me, that a Romish priest, who "was lately in the vicinity ef Tritchinopoly, "preached the atonement with great clearness and "force, to the astonishment of the people; and "that he had been removed by his superiors in con"sequence. I shall endeavour to find him out. If "I could make a confidant of a Jesuit, he would be "an admirable companion in my tour.

"I have just read the orders of the Madras go"vernment passed last year, excluding the French "and Italian Jesuits from ecclesiastical authority "in the Deccan, and granting the whole to the "Archbishop of Goa, and his ignorant native "priests. This circumstance renders my ap"proaches to the Jesuits more facile. I must look "into Goa. I have read in French, since I left "Pondicherry, La Croze's Christianity in India, a most admirable classical work. His chief subject "is the inquisition at Goa, and the Syrian Chris"tians; and his last pages are devoted to Ziegen"balg. He expresses a hope that some persons "will be sent from Europe on an embassy to the "Syrian Christians, to enquire concerning their "state, learning, and religion, after so long an in"terval.

"Joachim at Aughoor told me I should find "them in five days' march through the woods from "Travancore palace; he called them *schismatiques,* "whom no European or Romish priest had ever "visited."

During his stay at Tanjore, Dr. Buchanan wrote at considerable length to his venerable friend Mr. Newton. His letter contained a sketch of his journey up to that time, with a full account of the gratifying scenes which he had lately witnessed among the Christians in that quarter. The publicity which has been already given to that narrative renders the repetition of it in these Memoirs superfluous. Two circumstances only hitherto unnoticed may be mentioned as occurring in the letter to Mr. Newton. One is, that Dr. Buchanan, having heatd much of the sculptures at Vellore, had intended to have been there on the 8th of July, which was two days before the dreadful massacre took place. "But the Pro"vidence of God," he adds, "retarded my steps. "I was visited by-a fever, which confined me for "some time at a caravansera." This temporary detention was probably the means of preserving his life!

The other additional circumstance relates to the newly converted Christians;-" some of whom," observes Dr. Buchanan, "have suffered persecution. "This has, however, been so far useful, that it "shews the serious change of mind in the Hindoo "who can bear it. For it is often alleged in India, "that the Hindoo can never be so much attached "to Christ, as the Brahmin to his idol." The constancy of the native Christians in any instances of persecution for the faith is therefore a sufficient refutation of this calumny.

On the same day on which Dr. Buchanan addressed Mr. Newton at such length, and on so many important topics, he wrote a short letter to his two little girls, then only four and five years old, the affectionate simplicity of which will render it interesting, at least to parental readers.

"Tanjore, in India, 1st Sept. 1806, "My dearest little girls, Charlotte and Augusta, "I hope you are very well. Whenever you can both read the Bible, let me know, and I shall go home. I want little girls who can say to papa at breakfast, 'Papa, we will read the newspapers to you, while you take tea.' I want little girls who can read when papa writes to them *so;* and who do not oblige him to draw little letters till his fingers ache.

"I am happy, my dear children, to hear so good an account of you. Be very good, and I shall come to you soon.

"I saw the two little daughters of the King of Tanjore to-day. They are covered with pearls and diamonds; but their skins are black; and they cannot read one word, although they are about eight years of age. Therefore my own two little girls are more dear to their affectionate father than the princesses of Tanjore.

"C. Buchanan."

On the 4th of September Dr. Buchanan addressed the following letter to Mr. Henry Thornton, which is particularly valuable from the contemporaneous and almost local testimony which it contains respecting the cause of the unhappy massacre at Vellore, which was afterwards so invidiously brought forward to injure the interests of Christianity in India.

This refers to the first six lines of his letter, which Dr. Buchanan had taken the pains to write, or, to express it more plainly, to *print* in Roman characters.

"Seringham Pagoda, near Tritchinopoly, 4th Sept. 1806.

"Dear Sir,

"I had the pleasure of receiving at this place your letter of the 16th February 1806. I am concerned to hear of your frequent indisposition. You mention particularly that sedentary employment is inconvenient to you; and you notice this as a cause of your not writing to me. I do not expect that you should write, as you may perceive by my never entering fully into any particular subject. You have other and more important avocations to employ your pen, when you are able to sit down. I write to you sometimes, because I feel it natural that I should inform you from year to year that I am alive.

' In mentioning Mrs. Buchanan's happy death, you express a hope, that my last end may be like hers. And what can I better wish for you, than that when your hour cometh, you may die like your father, blessing your children?

"It is now four months since I left Calcutta, having travelled by land all the way, looking into Hindoo superstitions, and English manners in India. The officers of government, civil and military, English and native, have every where shewn me civilities, and aided my enquiries; and every where there have been many and serious subjects of enquiry.

"At most of the stations between Calcutta and Madras there is an evident disposition to favour the establishment of a Christian ministry. But they have no clergy of any kind. Two Presbyterian ministers arrived at Visagapatam last year, and the inhabitants have now built a house for them. They insisted on their reading the Episcopal Liturgy; which they had the good sense to do; and in return they are allowed to preach an extempore sermon.

"At Cuttack, Balasore, Juggernaut, Ganjam, Rajahmundry, Nellore, and the intervening stations, there is ' total eclipse.' And yet in all these places the residents would probably support a minister, if he were on the spot. 'We are indeed very bad,' they say; 'but if we had some encouragement, we should be better.'

"Lord W. Bentinck desired I would report my opinion on the best mode of ameliorating the state of the newly converted, in my progress through the Decean. And indeed their state demands the attention of government; for I find that the Company's servants in some districts consider the Christian as the lowest cast.

"The success of the Protestant mission during the last century has been very great. Something more perhaps will be done during the present. The Jesuits have hewed wood and drawn water for us. I am as yet on good terms with them; and their information is generally more important than that of the Protestant missionaries. Schisms and dissensions at present disturb both Protestants and Catholics.

"A rumour has for some months pervaded India, that all casts are to be made Christians. I know the alleged causes of the rumour, but I consider them as inadequate to produce the present effect, without a concurring Providence. This strange rumour of conversion is perhaps auspicious to the event itself; as the shaking of an old building announces its approaching fall.

"It was attempted to be shewn, that the massacre at Vellore, which happened when I was in the neighbourhood, was in some measure caused by this rumour. But it has been proved by the evidence of the conspirators, that the design of resuming the Mohammedan dynasty in Mysore was planned by the princes immediately on their hearing the joyful news that the Tiger Wellesley, as they styled him, had been recalled from India.

"I have been just conversing with the Brahmins of this celebrated Pagoda, (which, according to Orme, once maintained 40,000,) and they have been enquiring about Buonaparte. They have heard that on his arrival they are all to be made Christians. "I remain,

Dear Sir,

Very sincerely yours,

C. Buchanan."

"P. S. I have just measured the length of the granite stones of the Pagoda gate, which Orme says are five feet square, and thirty-three in length. But they are exactly forty-one in length."

The next letter of Dr. Buchanan is addressed to Mr. Grant, and is chiefly occupied with the state of the missions supported by the Society for promoting Christian Knowledge. The testimony at the close to the character of the native Christians, when compared with that of the unconverted Hindoo, is particularly gratifying.

"Madura, 14th Sept. 1S06.

"Dear Sir,

"I was lately favoured with a letter from Mr. Thornton, in which he mentions that you were yet well, and actively engaged in useful labours.

"Having been for upwards of four months past travelling in the interior of the country, I have heard but little of public affairs, and I do not desire at present to think of them. In consequence of my uncertain route, I am cut off from all correspondence, except that of the stations through which I have passed. This correspondence however is very interesting, as it usually refers to the suppression of idolatry, and the promotion of the knowledge of the only true God,

"As I suppose you are still connected with the Society for promoting Christian Knowledge,-I shall notice some particulars of their missions in these parts. I have now visited all the stations, and conversed with all the missionaries. At Tanjore I sat in conclave with three of them on the subject of the general mission, when they proposed that I should make a report to the Society of their present state. But this will not be necessary till I know what the Society has the power to do.

"I did not observe that the Gospel flourished any where but in Tanjore. In Tranquebar a holy remnant is left; perhaps also at Madras; but I heard not of many recent conversions. But from Tanjore streams will probably flow, like its own fertilizing rivers, throughout the neighbouring lands.

"Of all the missionaries, Mr. Kolhoff at Tanjore is the first and best; a man of meek spirit, but of ardent faith, and a worthy successor of the illustrious Swartz.

"Mr. Horst and Mr. Shveiffvogel appear to be zealous men, pure in their life and doctrine,

"Messrs. Pohle, John, and Rottler are now old men, and incapable of labour in the proper duties of the mission. Dr. John, and Dr. Rottler are conversant in natural history, which is often fascinating enough to become a study. Dr. Rottler is an amiable man, but seems to want energy.

"Mr. Pohl6 at Tritchinopoly, the senior missionary, is a learned man, but now stricken in years. He devotes himself chiefly to the *English* Church at Tritchinopoly, which of itself demands the whole labours of one minister.

"Three men of learning and piety are wanted to fill up the places of Swartz, Joenicke, and Gericke. But it seems that such are not now to be found in Germany.

"There is a great cry for Bibles throughout the Tamul land. The poor funds of the mission here cannot supply them. I have visited several Christian villages where there were but two Bible-houses. Mr. Kolhoff wishes this to be immediately represented. As the Tamul version is now finally settled, (like the English,) the Society might print the Bibles at home, and send out twenty thousand copies every year.

"I have conversed with many Hindoos of the Brahmin and other casts, who appear to be true members of Christ's body. I have seen in the feeble-minded native of Hindostan, truth, generosity, a spirit without guile, ardent zeal for the faith, and a love for those who love the Lord Jesus Christ in Nothing effectual appears to have been done towards supplying this pressing demand for Bibles till the year 1S10, when Mr. Brown preached a sermon at Calcutta upon the subject; and a subscription of one thousand pounds was in consequence raised towards the purchase of copies of the Tamul Scriptures, and the encouragement of a new edition. See Christian Researches, p. 80.

sincerity. I am satisfied that our Saviour hath a church here; and that in process of time all casts will come into it.

"I remain,
Dear Sir,
    Very sincerely yours,
    C. Buchanan."

On the 20th of September, Dr. Buchanan again wrote to Mr. Brown from Ramnad pooram, as follows.

"In the province of Madura, the Romish churches "are frequent. At Aour, or properly Aughoor, "near Tritchinopoly, is a church where the priest "reads the Syrian mass instead of the Latin, which "he does not understand. Nor do his people un"derstand the Syrian; for to them he preaches in "Tamul. He gave me a Syrian letter to his "brethren at Cranganore. At this church there is "an union of Romish ceremonies and Pagan super"stitions. They have their Rutt Jattra. I ex"amined the Rutt, which is built in the usual "manner with three cables to pull it. Only that, "instead of the Hindoo devices, it has hell and the "devils on the lower part, heaven and the blessed in "the higher, and above all, the Pope and the "Cardinals. The priest, my friend Joachim, is so "ignorant, that he did not seem conscious of any,, impropriety in having the Rutt. I asked him how many thousands of Christians attended the "festival: he said, generally about ten thousand; "which number corresponds with the report of the "collector of the district.

"The English here know little of these matters. "Mr. C. a Judge of circuit, told me he would pro"ceed immediately to Aughoor to see this sight. I "told him he might see it in many other places.

"I passed three days among the ruins and an"tiquities of Madura. This is a fine station for the "Gospel.

"I proceed from this place to the Juggernaut of "the south, Ramisseram. There Mussulmans and "Hindoos have consecrated the names of Adam "and Abel."

An interval nearly of a month occurred between the date of the preceding letter, and that of Dr. Buchanan's next communication to the same friend and correspondent; during which he had visited the island of Ramisseram, and from thence had crossed to Ceylon. Of his visit to the latter island, both at this time and again about eighteen months afterwards, Dr. Buchanan gave some account to the public in his Christian Researches; but of Ramisseram, as well as Ceylon, it may not be uninteresting to add the following particulars.

"Borders of Travancore, 18th Oct. 1806. "The Ranny of Ramnad gave me a letter to the "Pandarum or chief priest of the Pagoda of Ra"misseram, desiring that he would give me a ca"talogue of the Shanscrit books preserved in the "temple from time immemorial. The Ranny is "the patroness (by hereditary right) of the temple. "When I delivered the letter, the Pandarum in"formed the priests of its contents. They observed, "that no catalogue had ever been given before. "The Pandarum said he would give me an answer "next day. In the mean time I paid him a visit "of ceremony, and presented a nuzzur. The next "day he sent to acquaint me that the catalogue was "preparing, and would be ready for delivery in the "evening; when I was requested to proceed to the "Pandaruin's house. At live o'clock he came him"self to accompany me, attended by his elephants "and music, and the whole band of priests. In "this procession I moved round the temple to the "Pandarum's house, where all the books were ex"hibited in order. They are all written on ollas; "and had generally the aspect of antiquity.

"The Pandarum then presented the catalogue "written on four ollas. It contains ninety-six Shan"scrit volumes, and seventy-two Tamul.

"It was Mr. E. who suggested to me the attempt "to procure this catalogue.

"Ramisseram, or rather Ramacoil, or Ramacovel "that is, Rama's temple, is a noble building. The "aisles, or porticos of majestic height, are about six "hundred feet long. No abbey or cathedral in "Europe is of such magnitude. Like the other "temples in the Deccan, its revenues are wasting "away. But Juggernaut will fall, I think, before "Ramacoil. I saw no human bone in the island "of Ramisseram. Christianity in its worst shape "has civilized the Deccan. All descriptions of "people are more humane and intelligent than thr "Hindoos of Bengal.

"The Pandarum presented to me a fine shawl, "(the Ranny gave me two,) and then procured a "donie to carry me to Jaffnapatam. The wind "was fair, and

I was only one day on the deep. I "had letters to Mr. T. the civil magistrate of "Jaffna. I slept the first night on the island of "Leyden, at the house of Mr. T. the custom mas"ter. Next morning he shewed me three Roman "Catholic churches lately built, and assured me "that every person on the island was a Christian. "I passed through a bazar, and spoke to some "Christian women selling turtle, which they cut in "pieces to make curry. They were not so intelli"gent as Mr. Kolhoff's Christians.

"I next day visited the chief Romish church in "Jaffna town; built by Padre Leonardo, who now "presides in the island. This church is the largest "structure of slight building which I ever saw. "Every Sunday about a thousand or twelve hundred "people attend, and on feast days three thousand VOL. II. E

"and upwards. Leonardo introduced me to four "of his brethren, who all conversed very fluently in "Latin. There are five priests in Jaffna, and ten "in Ceylon. They are all of the same order, St. "Philip Nerius; and no priest of any other order "is ever admitted to the island.

"I passed half a day with Dr. S. mentioned by Thunberg. Dr. S. was at Japan, and brought "from thence a valuable collection of Japanese "books in print. They are chiefly on subjects "of natural history, having drawings of animals. "He has a very extensive museum of oriental cu"riosities. I went patiently through his library, "and found some information I wanted.

"Among the Dutch ladies are some examples of "serious religion. Mrs. M. is a pious woman. "She could not speak English; but she produced "a quarto Dutch Bible well worn, and we conversed with each other in texts.

"The chief justice spoke respectfully of Mr. Palm, "and so did the other gentlemen at Jaffna. They "wished me to go to Columbo, and report to. the "Governor: he has himself already visited Jaffna, "and Dr. S's collection.

"From Jaffnapatam I proceeded by land to " Manaar, through the woods; a journey of three "days. Elephants, bears, and buffaloes abound. "Every night two men preceded my palanquin, "carrying each a flaming log of gum-wood, to "frighten the wild beasts. In the open spaces in "the woods, I saw the Ryots guarding their cattle "with gum-wood torches. The cheetah is very "destructive here.

"Governor North built three caravanseras in "these desolate woods.

"At Manaar I found Captain B. commandant "of the Fort. He was a shipmate in the Bus"bridge. At his house I met Mr. M. son to the "old lady at Jaffna. He happened to mention that "he had Busching's Magazine in German, contain"ing Moen's (the Dutch Governor at Cochin) ac"count of the Jews at that place. This book is "referred to by Forster, who writes notes to Barto'' lomeo, as the last and most authentic account.

"Mr. M. has promised to translate the whole "into English, and send it to me in a fortnight.

"At Manaar I embarked in a donie, an open "boat, about the size of a burr, for Ramisseram. "A storm arose, and I went on shore at a fishing "village, situated near the north-west extremity "of the island Manaar. They were all Romish '' Christians, and I slept in their church. The "priest was absent; and his catechist had never "heard that there was such a book as the Bible. '' The dandies of my own boat were also Chris"tians, but had never heard of the Bible. They "had, however, a very good Christian custom. Be"fore they hoisted the sail, they all joined in prayer "to God for protection. Every man at his post "with the rope in his hands pronounced his prayer.

"Next morning I reembarked; and when we "were nearly out of sight of land, the wind began "to rise again. We could not gain any land before "it was dark. At four o'clock in the morning we "were alarmed by the noise of breakers; and in a "few minutes we struck on Adam's bridge. I had "expressed a wish to see it; and now I saw it in a "perilous situation. The boatmen leaped out, and "kept the boat's head to the sea till she floated, "and then forced her through the waves like a "Masoolah boat.

"At day-light I saw the towers of Ramisseram "near at hand, when we landed at Pomben, next "the continent. The boatmen offered up their "Christian thanksgiving for their deliverance from "the peril of the sea. One of Mr. Swartz's cate"chists, who accompanies me every where, ap"peared to be a good deal edified by the scene.

"My friends at Ramnad sent bearers to me on "my arrival at Pomben, and I was conducted once "more to Colonel M's hospitable mansion.

"Tell H. that in the island of Ramisseram I saw "Abel's tomb, which is about fifty feet long. It is "guarded by a Mussulman, as I expected would "be the case. In Ceylon the fable of Adam's "flight from the island is very current. The truth "seems to be this. The Hindoos called Ceylon "a paradise, on account of its spices and pearls and "precious stones. And the Mussulmans believing "it to be the Garden of Eden, introduced Adam "and his family immediately.

"At Ramnad-pooran there is a good Protestant "church and parsonage-house of stone, built by "Colonel M. and the Company about eight years "ago. But they have no minister, and long much "for a visit from some missionary.

"From Ramnad I proceeded to Tutycorin, where "there is a rich Romish church, and a Dutch Pro"testant church.

"At this place there is a tribe of Hindoos called "Parrawars, (not Pariahs,) whose chief is called "Prince of the Parrawars. The whole of this tribe, "without exception, are Christians in the Romish "communion. The wealth and dignity of the "prince support the church, and exhibit more mag"nificence than is now generally to be found in the "Romish churches.

"The Rutt is Attached to this church, as at Aug"hoor. The priest told me he walked before it in "procession. In the Hindoo temples it is usual to "ring bells and strike gongs the moment the idol "is unveiled. In analogy to this, bells are rung and drums beat at Tutycorin when the Virgin "Mary is unveiled. There are three bells within "the church of large size, which have a terrible "effect on the auditory nerves. I requested the "priest to undraw the curtain before the Virgin, "that I might see the golden image: but I was not "apprized of the thunder that was to accompany "the exhibition.

"I visited the prince in form, and enquired into "the moral state of his subjects. He was deno"minated by the Dutch the Prince of the Seven "Havens. The Dutch Minister shewed me his "library, in which I was happy to find Fabricius's "Lux Evangelii, in quarto. I went from Tutycorin "to Tinavelly in my palanquin, without taking my "eyes off this book.

"Here is the pearl fishery. I saw the shells in "heaps at the place where they are opened, and "Mr. M. the Dutch merchant at whose house I "lodged, made me a present of a large pearl, about "the size of a pistol bullet, but of little value from "its being clouded in various places.

"At Tinavelly I was hospitably received by the "Judge, the Collector, and the Register. In Pa"lamcotta Fort, which is close to Tinavelly, there "is a Protestant church and parsonage-house. "The Christians in the district are numerous, and "have suffered some persecution. Mr. Kolhoff "wished me to represent the subject to the Judge "and Collector, who have assured me that they will "afford them every protection and encouragement "in their power.

"Tell H. who gets all my natural history and po"litical remarks, that I write this at the bottom of "the lofty mountain, called Cape Comorin, whose "rocky head seems to overhang its base. The "birds which build the pendulous nests are here "numerous. At night each of their little habita"tions is lighted up, as if to see company. The "sagacious little bird fastens a bit of clay to the "top of the nest, and then picks up a firefly, and "sticks it on the clay to illuminate the dwelling, "which consists of two rooms. Sometimes there "are three or four fire-flies, and their blaze of light "in the little cell dazzles the eyes of the bats, which "often kill the young of these birds.

"I did not pass through Cape Comorin gate in "entering Travancore, but through another some "miles northward, called Arampalli gate. The "mountain called by sailors the Cape is again to "the north of this. Arampalli is thought to be the "Arguropolis of the Greeks. Here there is a for"tified pass, and lines of two miles in length, com"posed of stone walls and towers. The guard re"ceived me with frowning looks. I had unfortu"nately not yet received my passport from Colonel "Macaulay. I did not know, therefore, how I "should be received at the gate. But when I was "approaching it, I sent some of the armed peons "who accompanied me, to inform the commandant "that I expected he would be ready to receive "me at the gate, and to afford me an escort to the "Rajah's presence. And thus I passed without op"position.

"Next day I arrived at Cottate, the Cottonia "(hence the word cotton) of the ancients. It is "still a flourishing place. The day after I came to "Padmanburatn, a fort and residence of the King, "where his principal arsenal is established.

"From Padmanburatn to Trivandram is a road "shaded by lofty trees, called the King's Road, "whereon Brahmins and Nayrs alone are suffered "to walk. The lower casts do, however, walk on "it; but if they meet a Brahmin, they immediately "leave it, and seek a path in the woods. A person "sometimes precedes the Brahmin, to announce to "passengers that he is near at hand."

The date of Dr. Buchanan's next letter is on the 27th of October, from the palace of the Rajah of Travancore at Trivandram.

"I have received your letter of the 27th Sep"tember, in which you answer mine of the 1st from "Tanjore.

"I have not seen Geddes, but I am accustomed "to read quotations from him. I shall endeavour "to preserve some Syrian and Jewish relics for "you.

"On my arrival here, I found that Colonel Ma"caulay was a hundred miles off, at Cochin. But "I received a letter from him, tendering his services "in whatever way I wished to command them.

"I immediately informed his *Excellency* the Mi"nister (a noble Nayr of able and liberal mind) "that I wished to pay my respects to his *Highness* "the Rajah; for so are these illustrious personages "designated by the Company.

"The Rajah sent his Vakeel to announce that "he would receive me in form next day. In the "mean time he gave orders for my accommodation "and table. The Rajah's servants accordingly came "the next day to escort me to the gate of the fort "in which he resides. The military were drawn "out, and I was received on the steps of the palace "by the Minister and Secretary, who conducted me "to the Rajah's apartment. He was more gorge"ously "dressed than the Rajah of Tanjore. He was "twenty-five years old on the day I entered Tri"vandram; and of five subjects of compliment "which I had premeditated, this was one. He is "an affable sensible man. He conversed on poli"tical subjects for about two hours; and was ex"tremely desirous to have my opinion of the chief "persons, European and native, in Hindostan. His "grand subject, however, was to learn the particular "purpose of my various and extensive tour. No"body had been able to satisfy him on this head. "I was very candid with him, and declared my ob"jects plainly. He appeared to be a little thoughtful, "and I did not know what impression I had made "on his mind. His whole court of Brahmins and "Nayrs understood every word that was said. "When I was about to take my leave, he expressed "a hope that I meant to stay some days with him. "I told him I should.

"On the same day I sent to him the Rajah of '' Tanjore's list of books, and also the Ramisseram "catalogue. He read over both with great plea"sure. I then requested that he would order his "Brahmins to make out a similar list of their an"cient books. He assented immediately; but the "Brahmins resisted. The Minister told me this. "I asked whether the Brahmins governed the "Rajah. At my next audience the Rajah told me "the list was preparing.

"Understanding that I had the Rajah of Tanjore's "picture, he requested to see it. He was so much "pleased with the beauty of the painting, that he "desired to keep it for a day or two to shew it to "his ladies. It was three days before I could get "the Rajah of Tanjore out of the Zenana. I mean "to tell him this.

"Mr. Swartz's catechist, who accompanies me, "is called Pascal. He was heir to a person of pro"perty, who died some years ago at Trivandram. "He proceeded from Tanjore accordingly to claim "his inheritance about four years ago; but being "a poor man, and ill supported, he was told by this court that his claim was not just. Mr. Kol"hoff requested I would take Pascal with me, and "represent his case to the Rajah. I did so; but "having no hope of getting any thing for him, I "gave him an allowance as my interpreter. On "my second audience, I represented his case to ' the Rajah. The matter was investigated in pub"lic next day; and on the day following (to the "great astonishment of poor Pascal and all my "servants) the Rajah put him in possession of a "house and land in this place, and granted him "the option of inhabiting it, or selling it immedi"ately. He also delivered to Pascal bonds amount"ing to about six thousand rupees, and a great "number of jewels. Pascal says he must build a "church for all this."

Dr. Buchanan then mentions a second successful application to the Rajah in behalf of a small body of native Christians at Moiladdy, a district of Travancore, who had hitherto been refused permission to build a church.

"I asked the Rajah," says Dr. Buchanan, " whe"ther he had ever read of any people who were not "allowed to worship their God? The Minister was "willing. At last the Rajah told me, he would "himself soon visit the district of Moiladdy, and "would then point out a proper place for the church. The Brahmins, I hear, first opposed the "measure, alleging that the English would soon "have the country, if they were allowed to intro"duce their religion into it.

"At my last audience the Rajah was very gra"cious. He presented to me some shawls; and "when I was taking leave, he put an emerald ring "on my finger. He at the same time gave orders, '' that two of his officers (Nayrs) should attend "me throughout his dominions, wherever I was "pleased to go. This last favour was of a very "peculiar nature, and altogether unexpected."

Dr. Buchanan thus continues his correspondence.

"1st November, 1806"From Trivandram I went to Poontara on the "seacoast; and here I first saw a Syrian church "in the Romish communion. I mean in Travan"core; for I before mentioned to you that I had "visited one near Tritchinopoly. From Poontara "to Angengo I travelled by the sea-coast, and had "the pleasure to see a church every four or five "miles. From Cape Comorin to Cochin there are "about a hundred churches on the sea-shore alone. "Of these the chief part are the Syrian Latin, or "more properly the Syrian Romish churches. The "priest reads the Syriac Liturgy, not one word of "which the people understand, and then he walks "off; or he reads the Latin Liturgy, with which "the poor Christians are equally edified. Some of "them (the private Christians) have, however, the "prayers translated into Malayalim, or proper Ma"labar. The churches are snow white, and are "generally built in a grove of shady trees. Before "each, on the sand of the shore, is a lofty cross; "which, like the church itself, is conspicuous at a "great distance.

"There was an insurrection of the Nayrs in Tra"vancore last year, against the Rajah: three bat"talions of his Nayr body guards revolted, and "sought to kill the British Resident, and the Rajah, "and the present Minister. Colonel M. fled to "Cochin. The Rajah called in the *Christian* fish"ermen from the coast to defend him against the "Nayrs. They assembled at Trivandram in im"mense numbers, each man armed with a short "bludgeon. The bowmen from the hills appeared "at the same time in the Rajah's behalf, and the "Nayrs laid down their arms and fled. About fifty "of the ringleaders were seized and hanged. The "battalions were broken, and the Rajah accepted of "a subsidiary force from the English. This was a "dreadful blow to the Brahmins, whose influence in "Travancore is identified with that of the Nayrs.

"At Angengo I found apartments prepared for "me by the British Resident, Mr. H. who is ap"pointed by the Bombay government. Angengo "has been in possession of the English since "1628.

"At Quilon, Dr. M» nephew to the Colonel, en"tertained me. The subsidiary force is at present "encamped here. At this place I saw Dr. H. the "Hindostanee scholar. He told me, that though "he had been many months here, he had not yet "met with any one who could give an account of "the schismatic Syrians, as their churches were all "in the interior, where Europeans cannot go with"out permission from the Rajah."

The next letter, in which Dr. Buchanan announces his approaching departure to the interior of Travancore, will be read with lively interest by those who have followed him in his progress hitherto, and who are aware of the important result of his researches.

"Calycoulon, 4th Nov. 1806.

"I am now about to proceed northward and "eastward from this place to visit the Syrian "churches. There is one very near to Mavelicar. "The others are remote, situated (according to "Dr. L's account) in impenetrable forests, where "jungle fevers and tigers abound.

"The weather is dry and clear, and I have re"ceived a very different account of the regions I "wish to visit. I shall however proceed no farther "than may be prudent. I have told my servants, "that they may remain behind if they please. But "they choose to accompany me. The Rajah's men "encourage them. The Lord, who hath graciously "led me from Cambuslang to Calcutta, and from "Calcutta to Cape Comorin, will lead me in safety, "I trust, through the mountains of Travancore. "In many instances already mountains have been "made a plain before me; and I am ready to be"lieve that some good will result from a journey, "hitherto so remarkably favoured by Providence.

"I think it right, however, to ' put my house in "order' at this place, and leave the event to Him, "who disposeth of the lives of his servants accord"ing to his eternal purpose and righteous will.

"At a village near Calycoulon lives

Captain W. "an old officer of a former Rajah. He is now blind, "but his wife reads the Bible to him. Hearing of "my approach, he had prepared some questions to "ask me, which had long been on his mind, relating "to the doctrine of salvation. After supper, he "quoted several passages from the Epistles to the " Romans, Ephesians, and first of St. Peter; and "asked, how can these things be?

"After an hour's discourse, the old man said, "' It is even so, as I hoped.' And he began to weep "aloud."

It was surely worth a journey from Calcutta to Travancore to resolve the doubts and to shed light upon the path of this aged Christian!

On the 5th of December, Dr. Buchanan communicated to his excellent correspondent in Bengal a long and detailed account of his visit to the Syrian churches in Malayala. As it has been already observed with respect to Juggernaut and Ceylon, the narrative in this letter is substantially similar to that which has been long since published, and excited such general attention and interest. It will not, however, be deemed unnecessary to give a sketch of Dr. Buchanan's introduction to the Syrian Christians, and to add a few extracts, containing some circumstances which have not yet met the public eye.

"Cochin, Sth December, 1806.

"My last letter from Travancore informed you "that I was about to leave the sea-coast, and to "proceed into the interior of the country to visit "the ancient Syrian churches. I have been ena"bled to accomplish my purpose. I have visited "the remote churches situated amongst the hills at "the bottom of the great Ghauts. The scenery of "the country was every where delightful; the wea See the Christian Observer, vol. vi. and Christian. Researches, pp. 112—150.

"ther was cool and pleasant; and I have returned "from an expedition, which was represented to be " dangerous, in perfect health.

"Early in November I left the sea-coast, having "first supplied myself with plenty of gold and sil"ver. I directed my course towards Mavelicar, the "first Syrian church.

"The *kasheeshas* (priests) received me on my "arrival with much civility, perceiving that I was "accompanied by the Rajah's servants. Their cu"riosity to know the object of my visit was very "great; still greater when I took up their Syrian "books and began to read; and when I shewed "them my printed Syriac books, which they could "read. They produced the Scriptures, and their "Liturgy; also Lexicons and Grammars, Syrian "and Malayalim. The Malayalim, or proper Ma"labar, is a dialect distinct from the Tamul; but "the character is nearly the same. It is considered "by the learned Brahmins of this eoast as the eldest "and legitimate daughter of the Shanscrit.

"In the evening the church was lighted up for '(prayers, at which a good many of the people at"tended. Nothing objectionable appeared at this "service. The priests pronounced the prayers with"out book, and chaunted their hymns, having their "faces turned towards the altar. They have no "images, but on the walls were paintings from sub"jects of Scripture history,

"Next day being Sunday, I had an opportunity VOL. II. F

"of seeing the whole service, morning and evening, "as I sat in the chancel, with one of their books in "my hand. The people were very decently habited, "and filled the church.

"On Monday morning the four chief elders of "the church came with the priests to visit me. I "tcjd them I knew their history, and came as their "friend, and the friend of their religion; that I "knew they had been an oppressed people during a "long period. To all this they listened evidently "with deep thought and perplexity. They then put "a few questions to me. I told them I was about "to visit their remotest congregations, intending to "penetrate to Ranniel itself.

"Their countenances began now to assume great "distrust, and after a few civil sentences, they beg"ged leave to withdraw. I certainly appeared in a "most questionable shape among these simple peo"ple, who had so little commerce with the world. "In the evening I invited them to another con"ference. I told them I should set off the next "morning for the mountains; that I was much "obliged to them for their hospitable entertainment, "and begged they would accept something in re"turn. I gave each of the priests some gold, and "some to the elders of the church, for the poor; "and desired their benediction, that I might go in "peace. They then retired with apparent reluct"ance, looking at the money with dubious coun"tenances.

"I afterwards learnt that they immediately called "an assembly. An old man arose and said, ' What "if this stranger should prove to be a true Chris"tian, and a real friend? What proof have we "that he is our enemy? It is true no European "ever visited us before: but what say you to this "man's knowledge of our church at Antioch, to his "Syrian books, to his money? Besides it is said "that the Rajah put an emerald ring on his finger. "If he do not intend our good, he may have power "to hurt us.'

"They then conferred with Mr. Swartz's cate"chist, and my other servants of all casts, con"cerning my family, country, profession, my pre"sent journey, where I had been, and what I had "been doing, and what I intended to do.

"After this ordeal I was permitted to appear "before their tribunal once more. The old priest '' said he was afraid they had judged me too hastily; "but that there were some circumstances which he "would now communicate as an apology for their "suspicions."

Dr. Buchanan then relates the account which the venerable priest gave him of the various attempts of the Roman Catholics to force the Syrian churches to join their communion, as the ground of their suspicions respecting his present visit, and the manner in which he at length succeeded in removing their fears and gaining their confidence.

He next proposed to send a standard translation of the Scriptures in Malayalim to each of their fifty-five chinches, on condition that each church should multiply the copies, and circulate them among the people. To this they thankfully assented.

"One of the elders named Thomas, or Didymus, "stepped forward and said, ' To convince you, Sir, "of our earnest desire to have the Bible in the "Malayalim tongue, 1 need only mention that I "have lately translated the Gospel of St. Matthew "for the benefit of my own children. It is often "borrowed by the other families. It is not in fine "language; but the people love to read it.'

"'But how,' said the old priest, ' shall we know "that your standard copy is a true translation of "our Bible? We cannot depart from our own "Bible. It is the true book of God, without cor"ruption; that book which was first used by the "Christians at Antioch. What translations you "have got in the West we know not; but the true "Bible of Antioch we have had in the mountains "of Malabar for fourteen hundred years, or longer. "Some of our copies are from ancient times; so "old and decayed, that they can scarcely be pre"served much longer. I rejoiced when I heard "this.

"'But how,' repeated the aged priest, ' shall we "know that your Western Bible is the same as "ours?' 'I have here,' said I, a Western Syrian "Bible, which yourselves can read; and I have an "English Bible, which will be interpreted to you. "Let some portion of Scripture, selected at a ven"ture, be accurately examined. You can compare "the whole at your leisure hereafter.' They "turned over the leaves of my Bible with surprise, "having never seen a printed Syriac Bible before. "After some consultation, they proposed that the "3d chapter of St. Matthew's Gospel should be critically compared, word for word, in the Eastern "Syrian, Western Syrian, and English. St. Matthew "was selected, I believe, at the suggestion of "Thomas, who had got his Malayalim translation "in his hand.

"It was an interesting scene to me to behold the "ancient English Bible brought before the tribunal "of these simple Christians in the hills of Malabar. "They sat down to the investigation with great "solemnity; and the people around seemed to "think that something important depended on the "issue.

"I held a Greek Testament in my hand, and "proposed that the sense of the Greek copy should "be first explained, as the New Testament was first "given to the world in Greek."

Here a discussion arose respecting the comparative merits of the Greek and Syriac Scriptures, which Dr. Buchanan has given at length in his Researches After which he. adds, " Not thinking it "Christian Researches, pp. 114, 115. "prudent to proceed further in this argument, I "proposed that Jona (the aged priest) should first "read his own Syriac as the standard, with which "the other versions should be compared. We "accordingly began, and soon finished the colla"tion of the chapter. Jona was satisfied that the "English Bible was a faithful translation. As for "the Western Syrian, it agreed with the Eastern "nearly word for word. Thomas's Malayalim trans"lation alone was faulty.

"We next considered the establishment of "schools; the proposal of which seemed very ac"ceptable to them.

"My business was now done. The priests ob"served, that it would be necessary that their Bi"shop and Metropolitan, Mar Dionysius, now re"siding at Candenad, near Cochin, should be made "fully acquainted with all that had passed; as with"out his concurrence nothing could be done with "energy in so extensive a diocese. I told them I "had already ascertained that the good Bishop "would willingly give his sanction to measures so "beneficial to his people, and that he would signify "it to them officially in due time.

"The people now informed me they had deter"mined that one of the priests, and one of the "elders, should accompany me to the other "churches; and that letters should be sent before "to announce our coming.

"Next day we took our departure from Mave"lycar, and arrived in the evening at the church "of Chinganoor. The priests and people came out, "women and children in their holiday clothes, to "meet us at a little distance from the town. The "church is a spacious building, far superior to any "that I had yet seen. Near the altar are two "shrines of bishops who died here. I requested "Jesua the priest to select four of the chief elders, as representatives of the people, to hear what had "passed at Mavelycar. They received the proposal "for diffusing the Scriptures and establishing the "schools with the utmost cordiality.

"I was here told, that no European, or even "Romish priest, had ever penetrated farther into "the country than this place. Bartolomeo was not "here; for there is not a single Roman church in "this district of Malabar.

"Calicherry was our next church. It is built on "the top of a hill. The chief priest is Matthew, "aged eighty years. He gave me the history of "ancient times; and also a very accurate account "of the present state of the Syrian church. The "people here manifested the same favourable dispo"sition which had appeared at the former places.

"Still journeying towards the East, we arrived "at the church of Puttencow: from whence we "had a view of the delectable mountains, the ut"most bound of the Syrian churches. The church "of Puttencow was built by the present Bishop "about fourteen years ago. At this place I met "a greater number of aged persons than I had yet "seen. They suggested many useful improvements "in the plans to be adopted, and pointed out where "they were most liable to fail. Andrew, the priest, "appeared to be very zealous for Scripture trans"lation.

"We came the next day to Maraman, a small "church, over which presides the aged Zechariah. "I found him reading his Masmora (Psalms) in the "porch of the church. This part of the country is "interspersed with hills, round which the rivers "from the Ghauts wind their course. The Chris"tians go from place to place in little canoes. "Sometimes a woman may be seen with the oar "in her hand; sometimes a little boy; some of the "canoes being so small as to admit of two persons "only.

"The church of Colancherry was next in our "course. It is built in the bosom of the forest, "but not far from a river. The people were poor, "but very hospitable. An old lady wished me to "make a promise that I would come back again in a year or two, or at least that I would write to "them. She would take care that the Cassanars "did their duty.

"Next day we arrived at Ranniel, the remotest "church in these regions, and the limit of my pro"posed tour. This church is built on a steep hill, "or rather rock, in which a few steps are cut to "ascend. The people assembled from all quarters, -' and seemed delighted with the novelty of my ap"pearance, and that of my attendants. The two "priests were Lucas and Matthew; and the four "elders, Abraham, Thoma, Georgius, and Philip.

"I found Abraham to be rich; and to be withal "deeply interested in the success of our measures "for the extension of religion. He had travelled "a little. He said there was a great difference "between the religion of the heart and the doc"trines of the head; and it was to be lamented "that many priests were ignorant of this. 'You "were right,' said he, 'in taking a pledge of the "four chief elders, rather than of the young Cas"sanars. For want of colleges and places of re"ligious instruction, the young priests are sent "to teach us before they are taught themselves. "They are obliged indeed to lead moral lives, for "otherwise they would not be endured. But no "man should go forth to the ministry until he has "studied the whole Bible, and can quote it fluently "in his Christian discourse. For three hundred "years we have been quarrelling with the Romish "Church about supremacy, rites, and ceremonies, "but the Bible has been out of the question. The "Bible, Sir, is what we want, in the language of "our own mountains. With the Bible in his It may be gratifying to the reader to know, that Colonel Munro, the present British Resident in Travancore, has succeeded in procuring the establishment of a college for the better instruction of the Syrian priests.

"hand, every man can become the priest of his own "family.'

"While Abraham was thus discoursing, I thought "of that other Abraham, who was called ' the friend "of God' in a strange land. He gave me much "useful information, and conveyed it too with some "authority; for he seemed to consider me as a "young man who professed a good purpose, but "who was not likely to bring it to a happy issue, "without being well directed and well supported. "'After you are gone,' said he, 'evil men will en"deavour to frustrate your counsel. Nothing will "complete your success but the authority of the "English government interposed in our behalf. "Before any thing can be done in India on a great "scale, kings, and men in power, must range them"selves on God's side. When the Christian reli"gion is left to itself, as a thing indifferent, the "solid dominion of the devil will soon overwhelm "it; unless indeed it should please God to send "forth in these days his divine power in a miracu"lous way, as in the first ages. But this we are "not to expect, and therefore we ought to pray, as "in our Syrian Liturgy, 'that kings and ministers "would work with God.'

"I proposed to Abraham that he should corre"spond on these subjects with the most learned "and pious persons of his Church; and requested "he would inform me from time to time what was '' proper to be done. At parting I put a ring on "Abraham's finger, before the people. He said he "should ever wear it, and it should be a memorial "of what had passed. At the request of the priests "I recorded my visit in the church books, in the "Syrian language; being willing that there should "be the appearance of as much solemnity as pos"sible in my visit to this remote people; in order "that the objects of it might not soon be for"gotten.

"At all these churches I passed some time in "examining their Syrian books. At most places "there are ancient copies of the Scriptures, or of "some parts of them; for the whole Scriptures "are with them seldom bound up in one volume. "They are most generally in four: the *Or eta,* or "former part of the Old Testament; the *Evange"lion,* the *Praxeis,* and the *Egurta.* The Pro"phets are rarest.

"In the vicinity of Ranniel, there is a high hill, "from the top of which the people told me I "might have an extensive view of the country. "The hill was steep, and of laborious ascent, and "I left my servants below. When I had gained "the summit, I felt myself much fatigued, and "sat down to contemplate the delightful prospect, "The mountains of the Ghauts were at some dis"tance, but from their great height they appeared "to be close at hand.

"In a few minutes I saw a man coming up from "a village below, with a cocoa-nut in his hand. I "drank the cooling water, and was much refreshed.." He said he was a Christian; that seeing me "ascend, he thought the cocoa-water would be ac"ceptable. I said I was a Christian too. He "smiled doubtingly, looking at my English dress. "He said he was never farther from home than the "adjacent mountains, where he sometimes went to "fell wood. He did not seem to understand that "there were Christians in any other part of the "world than the mountains of Malayala. He "pointed out to me by name the Christian parishes "which I had visited, but most of the churches "were concealed by the trees. The Christians are "forbidden to have steeples, as they would appear "too preeminent among the pagodas of the heathens.

"While I surveyed the Christian districts all "around, I reflected on the inscrutable counsels of "God, in finding this asylum for the Bible during "so many ages; and yet in confining it for so long "a period to this region of the heathen world.-I "indulged the hope that the same Providence was "about to unfold itself by dispensing the Bible "throughout the East, by means of this people.

"I passed two hours on the top of this hill. I "do not know its name. But I called it Pisgah; "for I believed that I had a sight of kingdoms "promised to the Messiah in the second Psalm. " I will give thee the heathen for thine inheritance, "and the uttermost parts of the earth for thy pos"session.'

"On my return from Ranniel, I visited most of "the churches a second time, and then proceeded "to Nerenam, which was formerly the residence "of the Syrian Bishops. The episcopal chair, co"vered with red velvet, and decorated with copper "studs, is evidently the workmanship of a former "age. In a corner lay the pastoral staff. The "church itself is supposed to be nine hundred years "old. The chief Kasheesha here was Thoma, aged "62 years. He has five colleagues and one shum"shana, (student.) The Christians here are said "to be wealthy; but they must conceal their "wealth. Their chief elder is named Jacob Ter"ragon: the latter word is an addition conferred "by the Rajah on persons of condition. Jacob intimated to me, that he was ready to support "the cause with, money.

"Next day we arrived at Mavelycar, where I "received a better welcome than on my first visit "to that place.

"In all these churches which I visited, I found "the same zeal and affection for the religion of "their forefathers. In every church the elders "stepped forth with patriarchal simplicity and "zeal, as the natural guardians of the people. The "women in general were affable and courteous in "their manners, and appeared to be as much in"terested in the objects of my visit as the men. "The children shewed nothing of the Hindoo "shyness and alarm at a stranger. They used to "mount my palanquin, and sometimes get into it. "The manners indeed of the Nayrs of both sexes "have much of the same independent frankness. "As to the Brahmins, their families live in entire "seclusion, as in a Romish convent; unlike any "thing that is known elsewhere in Hindostan. "Romish Bishop at Verapoli, near Cochin; for "whose use, indeed, I chiefly intended it."

"From Mavelycar I went to Aleppe on the sea"coast; and thence I returned into the interior of "the country as far as Changanacherry, to visit "the Romish churches in that quarter. At Pu"lingunne is a Syrian academy for the Cassanars "of the Romish church. It is under excellent "management; and if its objects were well di"rected, it would become an useful institution. "The Romans were surprised at my condescension, "as they termed it, in visiting them, having under"stood that I had visited the Syrian congregations, "and favoured their religion. For it seems the "rumour of my progress to the mountains had "already gone far abroad. 'It is true,' said I, I am "a schismatic. Colonel Macaulay and the Governor "General, and all the English are schismatics from "the Romish Church.' The priests were very "polite, and would not allow that the English were "either heretics or schismatics. 'Indeed we are,' "said I, 'as much schismatics as the Syrians in the "mountains. It will be expedient for you, there"fore, to change the name for the future, if you "have any respect for the English.' This speech, "as I afterwards heard, was carried before me to the

Dr. Buchanan next directed his course to Candenad, the residence of Mar Dionysius, the Metropolitan of the Syrian Church.

"On my arrival," he says, " I found that a great "number of his clergy had assembled from dif"ferent parts of the diocese in expectation of my "coming. The old Bishop is infirm, being now "78 years of age, and received me in an upper "chamber. He saluted me with 'a holy kiss,' "after the apostolic manner. He said he had "learnt all that had passed in my progress through "his churches. His fears from the power of the "Romish Church had now subsided; and he was "satisfied that the English were the friends of his "Church. 'His joy was like that of the Jews, "when Cyrus sent forth his mandate to rebuild the "walls of Jerusalem.' "Next morning I delivered to him a paper con"taining some subjects for the consideration of him"self and his clergy."

This related to their disposition to an union with the English Church, to such extent as should seem practicable to both; to the translation of the Scriptures into the Malayalim language, and to the establishment of Christian schools in all the parishes of his diocese. Upon these subjects some very interesting discussions took place, the substance of which will be found in the Christian Researches, pp. 128—134.

"At the close of the conference the Bishop "added, ' I am in a declining state of health, and "cannot expect to live to see these pleasing pro"spects realized, which now open to our view. But "I am the father of fifty-five churches in a heathen "land; and I must soon give up my account to "the Bishop of souls. I have been thus explicit "in declaring to you my sentiments before my "clergy, that they may act wisely, and remember "them when I am gone.' He then introduced me "to two of the priests, whom he authorized to "communicate with me, as occasion might require, "on the subjects of the present conference.

"The next morning I visited the church of Udi"amper, which is only half a mile from Candenad. "This is the church in which the celebrated synod "was held in 1599, by Menezes, Archbishop of Goa. "It is a spacious edifice. "

From Udiamper Dr. Buchanan proceeded to Cochin.

'' On my arrival," he continues, " I slept the first "night at the house of Mr. V. the old Dutch go"vernor. Next morning I went over to an island "about two miles from Cochin, on which Colonel "Macaulay has a house. He received me with "great kindness, and has paid me much attention

"during my stay in Malabar. Colonel M. is a man "of letters; and had, previously to my coming, "collected various information and many manu"scripts, Syrian and Syrochaldaic, for my inspection. "He had also procured a copy of certain chapters' "of the Jewish Scriptures, which he understood I "wished to see.

"In a few days after my arrival, he accompanied "me to the Rajah of Cochin's palace, and thence "to Udiamper and Candenad. The old Bishop "was much gratified with this second visit, and "considered it as a proof of our affection for his "church. Colonel M. intimated to him that he "perfectly accorded with me in the measures that "had been proposed, and invited the Bishop to "dine with us at Cochin. This invitation his bad "health would not allow him to accept; but he "sent over two of his principal clergy to consult "with me further on the affairs of the Church."

From this place Dr. Buchanan visited Cranganore, the spot on which the Apostle Thomas is said to have first landed in India; Paroor, the church of which place bears the name of St. Thomas, and is said to be the most ancient in Malabar; and Verapoli, the residence of a Romish bishop, and the Pope's apostolic vicar.

"Before my arrival, the Bishop had lent some "books to Colonel M., one of which was ' La "Croze's Christianisme des Indes,' a book marked "in the Bishop's library as ' liber hereticus; pro VOL. H. G

"hibitus.' This book he wished to get back, lest "it should fall into my hands. Colonel M. re"fused to give it, knowing it was his intention to "burn it. I visited the Bishop at Verapoli, and "explained to him that I had not come to notice "*his* church, but to take care of a flock who seemed "to have no church of its own. It seems that he "and all the priests at Verapoli had taken it for "granted that my purpose was to Subjugate them "to the Church of England. 'How,' said, I,' could "I possibly think of effecting such a change?' I "shall not soon forget the answer. 'If the English "government should desire it, and threaten to "withdraw its protection if we did not comply, "what alternative would be left?' I answered that "I was glad to find they were so compliant, but "I had no proposition to make to them on that "subject. Only I should be much obliged to them "to give the Scriptures to the people. If they "were afraid of the inquisition at Goa, I could "promise that not one of them should be burnt.

"The Bishop has opened his library to me, and "shewn me many important records of his church. "He is indeed very cordial in his assistance, if I "may judge from his endeavours to afford me in"formation.

"You will perhaps think that my mission to "Malabar has terminated very satisfactorily with"out noticing *manuscripts*. These are certainly "of but secondary consideration with me, though "the learned will probably consider them to be of "primary importance."

Dr. Buchanan then relates his success in obtaining both Syrian and Hebrew manuscripts, and describes the brass tablets, fac-similes of which he procured at Cochin, and on which are engraved the privileges granted several centuries since to the Christians and Jews by the native princes of Malabar. But of all these circumstances a particular account is already before the public.

In the course of his tour, Dr. Buchanan made drawings of several of the Syrian churches on the spot; of which, though extremely simple, and with one exception exhibiting only the principal front of each building, it has been thought desirable to obtain engravings, as an accompaniment to this part of his Memoirs. They represent the old church of Paroor, those of Candenad and Udiamper, and that of Alangatta. The three former have been already particularly mentioned. Of the latter it will appear, that Dr. Buchanan merely states his intention of visiting it. It is said to be the largest of the Syrian temples, and a very handsome and noble building. The church of Paroor, as Dr. Buchanan remarked generally of the most ancient Syrian structures, is not unlike some of the old parish churches in England. The other three Christian Researches, pp. 128. 143. 232. 234. Asiatic Researches, *vol.* vii.

are more ornamented, and evidently in the style of architecture prevalent in Asia Minor and Syria. The sketches of these venerable buildings can scarcely be contemplated without exciting some tribute of applause to the Christian zeal and energy which prompted Dr. Buchanan to explore the recesses amidst which they had been for ages concealed, and to shed around them that scriptural light which poverty and neglect had well nigh extinguished.

The following miscellaneous extracts from his letter to Mr. Brown, dated Cochin, may next be added.

Colonel Macaulay has been fortunate enough to "incline the Travancore court to the belief, that "all the Christian churches are, and necessarily "must be, cognizable, in respect of interior ma"nagement, and the appointment of Bishops, by the ' Christian King, who is now Sovereign of India. "The Bishop of Cochin, lately appointed from "Goa, arrived while I was here. But he could not "enter on the duties of his office until he was "recognized by the British Resident, who gave "him his authority to be presented to the govern"ment of Travancore. The Bishop of Cochin ' presides over most of the churches on the sea"coast, towards the south.

"As to the Christians in the territories of the "King of Cochin, the Dutch constantly assumed "the entire management of the churches, and even "the collection of the revenues due to the Rajah "from the Christians. This was done to preserve "the people from oppression. It would be desir"able that a similar right were exercised by the "English government in relation to the Christians "in the territories of the King of Travancore.

"I was present the other night at the mar

"riage of the daughter of Nathaniel, the richest "Jew of the place. It was a very splendid solem"nity. The women were covered with gold and "silver Dacca and Surat muslins, that being the "costume on such occasions from time immemo"rial.

"The weather on the coast is still dry and plea"sant. I have had no cold as yet this year; an "indisposition which I never escaped in Calcutta "in the months of October and November. I "expect to leave Malabar in about a fortnight, and "shall probably be with you in Bengal about the "end of February. Swartz's catechist is still with '' me. I forget whether I mentioned to you that "one of Mr. Swartz's brass lamps is destined for "you. It is called the Halle University lamp. It "gives a bright and steady light, and a square "moveable canopy shade preserves the eyes. It is "worn thin by the midnight lucubrations of the old "man; for he was a hard student to the last year "of his life.

"I am now about to visit the interior of this "country a third time, and shall first proceed to "Angamalee, formerly an archbishopric of the Sy"rian Christians. I have written to you thus particularly of my tour through Malabar, in order, that if I should be long delayed in my return, you may know what has been done. I have succeeded certainly in the general objects of my enquiry beyond my most sanguine expectations.

"Mr. H. at Angengo has heard of an ancient history of Malabar in the Malayalim language, which his linguist has promised to procure. The Rajah's dewan tells me, that it is referred to in public acts. Mr. H. says, there are in the episcopal library at Verapoli some volumes on Shanscrit literature from the Propaganda, which, if possible, I shall procure for Mr. Colebrooke's inspection. I wish Mr. C. himself were here. The Brahmins still aver, that Malabar is the "cradle of Shanscrit science; and Colonel Macaulay has adopted that opinion fully. It possibly existed here at as early a period as in the north, but not with the same advantages of improvement,"

The date of Dr. Buchanan's next letter is December 14th, from Angamalee in Malabar. Though the name of this place occurs in the extracts published by himself from his Journal, the following account of it will be found to be fuller and more interesting.

a Christian Researches., p. 133.

"Angamalee was formerly the seat of the Archbishop of the Syrian churches in the mountains of Malabar. In the town of Angamalee there are three churches within a quarter of a mile from each other, in all of which service is still performed. The cathedral church is the largest, and contains the tombs of bishops and archbishops for many centuries. As I approached the town of Angamalee in the evening, I heard the "'sullen roar' of the great bell reverberating through the mountains. When the Romish Archbishop Menezes visited this place in 1599, the Christians strewed the way up the hill with flowers as he advanced. And yet he came to burn the ancient libraries and archives of Angamalee. As the flame ascended, the old priests wept; but they were obliged to hide their tears, dreading the inquisition at Goa. The Archbishop presented himself next day to the multitude, arrayed in his pontificals, resplendent with gold and precious stones. To this day they have a lively tradition of the splendour of his robes blazing in the sun, and forming a striking contrast with the plain white garments of their own primitive church. When Tippoo waged war with the King of Travancore in 1791, he sent detachments in every direction to destroy the Christian churches, and particularly the ancient edifices at Angamalee. Two thousand men penetrated into the mountains, and were directed to the place by the sound of its

"bells. They sprung a mine under the altar walls of each church, and the inhabitants who had fled to the higher mountains-witnessed the explosion. But the walls of the grand front being five feet and a half thick (I measured them yesterday), they did not attempt to demolish them for want of powder. In the mean time Tippoo, hearing that Lord Cornwallis had invaded Mysore, suddenly recalled his church-destroying detachments. Next year Tippoo was obliged to sign any terms that were offered him; but Lord Cornwallis forgot to desire him to rebuild the Christian churches. The inhabitants, however, have rendered them fit for public worship; and have proceeded some way in restoring the cathedral to its former state. The Archbishop's residence and all the other public buildings are destroyed. The priests led me over the ruins, and shewed me the vestiges of their ancient grandeur, asking me if I thought their Zion would ever be rebuilt. Angamalee is built on a hill. I told them, that their second temple would perhaps have more glory than their first.

"Two of the churches here are Roman, the third Syrian. But the two former would gladly return to their mother church.

"Colonel Macaulay accompanied me half way in my present excursion. I find the Syrian churches to the north much more splendid than those to the south. The books also are more numerous. I am now going to visit Alangatta and Edapalli, where formerly there was a Syrian monastery."

The preceding account of Dr. Buchanan's first visit to the coast of Malabar can scarcely be better closed than by the following letter to Mr. Henry Thornton, which comprises a brief but animated sketch of the whole; and which, notwithstanding the repetition of a few particulars which will be familiar to some readers, will not, it is presumed, prove uninteresting to any.

"Cochin, 24th December, 1806.

"Dear Sir,

"In August or September last I addressed a fetter to you from the Pagoda of Seringham, near Tritchinopoli. Since that period I have visited Ceylon, and many places in Southern Coromandel, and in the province of Malabar. I passed a week at the palace of the Rajah of Travancore, who aids me very liberally in all my pursuits. The Brahmins and present minister had taught the young man (he is only twenty-five) to oppress the Christians. But he promises milder treatment in future. This favourable change is produced by the exertions of Colonel Macaulay, the Resident, who I am happy to say is mUch alive to the interests of religion.

"From the sea-coast I proceeded into the interior of the country, to visit the ancient Syrian Christians who inhabit the hills at the bottom of the great mountains of Malayala. The weather was cool and pleasant. The country is picturesque and highly cultivated, diversified with hill and dale, and winding streams. These streams fall from the mountains, and preserve the valleys in perpetual verdure. The Christians received me courteously, seeing I travelled in some state, escorted by the Rajah's servants. But when they found my object was to look into their books and religion, they surveyed me with doubtful countenance, not well understanding how an Englishman could have any interest in the Christian religion. The contrary was only proved to them by long and serious discussion, and by the evidence of facts which for the first time came to their knowledge. But when their doubts had been dispelled, they sent deputies with me, who introduced me to all the other churches. No European, or even Romish priest, had ever, as they told me, visited that remote region. There are no Romish churches in its vicinity, and the Rajah gives no permission to Europeans to travel into the interior of his country.

"The Syrian is still their sacred language, and some of the laymen understand it; but the Malayalim is the vulgar tongue. I proposed to send a Malayalim translation of the Bible to each of the churches; and they assured me, that every man who could write would be glad to make a copy for his own family. They also agreed to establish schools in each parish for Christian instruction, which are to be under the direction of the four chief elders of each parish, and in which the Bible in the vulgar tongue is to be a principal class book.

"Their doctrines are not in essentials at variance with those of the Church of England. They desire an union, or at least such a connection as may be practicable or desirable for the better advancement of the interests of Christianity in India.

"As to manuscripts, I have succeeded far beyond my most sanguine expectations.

"It had been supposed that the Roman Catholics had destroyed in 1599 all the Syrian books. But it appears that they did not destroy.one copy of the *Bible;* and I have now in my possession some MSS. of the Scriptures of a high antiquity. The collation of these with our western copies is very interesting. There are some other MSS. which were not condemned by the Synod of Menezes. I have also found some old Hebrew MSS. biblical and historical.

"It is sufficiently established by the concurrence of oral tradition with written records, that the Jews were on this coast before the Christian era.

"I propose to send home some Syrian youth to England for education and ordination, if practicable. And I take with me to Bengal a Malayalim, a Syrian, and a Jewish servant. They will, however, be but nominal servants. I should have engaged them as moonshees; but I see there is no college now in Bengal.

"The Roman Catholics here were at first very jealous of my attention to the Syrians. The Romish Bishop, however, who is a *bon vivant,* perceiving that my chief object was to diffuse the Scriptures among the people, began to think that it might be politic in him to circulate them among his people too, and to please the English rather than the inquisition. Colonel Macaulay thinks the Bishop will adopt the measure the moment we seriously propose it. He lives in some state, and fires a salute of eleven guns on occasion.

"Cochin is rich in Hebrew literature, and I am purchasing what is to be sold. "The Rajah of Cochin has followed the example of the Rajahs of Travancore, of Tanjore, and the Ranny of Ramnad, and Ramisseram, in giving me catalogues of the Shanscrit books in the temples. I hope the Coorga Rajah will do the same.

"This opening of the Pagodas is a new scene in India. Mr. Swartz was the remote instrument. He opened the Rajah of Tanjore's heart; and the Rajah opened the Pagodas, those chambers of imagery, the emblem of the heart.

"The Rajah of Tanjore wishes me to visit him again. If practicable, I shall open a correspondence with him.

"I propose to leave this coast in a fortnight, and proceed to Bombay, from whence I shall probably go across to Benares, and thence down to Calcutta by the Ganges.

"Having arrived at the extreme boundary of my tour, and accomplished its object, I thought it would be acceptable to you to have some short notices of it. Be pleased to tell Mr. Newton that I am well. I wrote him a long letter from Tanjore. It is with pleasure I see that, amidst the agitations of the world, he is tranquil, and at peace, and nearly arrived at the haven where he would be. Mar Dionysius, the Bishop of the Syrians in the mountains, has somewhat of Mr. Newton's manner and appearance; only that the Bishop has a venerable long beard, which reaches below his girdle, and through which you may see a large gold cross beaming at intervals. He is now seventy-eight years of age, amiable in his temper, and devout according to his knowledge.

"I read at this place, in Hayley's third volume, Cowper's correspondence with Mr. Newton, and was pleased to see the name of the good man honoured.
I remain,
Dear Sir,
Very sincerely yours,
   C. Buchanan."

In his next letter to Mr. Brown, Dr. Buchanan announced his intention of shortly returning to Bengal, together with a farther plan which he was projecting respecting a visit to the Christian churches in Chaldea and Syria.

"Cochin, 23d January, 1807

"I am happy to hear that the first Gospel in "Chinese and Shanscrit is ready.

"I should have left Cochin before now, but some "splendid events have taken place. The Syrian "Church finding I was their friend indeed, opened "new sources of antiquity. I visited them once "more; and the Bishop presented to me an ancient "copy of the Old and New Testament in Syriac, "on thick vellum, reputed to be as old as the "Alexandrine. On the other hand, the Jews "were softened by gold, and a singular discovery "was made."

This referred to some valuable Hebrew manuscripts, of which Dr. Buchanan gave a full account in his Christian Researches, and which will be again noticed hereafter. The letter thus proceeds.

"I despatched on the 3d instant three chests "of books and MSS. to my own address, and to "your care. Be pleased to open them, and air "the contents. I shall carry round with me three '"chests more. My hands are so fully occupied "here, that I cannot proceed farther up the coast "at this time; besides I see you are desirous that "I should return. I therefore purpose to take my "passage in a large Danish vessel, now here and "ready to sail. I have promised to visit the Sy"rians and the Jews once more before I leave the "country, if practicable. The information I have "received from the Syrian Christians strongly inclines me to visit their fellow-churches in Chaldea and Syria. The ancient patriarchate of Antioch is just expiring, unless supported by the English Church. As it will be more convenient for a sea-sick traveller to go by land, I had always proposed to myself that route. And this new inducement will probably lead me to adopt it, about the conclusion of the present year, or whenever the monsoon will carry a ship rapidly into the Persian Gulph. These things I have thought of, not thinking that I can do much more in India; but I leave them to the issue which God in his allwise counsel shall be pleased to give. I have certainly no pleasure in the thought of returning to England, or of staying in India. The world (as the world) is equally distasteful to me every where. If I knew where it was the will of God I should pass my days, I should there lie down contented; and endeavour to do some good in a quiet and humble way.

"In one of the chests you will find some shawls. Let J. and H. choose one each; and each of the boys may choose a Hebrew book."

Dr. Buchanan's last letter to his friend, previously to his embarking for Calcutta, contained the important information of his having actually made arrangements for the translation of the Scriptures into the native language of Malabar. His success therefore, as to the great objects of his journey, had been complete.

"Cochin, 29th January, 1807.

"I received your letter of the 31 st ultimo, and am glad to hear that you have ended the year so well and so happily.

"I embark to-morrow in the Danish ship, Danesberg, for Calcutta; and shall touch at Columbo. I hope to be with you early in March. I send a chest of books and MSS. to England by the Bombay ships, which touch here.

"I am now about to encounter sea-sickness for a while. If I call at Mr. T's, in Columbo, it will be some relief, for I have much to do there. It is understood by all ranks here that I shall call on them six months hence on my way to the Persian Gulph. I have expended a large sum here. Mr. F. told me he had orders from his government (Madras) to supply me with any money I might want. But I did not avail myself of this kindness.

"My servant, who came from Calcutta, is still with me. He was formerly a ship-cook, and will be useful now by sea, as he has long been by land. Mr. Swartz's catechist, and other attendants, wait here to see me on board; as do various Syrian, Romish, and Jewish priests. I am glad to get out of the throng.

"I hope I have come to this place for good, and not for evil. The goodness is God's, and the evil is my own. It is wonderful that I should have travelled so far in safety; and that, after the strange events that have occurred, I now leave the coast in peace. If I should never see you, my testimony is gone forth to the world, and others must carry on what is now begun.

"The Tamul copy of the Scriptures (complete) is only arrived to-day from the Carnatic; I proceed with it to-morrow to the Syrian Bishop, who is now engaged with three learned Syrian and Malayalim scholars in the translation into the language of Malabar. The Bishop longed to see the Tamul, he being a good Malayalim scholar himself.

"I leave the three translators at monthly wages; and Colonel Macaulay superintends when I am gone.

"The Romish Bishop has consented to the circulation of the Scriptures throughout his diocese; so that there will be upwards of 200,000 persons who are ready to receive the Malayalim Bible."

Dr. Buchanan did not leave Cochin quite so soon VOL. II. H as he had anticipated in the preceding letter; but on the 6th of February he embarked on board the Danesberg, after having despatched the following letter to his valuable friend and coadjutor, Colonel Macaulay.

"My dear Sir,

"I have directed Messrs. Harrington and Co. at Madras to honour all drafts of yours for any sums you shall have the goodness to lay out on my account. I leave to you to settle the sum for the Verapoli Cassanar.

"Mr. Swartz's catechist stays a month at Candenad, to shew them the best plan of proceeding in the translation. If any obstacle to their progress should occur from the Tamburan, or Mar Thoma's fear, I shall be obliged to you to transfer the translation establishment to Tanjore, whither the chief man has no objection to go. If a Verapoli Cassanar, of Syrian and Malayalim learning, could be prevailed on to go to Tanjore also, the establishment would be complete.

"I cannot leave you without expressing my sense of the peculiar obligations I am under for your uniform assistance in every subject which has engaged my attention on this coast. Without your direct countenance, I certainly could have done little or nothing. Something beneficial to the country will, I trust, result from what has been done; though the circumstance of your leaving it presents but a doubtful aspect.

"Believe me to be,
My dear Sir,
Very sincerely yours,
C. Buchanan." CHAP. VI.

DR. BUCHANAN arrived safely at Calcutta, after a voyage of five weeks, on the 15th of March, having accomplished an arduous but most interesting journey of more than five thousand miles. On his return he found that the college of Fort William, which had flourished nearly seven years, and during that period had been productive of the most important benefits both to the service of the East India Company and to oriental learning and religion, had been reduced within very narrow limits on the first of January. The offices of Provost and ViceProvost were abolished, and the Professorships restricted to three; viz. the Hindostanee, Bengalee, and Perso-Arabic; it being intended that the students should only be attached to it, on an average, for a single year.

The public letter of the Court of Directors which conveyed this order was dated in May, and reached Calcutta in December 1806. On its arrival, Mr. Brown, deeply impressed with the importance of the moral discipline which had hitherto been exercised in the college of Fort William, and which was now superseded, felt it to be his duty to submit his sentiments upon the subject to the Governor General, and accompanied his representations with the offer of continuing to superintend the institution, and, if that were deemed necessary, to officiate without salary.

In making this communication to Sir George Barlow, Mr. Brown referred to his highly esteemed colleague, Dr. Buchanan, as follows.

"I particularly regret that there should be a "necessity for any material change during the ab"sence of the Vice-Provost, without his concur"rence or knowledge, from the consideration of his "having throughout so eminently devoted his su"perior talents, with the utmost zeal, and by every "exertion for the benefit of the public service, in "the success of the college. In his absence, I take "it upon me to communicate faithfully my thoughts, "and to submit them with respect and deference to "the consideration of the honourable the Governor "General"

Sir George Barlow, en receiving the representation and offer of Mr. Brown just referred to, expressed himself deeply struck and gratified by his philanthropy and disinterestedness, and assured him that " he should consider of his proposal." No farther notice of it, however, appears to have been taken; but the new modification of the college immediately took place, and the offices of Provost and Vice-Provost were accordingly abolished.

The labours, the influence, and the income of Dr. Buchanan were in consequence of this arrange Memorial Sketches of the Rev. D. Brown, p. 313. ment materially diminished. The reduction of the former was not only grateful to his taste and inclination, but necessary to his health; while that of the latter affected him only as it tended to abridge his means and opportunities of usefulness. The subject occurs but once in his various correspondence with his friends, and is then stated merely as a matter of information, in which he did not seem to be particularly interested.

His grand object was the promotion of Christianity in India. TlnVhe had kept steadily in view during the period of his Vice-Provostship; for this, as we have already seen, he made some provision when anticipating its abolition; and it was in pursuance of the same important object that he undertook the extensive journey through which we have lately accompanied him.

During his voyage, or immediately after his return to Calcutta, Dr. Buchanan had drawn' up a paper, under the title of " Literary Intelligence," containing a sketch of his proceedings on the coast of Malabar, which he was desirous of publishing both at Madras and Calcutta, for the information of those who were interested in the promotion of Christian knowledge in India. To the great surprise, however, of Dr. Buchanan, and of many of the most learned and respectable persons at both Presidencies, it was not thought expedient to per mit such a publication to be inserted in the government gazette. It was, in consequence, printed and circulated in a different form; and, without producing any of the ill effects which some had anticipated, it conveyed intelligence which was as gratifying to the friends of learning and religion in India, as the same information afterwards proved to persons of a similar character in England. It is to this circumstance that Dr. Buchanan refers in his subsequent correspondence with Colonel Macaulay; which will afford a connected view of his proceedings after his return to Calcutta. The following is an extract from one of his first letters to that gentleman.

"Calcutta, 4th April, 1807.

"The alarm of this government, *quoad suayyeXm,* "is subsiding. Your government also seems well "again. At least so writes the Rev. Mr. Thompson, "to whom Lord William declared, ' that the pro"motion of Christianity is on his heart, and that he "wishes for more missionaries.

"This Society anxiously anticipates the con"firmation of the report, that Lord Wellesley has The "Literary Intelligence" appears, however, to have been admitted into the Bombay gazette, by which means it reached Europe. It was afterwards published in England by the late Bishop Porteus. See Dr. Buchanan's Apology for promoting Christianity in India, p. 87 j and Owen's History of the British and Foreign Bible Society, vol. i. p. 320.

"been appointed a Secretary of State. I believe "it would be as agreeable to them, as to hear that "Buonaparte had *lost a leg;* which is also re"ported.

"Major Wilks's letter has been read here with "much interest. I think you are doing mqre in the "Deccan, than we in Hindostan.

"I send you a letter from the Bishop of Llandaff, "which has made some noise here. Had the Lite"rary Intelligence not been suppressed, the Bishop's letter would not have been published."

The letter thus referred to was afterwards inserted by Dr. Buchanan at the close of his Christian Researches. The extracts from it which follow, while they are honourable to the Christian zeal of the late learned and eloquent prelate whose name it bears, will not here be deemed irrelevant.

"Calgarth Park, Kendal, 14th May, 1S06. "Some weeks ago I received your Memoir of "the expediency of an Ecclesiastical Establish"ment for British India; for which obliging at"tention I now return you my best thanks. I "hesitated for some time whether I ought to in"terrupt your speculations with my acknowledg"ments for so valuable a present; but on being "informed of the noble premium, by which you "purpose to exercise the talents of Graduates in "the University of Cambridge, I determined to ex"press to you my admiration of your disinterest"edness and zeal in the cause of Christianity.

"Twenty years and more have now elapsed "since, in a sermon before the House of Lords, I "hinted to the then government, the propriety of "paying regard to the propagation of Christianity "in India; and I have since, as fit occasions of"fered, privately, but unsuccessfully, pressed the "matter on the consideration of those in power. "If my voice or opinion can, in future, be of any

"Weight with the King's ministers, I shall be most "ready to exert myself, in forwarding any prudent "measure for promoting a liberal ecclesiastical ". establishment in British India: it is not without "consideration that I say a liberal establishment, "because I heartily wish that every Christian "should be at liberty to worship God according "to his conscience, and be assisted therein by a "teacher, at the public expense, of his own per"suasion.

"The subjects you have proposed for the work "which shall obtain your prize, are all of them ju"diciously chosen, and, if properly treated, (as my "love for my Alma Mater persuades me they will "be,) may probably turn the thoughts of the legis"lature towards the measure you recommend.

"God in his providence hath so ordered things, "that America, which three hundred years ago was "peopled by none but Pagans, has now many mil"lions of Christians in it; and will not, probably, three hundred years hence, have a single Pagan in "it, but be occupied by more Christians, and more "enlightened Christians, than now exist in Eu"rope.

"Africa is not now worse fitted for the recep"tion of Christianity than America was, when it "was first visited by Europeans; and Asia is much "better fitted for it, inasmuch as Asia enjoys a "considerable degree of civilization; and some "degree of it is necessary to the successful in"troduction of Christianity. The commerce and "colonization of Christian states have civilized "America; and they will, in process of time, ci"vilize and christianize the whole earth. Whether "it be a Christian duty to attempt, by lenient me"thods, to propagate the Christian religion among "Pagans and Mahomedans, can be doubted, I think, "by few; but whether any attempt will be attended "with much success till Christianity is purified from "its corruptions, and the lives of Christians are "rendered correspondent to their Christian pro"fession, may be doubted by many: but there cer"tainly never was a more promising opportunity of "trying the experiment of subverting Paganism in "India, than that which has for some years been "offered to the government of Great Britain.

"Your publication has given us in England a "great insight into the state of Christianity in "India, as well as into the general state of learning "amongst you, and it has excited in me the warmest "wishes for the prosperity of the college of Fort "William. It is an institution which would have "done honour to the wisdom of Solon or Lycurgus. "I have no knowledge personally of the Marquis Wellesley; but I shall think of him and of his "coadjutors in this undertaking with the highest "respect and admiration, as long as I live.

"I cannot enter into any particulars relative to "an ecclesiastical establishment in India; nor would "it, perhaps, be proper to press government to take "the matter into their consideration, till this coun"try is freed from the danger which threatens it: "but I have that opinion of his Majesty's ministers, "that they will, not only from policy, but from a "serious sense of religious duty, be disposed to "treat the subject, whenever it comes before them, "with great judgment and liberality. May God "direct their counsels!"

A few days after the date of his former letter, Dr. Buchanan wrote to Colonel Macaulay as follows.
"Calcutta, 13th April, 1807.
"My dear Sir, "I have been favoured with both your letters, with their enclosures, and return you many thanks for your kind attention. Your first contained the Hebrew MS. I am perfectly satisfied with Levi's explanation of the cause of its detention. But I am not equally satisfied with his candour as to the opprobrious omission of the word *bo* in the last verse of the 27th of Deuteronomy. It is true, as you observe, that there is one 3 in that verse, ' all the people;' but there ought to be another, viz. 'all the words;' which the modern Jewish copies have not. But it is in the Samaritan copies, and also in the Syriac copy I brought from Travancore. I one day read the verse to Levi in a Jew's house in Mattinceri, and pointed out the omission. He ought, therefore, to have been candid enough to have recollected that. But poor Levi's ideas are always in a whirl.

"Your second letter, which I had the pleasure of receiving yesterday, contained Major Wilks's very interesting letter, and that of your writer, not less important. But what relates to yourself ought first to have my attention. I am much concerned to hear that your health is declining, and that you must leave India so soon.

"In November next I propose to sail for Cochin and Bombay; and thence to the Persian Gulph. My purpose is made known to government, and also the objects of a route overland.

"Since I shall be myself at Cochin in November or December, it will not be necessary for you to make any arrangement at this time for sending home the Syrian youths. I shall then be better able to judge of the prudence and importance of the measure.

"I could have wished to have a Syrian moonshee with me here for a few months before I go; but if it be not perfectly convenient to ship him off in time, you need not think further of it.

"I am happy to hear that the Malayalim translation proceeds with such spirit. Mr. Kolhoff writes to me, that he is very ready to undertake the superintendance of that work, if untoward circumstances should impede its progress in Travancore.

"The reason why I did not communicate to you the 'Literary Intelligence,' was, that you might be exonerated from the consequences of the publication of that paper, should there be any unpleasant result in a political way. The Madras government deemed it to be so dangerous, that they refused to publish it. The government here *par nobile)* refused also. This suppression of what almost all sensible men accounted to be merely 'literary intelligence,' has given great offence to the men of letters in the settlement. The consequence has been, that it is printed in the form of a pamphlet in large 4to, and in large type, with *Buhner s blaze,* and there is added something yet more offensive, viz. the Oxford and Cambridge notifications of the five hundred pound prizes, (which were also suppressed here;) and what is more offensive than the last, a copy of the second Latin letter addressed to me by the University of Cambridge, on the subject of diffusing a knowledge of revealed religion amongst the nations of Asia. This pamphlet of twenty-eight pages will be exposed for sale next week.

"and I, are on terms of high civility; but he is no friend to my evangelical purposes, and he does not like my (and your) steady adherence to the principles of Lord W.'s administration. But I wish to be at peace with all men; and I ever desire to conciliate my enemies. I mean enemies made by my evangelizing plans, for I have no other; and perhaps these are few in number.

"The Christian tablets, Syrian Bible, and Hebrew roll, are here objects of great curiosity. Mr. Carey beheld them with veneration. The public mind is strongly attracted towards Malayala; and the wall between Hinduism and Christianity seems to be tottering. You have applied the battering-ram to that wall with good effect in Travancore; and I sincerely wish that you could stay to give it a few more shocks. But you will be useful at home. I go home also; but only perhaps for a season. At least in the pamphlet now printed it is mentioned that I am going home overland, ' for the purpose of visiting the ancient Christian churches in Mesopotamia and Syria, and that I shall return to India in a short time.' Some were ready to *wish me a good journey;* but they did not expect this last clause, of *returning*. It has, however, given great satisfaction, I understand, to almost all the settlement. For you must know that 's per secution (as it has been called) of a good work, has procured It much success and many friends. is faithful. dubious of what is right. Sir H.

Russel, Sir J. Royds, and Sir W. Burroughs, are all friendly. So is Mr. Harington. The Malayala battering-ram is said to have given C. a violent and unexpected shock, which is likely to crumble his wall of hostility into the ruins of indifference. For so our Persians speak.

"I have had a letter from the Bishop of London, dated 1 st September last; in which he says, that it was too late last session to bring forward the proposition of an Ecclesiastical Establishment for British India; but that the Archbishop of Canterbury intends to move his Majesty's ministers on the subject next session.'

"His Lordship also says, that money will probably be sent out to support the great work of translating the Scriptures into the oriental languages. Lord Barham writes to the same effect on both subjects.

"I have placed the young Malayalim moonshee from Paroor, in the missionary school at Serampore, where he is very happy and in good health. I should be glad that your writer would communicate this to his mother. My Hebrew moonshee is well also. tdb/,

"Lord Minto's arrival is anxiously looked for by this settlement. I shall write to you again shortly, and remain,

"With much esteem,

Yours sincerely,

C. Buchanan."

The plan of a journey overland to Europe, mentioned in the preceding and in some subsequent letters, was proposed and long cherished by Dr. Buchanan, not merely as obviating his well-founded objection to a sea voyage, but as calculated to promote his benevolent researches into the state of the ancient and declining Christian churches in the East. It will, however, be seen, that, after many enquiries, he was at length reluctantly compelled, by political and military obstacles, to abandon this interesting expedition.

It may seem extraordinary, that of the addresses to Dr. Buchanan from the senate of the University of Cambridge, no more distinct or complete information should be contained in these Memoirs than the reference to the second of them in the foregoing letter. They probably expressed the sense which that learned body entertained of Dr. Buchanan's meritorious exertions in promoting the interests of learning and religion in the East, and of his munificent encouragement of those important objects by the series of prizes offered to the members of the University. No traces, however, of the letters in question have heen discovered among his papers; nor is it known that any copy of the pamphlet in which the second was printed in India has reached this country. It is therefore only to be regretted that no farther account can be given of documents which were, doubtless, highly valued by Dr. Buchanan, and equally honourable to him and to the distinguished body from which they proceeded.

Of the several objects of Dr. Buchanan's late tour it was stated to be one, to discover fit instruments for the promotion of learning, and for the dissemination of the Scriptures in India. It may now be observed, that it was in the course of his journey that he first thought of a plan which might effectually accomplish that object. The reader will probably recollect the meditation of Dr. Buchanan on the banks of the Chilka Lake; where, on the morning of the Sabbath, while reflecting on the painful scene which he had just witnessed, with the lofty tower of Juggernaut still in distant view, he conceived the design of some Christian Institution, which might gradually counteract, and at length extinguish, the idolatry of the eastern world. The historian of the Decline and Fall of the Roman Empire informs us, that he first conceived the a The Vice-Chancellor of the University, upon an application being made to him for copies of these letters, declined granting them.

VOL. II. I thought of his elaborate and eloquent work amidst the ruins of the Capitol. It was an association of a more sublime and sacred nature which suggested to Dr. Buchanan the design of the Institution, the general plan of which he then briefly described. Soon after his return to Calcutta, he employed himself in digesting and arranging its form and constitution; and on the 28th of May he thus adverts to the subject at the close of the following letter to Colonel Macaulay.

"My dear Sir, "I had the pleasure-to receive your letter of the 1st inst. two days ago, accompanying the Dutch translation.

"I am happy to hear that you have two Hebrew books for me. If any thing interesting in Hebrew '-or Syriac, printed or in manuscript, should offer while you remain on the coast, I shall be obliged to you to secure it for me.

"I presented the Bishop's" demand on Baretto's house, and enclose the answer. My compliments to the Bishop. I shall take care of his affairs, and send him *cauliflowers* when the season arrives.

"Dr. Leyden proceeds by sea to Madras to-morrow. He is in better health. He has been looking at a variety of my MSS. for some weeks past, but with little success. He can make nothing of the Of Verapoli.

Christian plates; but means to renew his attack on the Malayalim part of them when he arrives at Madras. He thinks the old Syriac Bible on vellum is as early as the fifth or sixth century. But that is certainly too high a period.

"The Indus sails as a packet for England in a few days. I have said in a letter, that you are meditating your return this season. By the Indus I send home a small work for publication; not in relation to Malabar, but to Juggernaut; nor to him directly, but to a Literary Institution, whose object shall be to promote Christian knowledge in Asia by means of books; which Institution shall be exclusively literary, and shall have no connection with any mission society. The Institution already exists, and is in extensive operation. I shall copy the heads of the sections on the opposite page. Nothing yet from England!

"I remain,
My dear Sir,
Very sincerely yours,
C. Buchanan."

Instead of inserting the short sketch to which Dr. Buchanan refers, it will be more satisfactory to give a fuller abstract of a work, which, though printed, it was afterwards deemed not expedient to publish. The title was as follows. "The Chris"tian Institution in the East: or the College for "translating the Holy Scriptures into the Oriental "Tongues."

The origin and objects of the Institution were described nearly in the terms of the preceding letter. It was dedicated to all good men, to be an instrument in their hands of extending the knowledge of revealed religion by the translation of the holy Scriptures, and was placed under the immediate patronage of the Archbishop of Canterbury, as President of the Society for the Propagation of the Gospel in Foreign Parts, and of the Society for promoting Christian Knowledge. One of its subordinate objects was to print small tracts on certain branches of art and science, fitted for popular use and improvement.

The various instruments of the Institution were next enumerated; comprising the venerable Bishop of the Syrian Church in Malayala; the British and Danish missionaries throughout India; Judah Misrahi, a learned Jew of Cochin, engaged by Dr. Buchanan as a translator of the New Testament into Hebrew; Professor Lassar for the Chinese language; and the late Rev. Henry Martyn, with two learned coadjutors, natives of the East, for the Persian, Arabic, and Hindostanee languages. With the exception of Mr. Martyn, who arrived at Calcutta during the absence of Dr. Buchanan, he stated that he had visited all the before-named persons at their respective residences, and had informed himself as to their abilities and principles.

It was not intended to form an expensive establishment; but that a professor should be stationed as a literary agent of the college in each of the principal provinces of the East, to study a particular language, to collect information, to correspond with the Society at home, to compose and to print books, and to instruct the natives in printing. The literary agents were in general to be paid for *work done;* that is, for translations or for printing, previously agreed for, and faithfully executed. Care was also to be taken, that, in cases where translations of the Scriptures should be entrusted to the members of any particular sect, their exclusive tenets should not find admission into the work.

Dr. Buchanan proposed, that the name of the Institution should not be derived from any church or sect in Europe, but from the religion itself, the knowledge of which it was intended to diffuse; and that the instruments which it would recognize in promoting this great design should be of all nations.

He next observed, that in order to secure its resources from failure, and that there might always be a copious supply of fit persons for the work, it was expedient, that the Institution should possess an organized body in England, and that its establishment should be sufficiently respectable to attach to it men of rank and learning. The college of the Propaganda at Rome owed its efficiency and perpetuity chiefly to its liberal establishment.

Dr. Buchanan grounded the necessity and importance of this Christian Institution upon a view of the present state of the Brahminical superstition at the chief temples of the Hindoos, and particularly at Juggernaut; and in order to convey to his readers in England some idea of the spirit and effects of the religion of Brahma, he added some extracts from the journal of his visit to that place.

Provision was made for the transmission of copies of every work published by the Institution in India to certain libraries in Great Britain; and it was stated, that thirty-one volumes had accordingly been forwarded by the packet which conveyed the work in question. It was added, that Dr. Buchanan would for the present continue to superintend the affairs of the Institution.

Such is the outline of the college for oriental translation conceived by Dr. Buchanan. His intention, in short, was to establish a British Propaganda, which, in proportion to the extent of its objects, should be superior to that at Rome, the fame of which still survives in Asia. Objections would probably have occurred to different persons with respect to some of the provisions of this Institution; and it was obviously never considered by its author as incapable of alteration and improvement. Its design and general plan were undoubtedly excellent, and would, probably, have been received with much approbation.

Upon its original formation, Dr. Buchanan proposed to the Baptist missionaries at Serampore, as extensively engaged in translating the Scriptures, that they should accordingly associate, merely in that character, with other fellow-labourers in different parts of India; that the missionary pursuits, properly so called, and the individual establishments of each society, should remain peculiar and private, as before; but that the translators of the Scriptures should act in concert, and maintain an amicable correspondence with each other, under the general direction of the superintendent, who would be responsible for the views and proceedings of the Institution at large. The intention of this proposal was clearly not to supersede the meritorious labours of the Baptist missionaries; but to render them more effective, by incorporating them in one great and comprehensive plan for the same important object, and by rescuing their operations from the appearance of any thing private or sectarian, and investing the united labours of the learned translators throughout India with a more public and national character.

It may readily be imagined, that the Society at Serampore might feel some hesitation and even reluctance in acceding to this proposition, after the publicity which Dr. Buchanan had given to their extensive plan of oriental translation; and it was, perhaps, expecting too much, that they should vo See his Apology for promoting Christianity in India, p. 70. luntarily abandon the " vantage ground" which they were thus occupying. However this may be, the Baptist missionaries declined the proposal; and the name of " the Christian Institution" was in consequence but partially assumed. The other branches of which it was intended to be composed, including, besides those already named, one of the most dis tinguished oriental scholars of the present age, the late learned and lamented Dr. Leyden, who undertook the translation of the Scriptures into the several dialects of the Malayan Archipelago, were generally associated after Dr. Buchanan's departure from India, under the superintendence of the late Rev. Mr. Brown.

The " Christian Institution" was, however, carried but very imperfectly into execution. On the arrival of the manuscript in England, though it was printed in pursuance of Dr. Buchanan's instructions, some of his friends, to whom the work was communicated, conceived that its publication was inexpedient, and might even produce consequences injurious to the general cause of Christianity in India. Under these impressions, they took upon themselves to suppress the publication of the work, more especially as Dr. Buchanan had announced his intention of returning to this country in the course of the following year. Their determination was, doubtless, guided by a sincere desire to promote the great object of his labours; and it will be seen that he acquiesced in their judgment.

With respect to the main design of the Christian Institution, as a college of acknowledged responsibility, embracing the associated learning and piety of the East for the grand purpose of sacred translation, and possessing commanding patronage, effective support, and enlarged superintendence and control, the failure of its establishment can scarcely be considered but as a subject of regret. The munificent donations of the British and Foreign Bible Society to its corresponding Committee in Bengal, combined with the exertions of its eastern auxiliary branches, and those of other societies, have undoubtedly promoted,4o a very splendid extent, the work of oriental translation. It is, however, well known, that various circumstances, inseparable from private and unconnected labours, have hitherto impeded its more complete and successful execution; nor is it probable that these will ever be removed, but by recurring to the general plan so ably and comprehensively conceived and developed by Dr. Buchanan in his " Christian Institution. "

Of the fate of this elaborate plan in England, its author was necessarily ignorant. He continued, therefore, to mention it, amongst other topics, in his succeeding letters to his friends, as if in the course of execution.

On the 9th of June, Dr. Buchanan thus wrote to Colonel Macaulay.

"My dear Sir,

"I yesterday received your letter of the 10th of May, enclosing the regulation against spiritual encroachments. It is admirably done, and the Bishop of Verapoli is saved. Your continuance in Travancore is important, if it referred to nothing else than the ecclesiastical concerns of the country.

"I am happy you stay a little longer on the coast. I shall hope to see you in November or December. All and every thing you have sent from the archives of Verapoli is interesting and important. Your account of the translation of the Scriptures gives me and others here much pleasure. *That work will prosper.* 'The Turk impedes my plan of route. I now propose to go through Armenia. I have ever been very desirous to visit the Armenian churches. But I have not determined what I shall do; for we may expect many a revolution before January next.

"The Tinavelly impostor is one of many who are lifting up their voices in the desert. This is an age for, ' Lo here, and lo there.' There is a luxation in all the joints of the Brahminical superstition, and the Wahabian philosophy is eating out Mohammedanism, as doth a canker.

"The copper-plates are arrived at the customhouse here. I shall have them to-day. I am greatly obliged to you for this rapid transmission of them.

"I thank Mr. Clephane for his friendly proposal as to the types. I shall confer with Mr. Kolhoff on that subject. A fount must be cut; that is certain. And from this fountain will flow a clear and living stream for the souls of men. I have despatched to the Archbishop of Canterbury, by the Indus, a copy of St. Matthew's Gospel in Chinese, and two of the Gospels in Shanscrit.

"I shall be obliged to your writer to inform Timapah Pulle, (who is now employed in translation at Candenad,) that I have received his letter; that I am pleased with his services; that if Colonel Macaulay deems it reasonable to add the Burdella Brahmin he speaks of to the list of translators, I shall approve of it; that I am happy he (T. Pull£) begins to consider the Christian religion the true faith; and that I will stand his godfather, agreeably to his request, if he should prove worthy; that I shall be glad to hear from him again, and that he may write to me in Malayalim, as I have an interpreter in Calcutta; and that the young man, his relation, who lives with him at Candenad, may receive from Colonel Macaulay six rupees per month, and arrears from the time of his own appointment, if he can shew that the lad is useful to him in his work. "I remain,

My dear Sir,

Very sincerely yours,

C. Buchanan."

In the course of the ensuing month, Lord Minto, who had long been expected, arrived as Governor General in Bengal. In a letter to Colonel Macaulay, on the 17th of August, Dr. Buchanan notices his Lordship's good example, and attendance on divine worship, and his civility to himself. "He ' wishes me," he adds, to communicate fully "with him on all the subjects which he knows have "long engaged my attention." A subsequent paragraph in this letter thus mentions another very meritorious ecclesiastical servant of the Company in India.

"I have not seen the publication of Dr. Kerr, to "which you allude." This was probably the account of the St. Thome Christians, the Syro-Romish, and the Latin church in India, which was drawn up by that excellent man by order of the Madras government.

"But," continues Dr. Buchanan, "I received "from him yesterday his ' Letter to Lord William "Bentinck,' on the subject of chaplains, printed "and sent home by the Indus. Dr. Kerr is an ar"dent and useful friend of the Christian religion; "and I think the Court will make him one of his u proposed vicars-general, or perhaps his suffragan "bishop."

It appears, therefore, that the necessity of an enlarged ecclesiastical establishment in India had oc See the Christian Observer, vol. vi. p. 751, and Christian Researches, p. 146. curred simultaneously to Dr. Buchanan and to Dr. Kerr. The latter zealous and laborious chaplain did not, however, survive long enough to receive any additional authority, even supposing that it would have been conferred upon him. His honour and his reward are in heaven.

Dr. Buchanan's next letter to Colonel Macaulay is dated September 15th, and contains some interesting notices respecting his intended journey overland to Europe, and the progress of the Malayalim translation of the Scriptures. It refers at the close to a painful subject, which is afterwards more fully explained.

"My dear Sir, "I had the pleasure to receive the copies of your correspondence with government regarding the discipline of the churches. Every additional letter you write on that subject is an additional pin to the tabernacle.

"If I should go by Persia, I am prepared to spend twelve thousand rupees in presents. But I hope to be able to travel by the route of Bussorah, Mosul, and Aleppo. I proceed to Bombay in the Metcalfe, Captain Isaacke, who will sail from this place about the 10th or 15th of the next month, October. If practicable, he will set me down at Cochin. If not, I shall first arrange matters at Bombay, and then For an account of this truly pious man, see the Christian Observer, vol. xi. p. 80. come down to Goa (which I wish much to visit) and to Cochin.

"I am greatly obliged to you for your letter of the 2d of August, containing Colonel Capper's sentiments on a journey through Persia and Armenia. His remarks are highly interesting, and may be useful to me hereafter. I am more afraid of the French than of the Persians.

"I am happy at the arrival of the Pontifical Bull. A Protestant Christian happy at the arrival of the Pope's Bull *I* Tell it not to the Church of England or to the Kirk of Scotland. Yea, I am happy, even though the object of it be a rosy bishop, who delights to quaff the essence of *sura;* for I hope through the medium of this bishop to diffuse the holy Scriptures among thousands of my fellow-creatures.

"Within the last few days arrived your eight packets of the holy Gospels, translated into the Malayalim language. They have been contemplated with mingled affection and admiration by the missionary corps. David Grant is now employed in reading them through, and prefixing the titles to the books, and numbering the chapters in English. People wonder here at this rapid fruit of my visit to Malayala. But yours is the praise, not mine.

"As we have no fount of Malayalim types ready cut in Bengal, I mean to take the MS. with me to Bombay, and to have it printed there under the superintendence of Sir James Mackintosh.

"The translators may take their rest now for a little while. Until we can ascertain the accuracy of the translation of the Gospels, we need not proceed to the Epistles. You may therefore settle accounts with the translators. I request you will thank them in my name for what has been done, and inform them, that I expect they will shortly resume their operations.

"I beg you will remember me to Dr. Macaulay, and to Mr. Hughes, the philosopher of the mountains. I fear he cannot tell me yet the mode in which a rock snake is killed by the hunters.

"I am on the eve, I fear, of a rupture with this government. The cause is the Gospel. They are endeavouring to restrain the exertions of the missionaries in Bengal. I have not yet interfered; and I trust it will not be necessary; for I love peace, and not war; particularly at the moment of my leaving the country. But I shall do my duty, and leave the event to God.

"I am,

My dear Sir,

Yours sincerely,

C. Buchanan."

On the 22d of September, Dr. Buchanan wrote to his two daughters. The following passage from his letter alludes to their lamented mother in a peculiarly affecting manner.

"I am now about to quit India, and to

go home "to see you. I propose to leave Calcutta in the "course of next month. If I find it dangerous to "go home overland, I shall proceed from Bom"bay by sea. I shall probably sail over those "waters where your dear mother lies. Do you "not know, that at the resurrection of the dead she "will come forth with a ' glorious body?' Though "it be ' sown in dishonour, it is raised in glory.' "Of this you may read in the Bible, and in the "Burial Service. Your mother will come forth "with a 'orious body;' for she was a good woman, "and remembered her Creator in the days of her "youth. Perhaps I shall die too before I reach "England. You ought therefore to pray that God "would preserve my life, if it be his will, (for I desire to do his will in all things,) that I may see "you, and shew you the affection of a father, and "receive the affection of daughters, and lead you "onward with myself to that happy state, whither "your mother is gone before you.",

It is gratifying to reflect, that this affectionate and pious father was permitted to realize the delightful prospect which he thus anticipated. The following extract is from a letter to Colonel Macaulay, which occurs shortly afterwards.

"Calcutta, 12th Oct. 1807.

"Your letters of the 13th and 15th ult. arrived "on this day. I have perused with pleasure and "pain your public letter on the subject of expen"diture at your residency; with pain, that your "resources have been so scanty, and your fortune "little; with pleasure, that you have upheld your "character with such dignity, and have repelled the "insinuations of ignorance with such temperance "and effect. The highest compliment I can pay "you, (and I seldom pay compliments,) is to say, "'That every word in your letter will be believed by ". the Honourable Court.'

"The attack I announced to you in my last has "not been yet made. I wish you were at my side "during the storm. I have friends, but they are "not soldiers. I am the forlorn hope, and yet I "have not twelve men. Nay more, my friends tell "me I shall certainly be killed.

"The assault however must be made, but whe"ther by silent escalade at the midnight watch, or "by heavy and hot battery at noon-day, I have not "yet determined. I think the latter. You shall "hear in a letter dated on or about the 1st of No"vember, *me vivente, et Deo volente.*"

The rupture with the supreme government, to which Dr. Buchanan refers in the preceding letters, was of so serious and unpleasant a nature, and is so closely connected with the illustration of his character, that it demands some farther explanation.

Not long after his return from the coast of Malabar, Dr. Buchanan preached a series of discourses in the Presidency church on the subject of the

VOL. II. K

Christian prophecies, which proved so acceptable to some of the congregation, that they expressed a wish that he would permit them to be printed; observing, that as he was about to return to Europe, they hoped he would bequeath these discourses, as a parting memorial to his friends. To this request Dr. Buchanan acceded, and accordingly made preparations for their publication. These sermons related chiefly to the Divine predictions concerning the future universal propagation of the Gospel; and were intended to excite the public attention to that important subject, as well as to animate and encourage those who from the purest motives were labouring to promote the knowledge of Christianity in India. Nothing could be more legitimate or laudable than such a design, conducted as it was by Dr. Buchanan, not in the spirit of violence and fanaticism, but of calm discussion, and reasonable and benevolent exertion. On transmitting, however, an advertisement to the government gazette, announcing the intended publication of his discourses, Dr. Buchanan was surprised to find, that the insertion of it was refused; and that an order had been issued to the printers of the other newspapers, forbidding them to publish the obnoxious notice. Shortly afterwards he received a letter from the Chief Secretary to the Presidency, desiring, that he would transmit the manuscript of his sermons on the Prophecies for the inspection of government. To this unexpected demand, Dr. Buchanan gave no immediate answer. It had long been the subject of painful observation to him, that on the departure of the Marquis Wellesley, during whose administration the spirit of promoting learning and religion in India had been general and ardent, a directly contrary disposition was manifested; as if it had been previously restrained by his presence. This first appeared under the administration of Sir George Barlow, and had been acquiring strength ever since. Lord Minto had now assumed the supreme government; and as several measures were adopted which appeared to Dr. Buchanan to operate very unfavourably for the interests both of learning and religion, he deemed it his duty, before he quitted Bengal, to address a memorial to his Lordship, in which he particularly directed his attention to the character and tendency of those measures; and, in so doing, explained his reasons for declining to comply with the wishes of government respecting his sermons on the Prophecies. The memorial was introduced to Lord Minto by the following letter.

To the Right Honourable Lord Minto, fyc. fyc. 8fc. "My Lord,

"I beg leave respectfully to submit to your Lordship some particulars regarding the present state of the Christian religion in Bengal, which I have thought it my duty to communicate for your Lordship's information at this time.

"I trust you will do me the justice to believe, that it is with the utmost reluctance I trouble your Lordship with a letter on such a subject so soon after your entrance on this government, when as yet few, if any, of the circumstances noticed in it can have come to your Lordship's knowledge.

"I have no other view in soliciting your attention to them, but the advancement of learning and religion. Perhaps no one has addressed your Lordship on the. subject since your arrival; and there are certainly many particulars, regarding their present state, which it is of importance your Lordship should know..

"Being about to leave India, I feared lest I should hereafter reproach myself, if I withheld any thing at this time which I conceived might be useful, particularly as I have been further encouraged to address your Lordship, by your known condescension in receiving any communications which are honestly intended.--.

"I have the honour to be,
My Lord,
With much respect,
Your most obedient,
Humble Servant,.-C. Buchanan."
"Calcutta, 9th Nov. 1807."

The memorial, which accompanied the preceding letter, and which was published some years afterwards by Dr. Buchanan, in his own vindication and defence, evinces, as it has been well observed, " the "temperate firmness of a man, who, knowing that "the Gospel is the power of God unto salvation, "is neither ashamed to profess, nor afraid to defend. it." It is introduced by a statement of the circumstances which have been just mentioned as having led to this address to the Governor General, Dr. Buchanan gave full credit to the officers of his Lordship's government, of whose conduct respecting the Christian religion he complained, that they were acting according to the best of their judgment; but adds, with much force and propriety of expression, "not to promote Christianity may, in certain cir"cumstances, be prudent; but to repress Chris"tianity, will not, I think, in any case, be defended." In proof of such a spirit of hostility to the progress of the Gospel in India, which is the main subject of his Memorial, Dr. Buchanan specified the four following facts. "First, the withdrawing of the pa"tronage of government from the translation of "the Holy Scriptures into the oriental tongues." "Second, attempting to suppress the translation of "the Scriptures." "Third, suppressing the enco"mium of the Honourable the Court of Directors on "the venerable missionary, the Rev. Mr. Swartz;" and, " Fourth, restraining the Protestant mission See his Apology for promoting Christianity in India. aries in Bengal from the exercise of their func"tions, and establishing an imprimatur for theolo"gical works."

The truth of the two first of the preceding allegations has been already proved in the course of these Memoirs, and needs therefore no additional confirmation. The third rests upon the simple fact, that the Bengal government, instead of following the example of those of Madras and Bombay, in giving publicity to the honourable testimony which had been recently borne by the Court of Directors to the merits of the venerable Swartz, in sending out to Fort St. George a marble monument to his memory, with a suitable inscription, which was ordered to be translated into the languages of the country, had chosen to pass over the whole transaction in silence; and had aggravated this neglect, by permitting the insertion of an article in the Calcutta gazette, "the obvious tendency of which "was to bring the character and labours of the "Christian missionary into contempt."

On the fourth head of the complaint preferred by Dr. Buchanan in his Memorial, it will be necessary to be somewhat more particular. The success of the Protestant mission in Bengal, Dr. Buchanan affirmed to have been long a source of uneasiness to those officers of government who did not think it right to attempt the conversion of the natives. ' And some of the native moonshees, attached to the public offices, knowing the sentiments of their superiors, were not backward in seizing any occasion to complain of the missionaries, which might be presented to them. Some clamour of this kind had been raised at two different times within a.few years, but had "passed away without offence to the Christian religion. The complaint of the moonshees against the missionaries on the latter occasion was, that they had in a certain tract "applied abusive epithets to "Mahomet." This tract, being an account of the life of Mahomet composed by a native convert, had issued from the missionary press at Serampore, but without the knowledge of the missionaries themselves.

In commenting on this charge, Dr. Buchanan observed, " the missionaries certainly mistake the "proper method of convincing the minds of men, "if they use epithets of abuse; the successful me"thod of pleaching is by argument and affectionate "address; and J presume this has been their ge neral method during the fourteen years of their "mission.

"At the same time, Christian teachers are not "to speak with reverence or courtesy of Juggernaut "or Mahomet; they must speak as the Scriptures speak; that is, of false gods as false gods, and of a lying prophet as a lying prophet. The Maho "metans apply abusive epithets and vulgar curses to "the idolatry of the Hindoos, and to the faith of "Christians; and these epithets are contained in "books; the government might, on the same prin"ciple, have been assailed with the petitions of "Christians and Hindoos against the Mahometans.

Trie complaint, however, of the Mohammedans produced various restrictions on the proceedings of the missionaries, which were defended on the plea that the public faith had been pledged to leave the natives in the undisturbed exercise of their religions. If by not disturbing the natives in the exercise of their religion, it is meant that we are to use no means for diffusing Christianity among them; then, observed Dr. Buchanan, " this pledge has been vio"lated by every government in India, and has been "systematically broken by the East India Com"pany, from the year 1698 to the present time, "The charter of 1698 expressly stipulates that they shall use means to instruct the Gentoos, &c. in "the Christian religion. Nor in this is there any "thing at variance with the pledge in question. It "is a very different thing to apply arguments to the "mind, and violence to the body; to civilize and "humanize, to address the understandings and affec"tions of subjects, and to interfere with their su"perstitions by compulsory acts."

After various illustrations of the countenance afforded by the Company itself to Christian missionaries, and of their successful efforts in different parts of India,-Dr. Buchanan adds the following observation. -.

"It has been '-the usual conduct of Asiatic governments to let Christianity alone. In the annals of the British administration in India, has there been no instance of the suppression of a Christian mission."

Having presented the preceding considerations to the notice of Lord Minto, Dr. Buchanan recurs to the subject of his discourses on the Prophecies. He had at the opening of his Memorial professed that he would willingly transmit them to the perusal of the Governor General, and that he should be happy to receive such observations on them, as his Lordship's learning and candour might suggest. But, adds Dr. Buchanan, " I now beg leave to submit to your Lordship's judgment, whether in "the view of the temper of mind displayed above, ' it would be proper in me to submit my compositions to the opinion and revision of the officers of your Lordship's government. I incline not to commit them to the hands of those officers from another consideration: it would be a bad precedent. I would not that it should be thought,.' that any where in the British dominions there exists any thing like a civil inquisition into matters purely religious..-..

"It is nearly two months since I received the letter from government on this matter, and I have not yet communicated ray intentions. I now beg leave to inform your Lordship, that I do not wish to give government any unnecessary offence. I shall not publish the Prophecies.

"At the same time I beg leave most respectfully to assure your Lordship, that I am not in any way disappointed by the interference of government on this occasion. The supposed suppression of the Christian prophecies has produced the consequence that might be expected. The public curiosity has been greatly excited to see these prophecies; and " to draw the attention of men to the divine predictions could be the only object I had in view, in noticing them in the course of my public ministry. Another consequence will probably be, "the Prophecies will be translated into the languages "of the East, and thus pave the way, as has sometimes happened, for their own fulfilment."

Dr. Buchanan closed his Memorial with entreating Lord Minto, in case any circumstance should afford a pretext for renewing the attempt to suppress the translation of the Scriptures, that the Chinese translation, in which, as its original proposer and patron, he felt peculiarly interested, might at least be spared; and with offering any farther evidence or explanation of the facts asserted in his letter, which his Lordship might require. This offer, however, Lord Minto did not condescend to accept. He did not even honour Dr. Buchanan with a single word of reply. Instead of considering the Memorial as a communication intended to inform his Lordship on subjects with which he was likely to be unacquainted, he viewed it as disrespectful to his government, and transmitted it by the very fleet which conveyed Dr. Buchanan himself to England, to the Court of Directors, accompanied by a commentary, of which Dr. Buchanan remained perfectly ignorant till some years afterwards;' when, with many other documents relative to Christianity in India, it was laid upon the table of the House of Commons. It then attracted his notice, and called forth some remarks, which will be better considered, when we arrive, in the course of this narrative, at the period of their publication. The Bengal government, however, not having thought proper to pay any attention to his Memorial, Dr. Buchanan deemed it to be his duty to transmit a copy of it to the Court of Directors, which he did immediately before his departure from Calcutta, accompanied by a letter, in which he expressed his hope, that some general principles on the comparative importance of religion in political relations in India, might be established at home, and transmitted to our eastern government for their guidance. Dr. Buchanan concluded his address to the Honourable Court, by recalling to their notice the solemn charge which he had received about eleven years since from their chairman, the late Sir Stephen Lushington, the tenor of which has been already stated. "In obedience to these instructions," observes Dr. Buchanan, " I have devoted myself much to the advancement of the Christian religion, and of useful learning, since my arrival in India; using such means as I was possessed of, and directing the Opportunities which have offered, to the accom

"plishment of that object. I am yet sensible that "I have' fulfilled very imperfectly the injunctions of "your Honourable Court. It suffices, however, for "my own satisfaction, if what I have done has been well done; that is, with honesty of purpose "and with the sanction of truth. In my exhibition "of the religious and moral state of British India, "I might have palliated the fact, and presented a "fair picture, where there was nothing but deformity. "But in so doing, I should not have done honour "to the spirit of the admonitions of your venerable "chairman, now deceased. And however grateful "it may be for the present moment to suppress "painful truths, yet as my labours had chiefly reference to the benefit of times to come, I should "not, by such means, have conciliated the respect "of your illustrious body twenty years hence."

Under these impressions, Dr. Buchanan requested that the Court would be pleased to investigate fully his proceedings, with respect to the promotion of Christianity in India, that the Company at large might be enabled justly to appreciate them; and that he might be encouraged (if it should appear that encouragement were due) to prosecute an undertaking which seemed, he said, to have commanded the applause of all good men, and which had certainly commenced with omens of considerable success.

The preceding letter to the Court of Directors was not published with the Memorial to the government of Bengal, nor does it seem to have been noticed by the Court. Neither of those addresses, however, though unacknowledged at the time, was unproductive of effect. In

Bengal, a more favourable disposition on the part of the government, towards the promotion of Christianity, shortly afterwards appeared; and the reply of the Court of Directors to the representations of the Governor General in council, though not friendly to Dr. Buchanan, was, as we shall hereafter perceive, strongly marked by those enlightened and liberal views, which he had been so anxious to see established for the guidance of our Indian governments. The favourable change which took place in the conduct of the Bengal government towards the mission of Serampore, is, however, chiefly to be ascribed to the Memorial presented by the missionaries themselves to the Governor General in council; which, when published a few years afterwards in this country, excited general admiration.

The painful transaction which has been thus detailed was nearly the last of a public nature in which Dr. Buchanan was engaged in Calcutta. The; time was now approaching for his second and final departure from that city. Accordingly, in the month of November he preached his farewell sermon to the congregation at the mission church from the words of St. Paul to the Philippians, chap. i. *17.* "Only "let your conversation be as it becometh the Gospel "of Christ: that whether I come and see you, or else be absent, I may hear of your affairs, that ye "stand fast in one spirit, with one mind, striving "together for the faith of the Gospel." From this appropriate and interesting passage, Dr. Buchanan delivered a discourse remarkable for the importance of the practical truths which it enforced. After an introductory view of the origin and progress of the Church at Philippi, Dr. Buchanan considered the two particulars, of which the parting request of the Apostle to his favourite converts consists. The first respects the holy practice which they were exhorted to maintain.

"Without a highly moral conversation," observed Dr. Buchanan, " a congregation of Christians can"not be said to have substance or being; for faith "without works is dead. Unless the world see "something particular in your works, they will give "you no credit for your faith; or rather, they will "not care what your faith may be. In such cir"cum"stances, your faith will give them no trouble. But "when ' wonderful works' appear, they will begin to "ask what power hath produced them.' In this "very Epistle, the Apostle calls the Christians at "Philippi, ' the sons of God,' and the lights of "the world;' and he expresses his hope, that their "conduct would be correspondent with these noble and distinguishing appellations.

"Now," continues Dr. Buchanan, "when this "light shineth to the world, even the light of a holy "life and conversation, it will be manifested by these "two circumstances. First, it will not be agreeable "to some. And, secondly, some will misrepresent "your motives, or attach to your conduct an evil "name; accusing you of hypocrisy, or of unnecessary "strictness. And if no man allege any thing of this "kind against you, if the worst of men make no "derogatory remark on your conduct, then may you "doubt whether you are walking in the steps of the "faithful servants of Christ. They all were marked "out by the world, as being in a greater or less "degree singular and peculiar in their conduct, as "persons swayed by other principles, and subject to "other laws. If these things be so, you will per"ceive how little concerned you ought to be about "the praise of man, or the honour which cometh "from the world.'

Dr. Buchanan then proceeded to the second part of the Apostle's exhortation; and in urging the duty of " striving for the faith of the Gospel," he observed, "This will appear strange to nominal "Christians, both preachers and hearers. But when "once a man's heart comes under the influence of "the grace of God, he will discover (perhaps in old "age for the first time) that it is his duty, and it will "be his pleasure, to promote the faith of the Gos"pel, by every way; by his means, by his influence, "by his exhortation, by his example. Every-true "disciple of Christ, however humble his situation, "or peculiar his circumstances, will find opportu"nities of doing something for the faith of the "Gospel. And, indeed, the poor often enjoy means "of usefulness, which, from many causes, are denied "to their superiors."-.."'

Dr. Buchanan next directed the attention of his hearers to the Apostle's rule for the successful pursuit of this great object, "that ye stand fast "in one spirit, with one mind—that they should "preserve *unity;* unity in the faith, and in the "Church." The following passage, relative to this important point, displays considerable acuteness of observation.-, You will generally observe in the present day, "that new opinions concerning forms and doctrine "are chiefly introduced by men who have had little "learning in their youth; so that when in advanced "life they begin to be serious and to acquire know"ledge, the novelty flatters their understandings for "a time, and leads them to adopt new systems, as "they acquire new knowledge. This is very natu"ral. Whereas those in whom serious piety and "sound learning have united in early life, are sel"dom subject to such changes. But the unsettled "man is designated by St. Paul under the appella"tion of a ' novice,' whatever his age may be; one "who being lifted up for a time in his own conceit, »" gradually loses his reputatiaSfjDr perhaps has a "fall in the face of the church. And when his "pride has been thus humbled, he generally returns "to meekness of conduct and sobriety of speech."

Dr. Buchanan noticed, in the third place, the nature of that faith for which Christians ought to strive.

"With respect to this," he observed, " it is not "necessary for me now to declare it. It hath often "been described to you from this place, even that "faith which was once delivered unto the saints;' "and which hath descended from age to age, like "a pure stream of the water of life, gladdening the "hearts of men, and nourishing their souls unto "everlasting life. Amongst yourselves, have there "been some, who drank of it deeply, and have now "passed away into glory; good and holy persons, "who bequeathed to you an illustrious testimony, "and pointed out to you the true way.' These "all died in faith, and now inherit the promises. "These are your 'cloud of witnessesthat you "should ' run with patience the race that is set be"fore you.' These once, like some of you now, "endured suffering for conscience sake, some "trouble of body, or some distress of mind. But "all was sanctified to them, as it will be to you; "they endured unto the end, and their names shall "be had in everlasting remembrance."

The sermon was concluded by a faithful and solemn exhortation to the young and to the old, to those who doubted as to " the true way," to the sinner and the saint, to strive to obtain, and, having obtained, to adorn and recommend the faith of the Gospel. "It only remains," added Dr. Bu VOL. II. L chanan, " that I implore the solemn benediction "of God on this congregation.

"I pray, that the word of Christ may ' run and "be glorified' amongst you; that from this place, "as from a fountain, streams of truth may flow far "and wide; that you may be ever blessed with "wise and learned instructors, ' able ministers of "the New Testament,' who shall take delight in "dispensing the word of life, and in tending the "flock committed to their care; and finally, that "the honour of your church may ever be preserved "pure from any stain, that ye may uphold a con"duct 'blameless and harmless,' as examples to "men, as 'the lights of the world; striving to"gether with one mind and in one spirit, for the "faith of the Gospel."

Such was the simple but impressive strain in which Dr. Buchanan took leave of the congregation which contained the greater proportion of religious persons in Calcutta. His farewell at the Presidency church was probably of a different nature, though characterized by the same pastoral fidelity and practical wisdom, as that which we have just observed. There were, doubtless, some in each congregation from whom he would regret to be separated, and many who would lament his departure. Mr. Brown would particularly feel the loss of his able and affectionate coadjutor and friend, with whom he had taken " sweet counsel" in the house of God, and had shared the burden and the heat of many a laborious day. Of the sentiments entertained by this excellent man respecting his learned and valuable colleague, the following brief extract from a confidential letter to his brother, written just as Dr. Buchanan was on the eve of his departure from Calcutta, will be a sufficient testimony.

"You ask me," says Mr. Brown, " if Dr, Bu"chanan is my friend? I answer, I know no man "in the world who excels him in useful purpose, "or deserves my friendship more. Perhaps there "is no man in the world who loves him so much "as I do; because no man knows him so well. "Further, no man I believe in the world would do "me service like him. We have lived together in "the closest intimacy ten years, without s shade "of difference in sentiment, political or religious. "It is needless to add, without a jar in word or "deed. He is the man to do good in the earth, "and worthy of being Metropolitan of the East."

The private and unaffected nature of the letter from which the preceding passage is extracted, the well known simplicity and integrity of the writer's character, and the perfect competency of his testimony, render this warm and energetic tribute to the merit of his friend peculiarly valuable. To separate from such a colleague must have been a subject of sincere regret to him. But, with this and a few other exceptions, Dr. Buchanan's ties to India were neither strong nor numerous. The society of Calcutta is necessarily fluctuating. One of the most important branches of his employment no longer existed; he had laid the foundation of a great work for the promotion of Christianity in India, which he could in future more advantageously forward and defend in his native country; and thither he felt attracted by the associations of early and maturer life, by filial duty, and paternal affection. For this return, therefore, after making a variety of arrangements to ensure the continuance of the works carrying on under what he considered to be the " Chris"tian Institution," more particularly of the Chinese class at Serampore, he at length prepared.

On the 27th of November, Dr. Buchanan left Calcutta, and reached Fulta the next" day; and from this place he wrote to Colonel Sandys as follows.

"Dear Sandys, "I am thus far on my way to Europe. I sail in the Baretto to Goa, to look into the inquisition there, and examine the libraries. Thence I proceed to Bombay.

"A few days ago I received your letter of the 28th of May 1807, dated from Northwold, containing the signatures of the little girls. They write very well, and have made a flattering progress in their education. I am much obliged to you for your particular account of the two children, which is very correct, I believe, and very pleasing. Being long estranged from them, and hearing none converse about them, I seldom think of them now comparatively. But when we meet again, I suppose we shall fall in love.

"You observed in some of your late letters that you heard I was likely to be married again. It so happens, that I have not once thought of it. It is possible that I may marry some time after my arrival in England. But yet I would avoid it, for some reasons. It is a subject I think not of.

"Instead of love and marriage, I am engaged in war and fightings. I have been obliged to address this government publicly on its hostility to religion and to its progress in India. All Calcutta wondered what step government would take. In the midst of this strange scene, I paid a farewell visit to them all, and left every creature from the Governor General to the pilots, on good terms.

"I have now finished my labours, and pray that God may bless them.

"I have been down here for eight days, waiting the despatch of the ship. The Calcutta people have not been uninterested in my late contention with the government; and I hear some of them have called a ship by my name, since I came down here. The ' Christian Institution in the East' is unknown in Calcutta to this hour, though active in its operation.

"Yours affectionately,

C. Buchanan."

The ship in which Dr. Buchanan sailed left Saugor on the 9th of December; but no memorial of his voyage occurs until the 23d of that month, when he wrote to Mr. Brown as follows, from Columbo, in the island of Ceylon.

"Ceylon again'. In crossing the Gulf of Manaar, "we encountered a gale, and put into Columbo. I "had requested the captain to touch here when I left "Calcutta; and now he was obliged of necessity. "I have been well on board, and well treated. "Many causes for thankfulness, as usual. The Adele "was taken by the Russell the day before we came "up to her, and we had parted convoy. In the "Gulf of Manaar we were about to throw over our "cargo, when the gale abated.

"On my arrival here, many of the chief persons "waited on me. From my having touched last year "at so many Dutch settlements, I found all the fa"milies knew me. I have only been here three "days, having arrived on Monday last, and the ship "proceeds on her voyage on Friday. I have some "thoughts of letting her go, and following at my "leisure; for I find there is something for me here "to do. What a field for English, Dutch, and "Cingalese preachers in this fertile and renowned "land!

"I propose to proceed straight to Cochin from "this place. Sir James Mackintosh is on the Ma"labar coast, I hear, with his family. Two Bombay "civil servants now here wish me to travel by land "from Cochin to Goa. They have been judges and "collectors for fourteen years on that coast, and al"lege they know more about the Christians than "any other persons in India. They complain much "of the undue influence of Goa, exercised some"times cruelly on all Christians who are not Ca"tholics. Mr. B. carries me out to-day to his "country house, to visit some of the Cingalese "Christian churches.

"My affectionate regards to all your family."

By the date of his next letter, Dr. Buchanan appears to have left the Baretto, in which he originally embarked from Calcutta, and to have exchanged that ship for the Canton, from which, on the 26th of December, he thus wrote off Cochin, to Colonel Macaulay.

"I had flattered myself with the hope of being "landed here, but the commander of the ship can"not wait, and I am disappointed. He has engaged "to put me down at Goa, where I propose to remain "some time, and from whence I shall write to you "particularly. I left Calcutta on the 8th inst. and "touched at Columbo, where I staid some days, and "found flattering assurances of support in our evan"gelizing plans for that island. There is less pre"judice there than in the Company's settlements.

This is the third time that I have visited Ceylon; so that the people begin to think I have some se"rious design against them.

"In my last I believe I informed you that I was "*standing in the breach.* I have now the pleasure "to announce that the battle has been fought. "Long consultations were held how to proceed. It "was at last decreed, that I should be permitted to "depart in peace.

"I have the copy of the Malayalim Scriptures "with me, and mean to print when at Bombay: "five thousand copies will suffice for a beginning, I "suppose.

"I left Misrahi, my Jew, in Calcutta, with his "own consent. I have advanced him in the whole "a thousand rupees; so I suppose he will trade "there.

"I hope to see you before I leave India; but I "do not know at this moment where or how. May "all our resolves and purposes be acceptable to the "Divine will!

"Mr. Johnston, Judge at Columbo, will furnish "me with some important official documents re"lating to the state of Christianity in that island. "The Governor was absent; but Major Maitland "(Lord Lauderdale's son) came to inform me, that "he would return in two days, if I would stay to see "him. I could not stay; but I communicated to "him, that if he would give to the Cingalese trans"lation of the Scriptures his *countenance,* I would "give *money;* and Judge Johnston would find in"struments. Mr. J. is an excellent Cingalese scho"lar himself."

Notwithstanding the disappointment of which Dr. Buchanan expressed his expectation at the commencement of the preceding letter, we find him twd days afterwards safely landed at Cochin, and under the roof of his friend, Colonel Macaulay. He thus writes to Mr. Brown.

"Cochin, 28th Dec. 1807.

"On the 24th, Christmas-eve, we left Columbo, ' crossed the Gulph of Manaar on Christmas-day, "and arrived here on the 27th, yesterday. I found "all my Jews and Christians in fine health and spi"rits, and highly gratified at my unexpected arrival. "I reside with Colonel Macaulay. After passing "some time in these regions, he accompanies me up ' the coast, by land, through all the Christian terri"tories, as far as Cananore, perhaps Mangalore, "whence I proceed by sea to Goa.

"The Jews have lately had a meeting about the "prophecies. And I am about to call another San"hedrim on the subject before I go. It is a strange "event.

"I am happy I have visited this place a second "time. May God direct all these things to his own "glory, and to the good of men! I have need of "watchfulness and prayer. Much lies before me, ere "I leave India yet; if ever I leave it.

"Tell H. that the poor Jews, blind, lame, and "halt, are come this morning, exclaiming, as usual, "' Jehuda Ani.' I wish I could impart a better "gift than silver or gold. The Rajah of Travancore "has desired I will visit him. I do not know what "to do. The Rajah of Cochin has offered to come "over to see me. Ambassadors from the Syrian "Christians are expected to-morrow."

On the 2d of January 1808, Dr. Buchanan left Cochin, accompanied by Colonel Macaulay, on a second tour upon the coast of Malabar. The following letter to Mr. Brown will afford an interesting account of their progress.

"Tellicherry, 14th January, 1808.

"I write this from the fort which the English "first built in India; and where, as Tippoo ob"served in his official manifesto, the English ped"lars first exhibited their scissors and knives.' "Tellicherry lines enclose nine miles in circumference; and the natives have enjoyed the protection of the English for about one hundred and sixty years. The enemy was never suffered to destroy them. *But no English church, or house of prayer, has yet been built.* From this spot we extended our power to the utmost limits of India.

Colonel Macaulay has accompanied me thus far. We first proceeded from Cochin to the famous Shanscrit college at Trichiur; and thence to a district of the Syrian Christians which I had not before visited. It was named by Hyder, Na*zarani Ghur, or the city of the Nazarenes. It is a beautiful place, fertile and populous. The town is four square, having four gates, built on the side of a hill, with steps cut in the rock from street to street, surrounded by lofty groves of palm and other trees. A verdant meadow winds about the foot of the hill, and the whole country is a scene of hill and dale. The priests and people, knew me, and received us with great affection. Colonel Macaulay accompanied me to the principal church. Having signified my intention of presenting a large gold medal to this church, in the name of all the Syrian churches in Malayalim, a vast concourse of people assembled. There is no person in the town but Nazarenes. The medal which I presented to them, was that which Mrs. J. gave me before I left Calcutta. It is about three times as large as a college gold medal, and exhibits the baptism of Jesus in Jordan, elegantly executed; and on the reverse, a child brought to be baptized. I placed it on the altar, in the presence of the people, with due solemnity; and beside it, a gift to the poor. This town is in the territories of the Rajah of Cochin, whom I visited a fortnight ago. Tippoo invaded this Syrian colony in 1789. The people pointed out to me the grove of trees on which the Christians were hanged. They are now so respectable for number and opulence, that the Rajah of Cochin is obliged to treat them with indulgence; and the more so, as they are within four miles of the English territories in Malabar. Nazarani Bazar (as it is sometimes called) is due east from Paniani, and is near Palghutcheri. This second visit to the Syrian churches has been useful.

The Jews at Cochin are very unsettled in relation to the prophecies. They wonder at the attention paid by the English to these subjects for the first time. You will read in the Bombay courier an account of a ceremony in the synagogue at Cochin, which took place at Christmas last, a few days before I arrived. Some of the Jews interpret the prophecies aright, and some in another way; but all agree that a great era is at hand.

I visited Mahe, a beautiful place, formerly a French fort, but now in ruins, and Calicut. At this last place Vasco de Gama landed in 1497, at a fine bay a little above the town. I saw the ruins of the Samorin's palace, in which he was first received. The Mahometan towns on the sea-coast are large and populous. The Romish Christians are numerous. The English Christians complain that there is no Protestant church or minister on this coast, except a chaplain to the garrison at Cananore.

The march of Menou prevents my going home by land.

I propose to proceed to Goa in a day or two, and thence to Bombay, if time permit. I reside here at the house of Mr. C, the Judge of the province.

I enjoy good health in this favoured land. Amidst all my researches, the importance of the Gospel appears every where conspicuous. Every evil I witness, and every defect, might be remedied by the Gospel, whether among the natives or the Europeans."

Dr. Buchanan's next letter to Mr. Brown is dated, " Goa, 25th January, from the great hall of the Inquisition. " It contains an account of his bold and interesting visit to that metropolis of the Roman Catholic religion in the East, and is similar to that with which the public in general is already well acquainted. Instead, therefore, of repeating that admirable narrative, in which the ardour of Christian research, and of Christian courage and benevolence, are strikingly displayed, a sketch only of this enterprising expedition shall be given, which occurs in a letter to Colonel Macaulay.

"On my arrival at Goa, I was hospitably entertained by Captain Schuyler. He and Colonel Adams introduced me next day to the Viceroy, who affects great pomp, rails at the French, and is a true Frenchman at heart. Next day Major Pareira went up with me to old Goa. The Archbishop received me cordially. I professed a purpose of remaining some days there. This, it Christian Researches, pp. 155—178.

seems, was unusual, and it occasioned some discussion and difficulty. At last I was received by one of the *Inquisitors;* not *your* friend, (who lives at a distance from the place, but by the second Inquisitor, Josephus a Doloribus, the chief agent of the Inquisition, and the most learned man of the place. By this *malleus hereticorum* was I received in his convent of the Augustinians, in a suite of chambers next his own. He was extremely communicative. All the libraries were opened; and were extensive and valuable beyond my expectation. That of the Augustinians alone appeared to be larger than the library of the college of Fort William.

"My object all this time was the Inquisition; and I gleaned much information imperceptibly. I disguised my purpose for the first three days, and the Inquisitor referred me to various books and documents elucidating the very subject I wanted to investigate; so that, on the fourth day, I attacked him directly on the present state of the Inquisition.

"I had already discovered that it was abolished in 1775, by the court of Portugal, on account of its inhuman rigour; that in 1779 it was restored on the accession of the present Queen; and that it has been in operation ever since. On its restoration, its rigour was qualified in some points. It was not to have a public Auto da Fe; but it was permitted to have a private one annually. The dungeons and torture remain the same. It has power to incarcerate for life; and there are now victims in its cells. The tribunal is supported in its ancient pomp; and its establishment is full. In fact, it is the only department which *is alive* in ancient Goa.

"Josephus a Doloribus was alarmed when he discovered the real drift of my enquiries. I told him, that he had now said so much, he might as well tell me all; and that I should not leave Goa till I had seen the Inquisition. He at last consented to shew me the great hall. I accompanied him, clothed in the solemn robes of his office. When I had surveyed the place awhile in silence, I desired that he would now let me go below and visit the dungeons. He refused; and here our first contest began. I told him, that if he did not open the dungeons, and let me count the captives, and enquire into the periods of their imprisonment, and learn the number of deaths within the last year, I should naturally believe that he had a good reason for the concealment; and that the ancient horrors of the Inquisition still subsisted. Whereas, if he would now unbar his locks, I could only declare to the public the truth as it was; and nothing would be left to imagination. He felt the force of this; but answered, that he could not oblige me, consistently with his oath or duty as an Inquisitor. I observed, that he had broken that oath frequently, during the four last days; and that he had himself noticed in his own justification, that the ancient regulations of the Church were in many instances obsolete. I then put the following question solemnly; 'Declare to me the number of captives which are at this moment in the dungeons below.' 'That, Sir, is a question,' said he, 'which I must not answer.'

"I was now in the hall where the captives were wont to be marshalled when they proceeded to the flames. I contemplated the scene awhile with mournful reflection, and then retired. The alcaides and familiars of the holy Inquisition stood around me, wondering at my introduction into the hall, and my conversation with the Inquisitor. I went into a neighbouring church, and ruminated on what I had seen and heard. I resolved to go again to the Inquisition. The familiars thinking I had business with the Inquisitor, admitted me. I immediately saw a poor woman sitting on a bench in the great hall. She appeared very disconsolate, and was waiting to be called before the tribunal in the next room. I went towards the tribunal, and was met at the door by Josephus a Doloribus, who seemed to have lost his temper at this intrusion, and exclaimed, '*Quid vis tu, "Domine?*' All our discourse was in Latin. I told him I wanted to speak with the chief Inquisitor, who was on the bench. I then looked at the poor woman very significantly, and then at him—And what has this poor woman done? He was silent, and impatient to lead me out. When we came to the head of the stairs, I took my last leave of Josephus a Doloribus, and repeated once more in his ears, what I had pleasantly pronounced before in our amicable discussions about the Inquisition, '*Delenda est Carthago!*' Before I left Goa, I communicated to him my intention (I first declared it to. him in his own cell) of addressing the Archbishop in a Latin letter, which would probably be published, on the four following subjects:

"1. The Inquisition.

"2. The want of Bibles for the priests.

"3. The disuse of public preaching and instruction in his diocese.-.

"4. The state of the public libraries.

"This letter I began and dated from the convent of the Augustinians, 25th January 1808. I shall probably print it before I leave Point de Galle.

"My visit at Goa has excited a very general alarm among the priests. The Viceroy wishes success to my endeavours. The English at Goa seemed to know little or nothing about the subject. The whole Catholic body there are awed by it; and it was said, that some would suffer in consequence of my visit; for Major B. and others of the Viceroy's household were known to furnish me with every information in their power. But VOL. II. M

"at last I perceived, that even B. himself, the philosophic, liberal, learned B. was cowed, and endeavoured to draw off."

On quitting his friend, Josephus a Doloribus, whose favour and forbearance had perhaps been conciliated by the present of a small purse of moidores, previously to his admission into the *santa casa,* Dr. Buchanan confesses in his letter to Mr. Brown, that his own mind was much agitated.

"I began to perceive," he says, " a cowardly fear of remaining longer in the power of the Inquisitors. My servants had repeatedly urged me to go, and I set off about twelve o'clock, not less indignant at the Inquisition of Goa, than I had been with the temple of Juggernaut."

Dr. Buchanan's great object in this, as in all his researches, was not so much the gratification of personal curiosity, as the discovery of useful and important information, with a view to the detection and the removal of spiritual and moral evils. The suggestion in the published extracts from his journal, as to the propriety of an interference on the part of the British government with that of Portugal, for the abolition of the dreadful tribunal of the Inquisition, had been happily anticipated, but did not render his animated appeal upon that subject superfluous; while his enquiries relative to the moral and religious state of the Romish and Syro-Romish churches on the coast of Malabar, led to efforts to disseminate the Holy Scriptures, for the instruction and illumination of that numerous and long neglected body of Christians.

"In two hours," continues Dr. Buchanan in his letter to Mr. Brown, " I reached New Goa. The alarm of my investigations had gone before me. The English came to enquire what I had seen and heard, and I told them all. I staid a day or two with them, and embarked in a pattamar (an open boat) for Bombay. The wind was contrary, and I was ten days on the voyage. I touched at three different places on the Pirate coast; Gheria, the celebrated fort of Severndroog, &c. One day we were driven out to sea, and in considerable danger. At length, however, on the 6th of February, I reached Bombay."

On his arrival at this Presidency, Dr.

Buchanan was kindly received by Governor Duncan, and took up his abode at the house of Mr. Forbes. He experienced the utmost civility from the principal persons of the settlement, and was particularly gratified by the attentions of Sir James Mackintosh. "I passed five hours," he observes in a letter to Colonel Macaulay, " with Sir James in his library. "It is uncommonly numerous and valuable. He is "a friend to religion; and professes a desire to sup"port me in all useful plans for India. "

Dr. Buchanan had taken with him to Bombay the manuscript translation of the four Gospels into the Malayalim language, which had been completed by the Syrian bishop and his clergy, and transmitted to Colonel Macaulay, intending to print it at his own expense; an excellent fount of types having been recently cut at that place. When Mr. Duncan, however, heard of this intention, he intimated his wish, that Dr. Buchanan would address a letter to the government upon the subject, promising to give it his countenance and support. He accordingly availed himself of this hint, and, in an address to the Governor in council, briefly detailed the circumstances of his visit to Travancore, and its result relative to the version of the Scriptures into the Malabar language. He also stated, that, on his arrival at Bombay, he had submitted the translation of the four Gospels to the judgment of Dr. Drummond, of that Presidency, author of the Malabar Grammar; who had reported, that he considered it to be a faithful version of the sacred original, and easily intelligible by the common people. Dr. Buchanan took the same opportunity of representing the importance of a cheap edition of the English Bible for the use of the army, and of the English inhabitants generally, of that country. In reply to this communication, the Secretary to government informed him, that the Governor in council readily extended his countenance to the good work which he was so laudably meditating, and would for that purpose be disposed to accede to such ulterior measures as might tend to promote it; but that the communities of Malabar Christians to whom he had adverted, being chiefly within the jurisdiction of the Presidency of Fort St. George, the Governor felt it to be his duty to transmit thither his representations upon that subject. With respect to the supply of the English Scriptures, the Governor expressed his intention of shortly recommending that part of Dr. Buchanan's suggestions to the consideration of the Court of Directors, who, he doubted not, would be desirous of ensuring to the Europeans at Bombay the edification to which the dissemination of the holy Scriptures must materially contribute.

In consequence of this favourable disposition of the government, Dr. Buchanan drew up an advertisement for a subscription towards defraying the expenses of the printing of the Gospels in the Malayalim language; the Governor himself professing his intention to subscribe, and to lead the way in this laudable design.

"I took no steps, however," says Dr. Buchanan in a letter to Colonel Macaulay, dated off Calicut, February 27th, " till the last day of my stay at "Bombay; when I tqld Mr. Money that I had a "delicacy in pressing the subscription when I was "on the spot, but that I should leave it in his "and Mr. Forbes's hands, and trust to them for its "success.

"I left a note of instructions with Messrs. "Forbes regarding the appropriation of the funds; "and they are authorized to pay all bills relative to the expense of translating the Scriptures into "the Malayalim language, and of sending learned "persons to Bombay to superintend the printing, "which shall have received your signature.

"The types are ready, but they have not one "Malayalim learned native in Bombay. The first "thing that I request of you is to send round two "persons qualified to superintend the printing. "Mr. Diummond will superintend *them*. It will "be expedient that one of the moonshees be a "Romish or Syro-Romish priest, for the reasons "mentioned in the advertisement. The prefaces peculiar to the Syriac may be "omitted; and it may have a general conformity to "the Vulgate.

"Some of the Romish priests will, perhaps, op"pose the design; but I have warned the gentlemen "at Bombay of that circumstance. A Padre L. is Italian instructor in Sir James Mackintosh's family, "and assumes consequence. Mr. Duncan told me "that this priest (who occasionally visits him) had (' come to him in evident alarm, and announced "that I was about to destroy the Inquisition, and to "declare to the world that the old horrors still exist; "which, said he, is not true. I took this opportu"nity of giving Mr. Duncan some account of my "enquiries; when he expressed his approbation "fully of my intention, and urged me to weaken the "Romish interest as much as possible in India. It (' seems the priests have given government some "trouble lately; and he has proposed something to "the Madras Presidency on the subject.

"It would take a fortnight to detail what passed "during my fortnight at Bombay; and therefore "I must conclude.

"I have taken my passage in the Charlton, and "have secured the first officer's cabin, which is "large and commodious, for myself and Master "Drummond. We have ten ladies on board, and "Dr. Pouget, of Surat, a man of information.

"If you write a note to Point de Galle, I shall "probably receive it.

"I have often recommended your going home, "and now I wish you to stay two or three years. "If your health will allow this, your stay will '' accomplish a great object for the Church of "Christ.

"Your friend Ribeymar, the chief Inquisitor, re"ceived me very kindly, and made a feast on the "last day but one of my stay; at which were pre"sent the whole staff of the Santa Casa. He said "he would answer your letter. The 'thieveless "errand' I had to visit the Inquisition a second time, "was to enquire, whether the chief Inquisitor had written his letter.

"I did not touch at Cananore or Mangalore. I "was afraid of losing the Inquisition and my pas-"sage.

"On my arrival in England, I shall not fail to give you some account of affairs, if I mix with "men, which I much doubt; for I am tired of "fighting, and sigh for quiet and retirement. "I remain,

"My dear Sir,

"Very sincerely yours,

"C, Buchanan."

It may be satisfactory to add, that the letter from the chief Inquisitor to Colonel Macaulay above referred to, strongly expressed his respect for that gentleman, and the pleasure which he had received from Dr. Buchanan's visit, notwithstanding the freedom of his enquiries and observations.

In another short communication to Colonel Macaulay about the same time, Dr. Buchanan mentions a pleasing mark of kindness which had been shewn him by one of his friends at Calcutta, and informs him of a proposal which he had made relative to one of the most stupendous and interesting objects of curiosity in India.

"Mr. Speke has sent a beautiful large quarto "Bible after me, as a keepsake. He had heard "that I complained of my sight in reading small "print at night. . And this is my last communi"cation with the learned of Calcutta. *Hoc Deus "fecit.* "I have put them on restoring Elephanta at "Bombay. I found the cavern and figures in a state "of progressive annual dilapidation. Mr. Money "has taken up the subject warmly. If government "does not execute it, I have proposed a subscription, "with a promise of five hundred rupees as soon as "the work shall commence under a scientific super"intendant. I have left a memorandum of the "subjects of improvement, and reedification, accord"ing to my idea. I have a reason for wishing that "the Trinity in Unity at Elephanta may remain while "this lower world exists."

Dr. Buchanan thus adverts to the same extraordinary remains of antiquity, in writing to Mr. Brown.

"I have visited Elephanta; a more wonderful "work than the Pyramids of Egypt. But the works "of Providence are yet more wonderful; at least so "I should esteem them; for in every region, and "in every clime, the lovingkindness of God is mag"nified in my experience. May his grace also be "magnified in me! My love to all your family."

On the 13th of March the Charlton arrived off Point de Galle, from which place Dr. Buchanan again wrote a few lines to Mr. Brown.

"I had intended," he says, " to have published my "letter to the Archbishop of Goa at this place. But "if we do not go on shore, I shall have no op-por"tunity. I shall therefore publish it at home.

"I have just been on board the Piedmontaise fri On his arrival in England, Dr. Buchanan found it unnecessary to publish this letter, the Inquisition at Goa having been abolished.

"gate, which has been captured by the St. Fiorenzo. "The Piedmontaise lost one hundred and sixty-five "men killed and wounded, and exhibited a scene of "vast carnage. Captain Hardinge of the St. Fio"renzo is killed.

"I have extensive commissions for sending good "books and Bibles to Bombay, Malabar, and Ceylon. "For if they have no preachers, they must read.

"All is well on board this ship, and I hope some "good will be done.

"With unfeigned prayers for the best of spiritual "blessings on you and your family, "I remain, "My dear Sir, "Very affectionately yours,

"C. Buchanan."

To Colonel Macaulay Dr. Buchanan wrote the next day, as follows. "My dear Sir,

"We have just arrived at this place, and see the Bengal fleet ready to sail; so that I have only time to bid you farewell. We staid three days at Columbo; one of which I passed with General Maitland at Mount Lavinia. After long and interesting conversations, he was pleased to promise that he would recommend to his Majesty's government an Ecclesiastical Establishment for the island of Ceylon.' By the next despatch he will send me, under cover to the Bishop of London, copies of all the papers I wanted relating to the ecclesiastical state of the island for the last two centuries. He has agreed to support the translation of the Scriptures into the Cingalese language. I resided with the Honourable Mr. Twisleton, whom I found well disposed to second all my views. Mr. Heywood did more. I think he is inclined to be zealous as a pastor to his people. I shall correspond, I hope, with both. They are surprised at the Governor's full acquiecence in the above important measures. I hope he will not retract.

"I received your letters for your brother, which I hope to deliver into his hands. I am much obliged to you for your introduction to him.

"The fleet is now under weigh for St. Helena. Farewell.

C. Buchanan."

"H. C. Ship Charlton, Point de Galle, 14th March, 1808"

Here we also must for the present take our leave of Dr. Buchanan; and, while he is pursuing his homeward voyage, resume our account of various events and circumstances connected with his history, which occurred during the interval between the publication of his Ecclesiastical Memoir, and his return to this country.

MEMOIRS OF THE REV. DR. BUCHANAN. PART III. CHAP. I. OF the events referred to at the close of the preceding division of this narrative, the first in order of time relates to the determination of the munificent prizes proposed by Dr. Buchanan to the Universities of Oxford and Cambridge, in the year 1805. It has been already stated, that the time assigned for this purpose was the 4th of June, 1807; on which day, the prize was adjudged at Oxford to the Author of these Memoirs. At Cambridge some circumstances occurred which prevented any decision upon the subject; and which the following letter from the Vice-Chancellor of that University to Dr. Buchanan will sufficiently explain. "Reverend Sir,

"The sum of five hundred pounds proposed by you for the best Essay on 'The probable Design of divine Providence in subjecting so large a Portion of India to the British Empire,' &c. was accepted by the University; and Dr. Milner, Dr. Jowett, and Dr. Outram, appointed to read the compositions, and decide upon their respective merits.

"Of all that were sent in within the appointed time, not one was deemed worthy of so magnificent a prize. Another came a few days after the time, which was unanimously preferred to all the rest; and to which the examiners would without the least hesitation have adjudged the prize, but did not think themselves authorized to do so, without your special permission, as one of the conditions, the presenting the composition within such a time, had not been complied with.

"The author has since avowed himself to be the Rev. J. W. Cunningham, M.A. of St. John's college.

"Dr. Pearce, Vice-Chancellor at the time when the examiners made their report, having heard that you were on your passage to England, deferred writing, as he daily expected to have a personal interview with you: and thus has devolved to me the office of communicating to you the thanks of the whole University for your very liberal offer, and their regret that your design has not been completely carried into execution.
,, Though I have not the honour of being known to you, yet in admiration of your character as the munificent PatTon and Promoter of literature, '(I subscribe myself,
With the greatest respect,
Your very humble Servant,
Francis Barnes."

"St. Peter's College, Cambridge, Jan. 19th, 1808."

It appears that Dr. Buchanan did not feel himself at liberty to make any decision upon the point stated in the preceding letter, and that the University was unwilling to resume the official consideration of the subject. Dr. Buchanan, however, offered to bear the expense of printing Mr. Cunningham's work.

On the 10th of May and the 28th of June, 1807, two sermons were preached before the University of Cambridge, by the Rev. Francis Wrangharn, of Trinity College, and the Rev. John Dudley, of Clare Hall, pursuant to the proposal of Dr. Buchanan in the preceding year, on the translation of the Scriptures into the oriental languages. Two discourses on the same important subject were preached before the University of Oxford, on the 8th and 29th of November following, by the Rev. Dr. Barrow, of Queen's College, and the Rev. Edward Nares, of Merton College. The two former of these sermons were published in the course of the year 1807, and the two latter early in 1808. All of them, with different degrees of ability and eloquence, and by various considerations and arguments, supported the duty and expediency of translating the sacred records into the principal languages of the East; and all strenuously maintained the general obligation of this country to attempt, by every wise and rational method, to promote the knowledge of Christianity in India. But the authors of these excellent discourses, like those of the first series of prize compositions, though a most able and efficient corps, formed the advanced guard only, if the expression may be allowed, of the main body which was now hastening to its support, and whose united exertions were eventually crowned with the most gratifying and decisive success.

Dr. Buchanan's Memoir on the expediency of an Ecclesiastical Establishment for British India, produced, as might be expected, a considerable sensation on the public mind. The subject was not only highly important, but it was new. The world had, indeed, heard much of East Indian commerce, policy, and conquests; but of East Indian religion, little or nothing. Now and then the name of a chaplain to the Company had been mentioned, and, still more rarely, that of a missionary to the Hindoos. But, generally speaking, the whole subject of the religion of India was little known, and still less regarded. Its European population was presumed, without thought or enquiry, to be sufficiently provided with the means of Christian Instruction; and as to the natives, they were considered as a race so completely separated from ourselves, and at the same time so religious and even moral in their own way, that, with the exception of those who had heard something of the Danish mission on the coast of Coromandel, the idea of converting any considerable number of the Hindoos was either treated as altogether unnecessary, and even unjust, or deemed in the highest degree visionary and impracticable. The admirable writings of Sir William Jones had illustrated the history, the antiquities, and the laws of India, and had excited some degree of literary and even political interest in favour of its native-inhabitants; but the peculiarly Christian consideration of them and of their country was a topic which had hitherto been but incidentally noticed. In this state of things, a work like the Memoir of Dr. Buchanan, exclusively devoted to this momentous and unusual subject, and characterized by great boldness, decision, and ability, might naturally be expected to produce a powerful and various impression upon the public. The more religious part of it hailed this production as presenting facts and arguments of a most important nature, and as opening a boundless sphere of exertion to the newly awakened and expanding energies of Christian benevolence and zeal; while others, and those a numerous and respectable class, considered it as at best a rash and unauthorized publication, and even deprecated it as tending to excite dissatis VOL. II. N faction at home and disturbance abroad. The growing extent and influence of the British and Foreign Bible Society, and the anxiety which it had evinced to promote the translation of the Scriptures into the oriental languages, added materially to the displeasure and alarm of the persons last alluded to.

It was not long before sentiments and feelings of a hostile nature were publicly avowed; and it forms a very remarkable coincidence of events in either hemisphere, that while attempts were, as we have already seen, making at Calcutta to arrest, or at least to impede, the progress of Scriptural translation, and to restrain the efforts of Christian missionaries, a formidable attack was carrying on in this country, with a view to check the ardour which had been kindled in the minds of multitudes in favour of both those great and interesting objects, and to provoke the authoritative interference of government to extinguish at once their hopes of effectually promoting them. The attack in question originated in a pamphlet published in the month of October 1807, under the title of "A Letter to the Chairman "of the East India Company, on the danger of in"terfering in the religious opinions of the natives "of India, and on the views of the British and Fo"reign Bible Society, as directed to India." This pamphlet, though at first anonymous, was shortly afterwards avowed by Thomas Twining, Esq. a senior merchant on the Bengal establishment; who announced it as only the precursor of a motion, which he intended to bring before the Court of East India Proprietors, for expelling from Hindostan all the Christian missionaries, who were then labouring in that extensive but neglected field; and for preventing the holy Scriptures from being circulated in the languages of the East. The alarm of this gentleman, which could excite so formidable an intention, was no doubt genuine and extreme; though the changes which have taken place since the date of his publication, both in the religious state of India, and in the opinion of the public at large respecting the propagation of Christianity in the East, may be said to give to his distorted representations the air of irony and satire, rather than of grave complaint and serious expostulation. Mr. Twining's pamphlet was chiefly composed of partial extracts from the Reports of the British and Foreign Bible Society, and from Dr. Buchanan's Memoir, which undoubtedly indicated the wish and the design to promote the knowledge of the Gospel throughout the world, and, amongst other quarters, in which that knowledge was particularly needed, throughout the British dominions in India. This laudable intention Mr. Twining interpreted as evidence of a strong disposition to interfere, in some violent and unwarrantable method, with the religious opinions of the native inhabitants, and as exposing our eastern possessions to the most imminent and unprecedented danger.

With respect to the share of the British and Foreign Bible Society in this extraordinary charge, it is only necessary to refer to the able reply published by the Rev. Mr. Owen, in the month of December following, and to that part of his History of the Society, which relates to this controversy.

The attack of Mr. Twining upon Dr. Buchanan « was founded partly upon some passages in his Memoir, in which he discusses, in the most calm and benevolent manner, the duty, the practicability, and the advantages of endeavouring to promote Christianity in India; and partly upon the misconstruction of one sentence, in which the acute sensibility of the former gentleman led him to imagine, that Dr. Buchanan, in expressing his opinion as to the expediency of *coercing* the contemptuous spirit of the *Mohammedans,* was desirous of exercising some species of *compulsion* with respect to the religious sentiments of our native subjects in general. The term thus used by Dr. Buchanan may perhaps be considered as unfortunate, and he himself, on being informed of the perversion which it had suffered, omitted it in a subsequent edition of his Memoir; but even as it originally stood, no one, who had read that publication with common attention and candour, could so far mistake the whole object of the writer, as to suppose him guilty of the absurdity of recommending, that'the natives of India should be converted to the Christian faith by *farce.*

Notwithstanding the vague and unsatisfactory nature of this attempt to arrest the progress of Christianity in India, there were not a few, who, from the respectability of the quarter from which it issued, from ignorance or miscQnception of the subject, from mistaken views of worldly policy, from the want of any lively sense of the infinite value of the Gospel, and from a morbid dread of every thing which was pronounced by persons affecting local knowledge as likely to endanger the security of our eastern empire, were disposed to favour and support it.

The prejudice and alarm which began to be excited by Mr. Twining's pamphlet were inoreased by the publication of one, and subsequently of a second, by Major Scott Waring; who inveighed with even greater warmth and violence against the Bible Society, the missionaries in Bengal, and the Memoir of Dr. Buchanan; and, in addition to the misrepresentation of his sentiments which has been just referred to, discovered in his benevolent recommendation of adopting destitute Hindoo children, with a view to their education in Christian principles, another proof of his wish to introduce a sysr tern of compulsion in India!

But the exertions of the friends of religion were successful in checking the rising spirit of jealousy and opposition occasioned by these publications; so that on the 23d of December, when the Court of Proprietors met at the India House, Mr. Twining found so little encouragement to propose his threatened motion, that he withdrew it, and the Court in consequence adjourned.

The important controversy, however, which had been thus begun, did not terminate here. Early in the year 1808, it was renewed by the publication of a pamphlet, entitled, a "Vindication of the Hindoos "from the aspersions of the Rev. C. Buchanan, "M. A.; with a refutation of his arguments for an "Ecclesiastical Establishment in British India. By "a Bengal Officer." This extraordinary publication was distinguished by the bold avowal, that the Hindoo system little needs the ameliorating hand of the Christian dispensation to render its votaries a sufficiently correct and moral people, for all the useful purposes of civilized society. Its military author, therefore, endeavoured strongly to maintain the excellence of the moral and religious doctrines of the Hindoos, and of the moral character of the Hindoos themselves. With much pretension, however, to local knowledge, he, in fact, betrayed much local ignorance, and with some partial information as to the speculative system of the Brahminical religion and morals, great disregard to its practical influence, and total deficiency in all large and general reasonings.

The " Bengal Officer," like his predecessors in this warfare, dealt much in general abuse of Dr. Buchanan's statements in his Memoir, but adduced no one definite proof of their incorrectness. And here it may be right to observe, that while a few expressions in that work relative to the apparent absence of religious views and feelings in the Europeans generally resident in India, might be considered as somewhat too strongly and indiscriminately hazarded, no well-grounded objection to his representations upon any point connected with his main argument was ever substantiated. So convinced was Dr. Buchanan himself of his correctness and integrity as to the statements contained in his Memoir, that in a note to his letter to the Court of Directors from Calcutta, in December 1807, which has been already mentioned, he ventured to make the following appeal upon this subject.

"The Memoir of the expediency of an Ecclesi"astical Establishment for British India has now "been in the hands of our Indian governments for "a year and a half, and I have not heard that any "one fact or deduction contained in that volume "has been disputed or disproved; which in this "countrv, where the merits of such a work can be "best understood, and where only just information "of the local circumstances therein detailed can be "obtained, and where moreover there are *fourteen* "weekly publications to animadvert on that infor"mation, may be considered as some testimony to "its general accuracy, as well as some acknowledg"ment of the necessity of the great measure therein "proposed."

The labours of the friends and advocates of diffusing Christian knowledge in India more than kept pace with those of its adversaries. Amongst others, the venerable Bishop Porteus wrote some remarks on Mr. Twining's pamphlet, which were published anonymously, and which, in a strain of animated and well-directed irony, defended the measures of the British and Foreign Bible Society, and what his Lordship termed " Dr. Buchanan's invaluable Memoir."

Early in the spring appeared Mr. Cunningham's "Essay on the duty, means, and consequences of "introducing the Christian religion among the "native inhabitants of the British dominions in "the East;" forming a part of the work which he had submitted to the University of Cambridge, as a candidate for Dr. Buchanan's prize. The main argument of this able and elaborate publication was founded upon the malignant and pernicious nature of the Hindoo superstition; which was here *So* completely developed, as not only to form a decisive answer to the statements of such writers as the Bengal Office,!-, but to prove the obligation of Great Britain to communicate that divine system of faith and morals, by which alone the civil and religious character of the natives of India can be effectually improved.

Mr. Cunningham's Essay was followed by the Prize Dissertation of the Author of these Memoirs; See Owen's History „i the Lritich end ibreign Bible Society, i. p. £50.

of which he will only observe, that he shall ever esteem it one of the chief privileges and blessings of his life to have contributed, in whatever degree, to the accomplishment of the great end which the admirable proposer of the subject had in view; the infinite importance of which is confirmed by every year's experience, and cannot fail ere long to be universally acknowledged.

One other work remains to be mentioned of singular excellence and authority; and of which it may be justly remarked, that had it appeared in an earlier stage of the controversy, it would have superseded every other. This was the production of Lord Teignmouth; who, together with the principles of Christian piety and benevolence, brought-.' to the consideration of the weighty subject in question the correct and extensive local knowledge and the practical wisdom and experience which were the result of the high stations he had occupied in India. The temperate and dignified manner in which his Lordship discussed the various topics connected with the controversy before us, deserve the highest admiration; nor is it too much to assert, that his "Considerations on the practicability, policy, and "obligation of communicating to the natives of "India the knowledge of Christianity," were not only conclusive of the temporary contest in which they appeared, but will remain a standing testimony to the duty of a Christian nation towards its ignorant and unconverted subjects.

It would be unjust to close this brief enumeration of the principal writers in this controversy, without mentioning the eminent services of one periodical publication, distinguished by the zeal and ability with which it originally embraced and steadily supported the great cause of Christianity in India. It is scarcely necessary to add the name of " the Christian Observer;" which, whether in the examination of the productions on either side of the question, or in original communications, may justly claim a very considerable share of the praise which belongs to its successful termination.

Thus, as in the instance of the rising opposition at Calcutta, the storm which threatened to overwhelm the efforts of Christian benevolence in this country to diffuse the knowledge of the Gospel in the East was quickly dispersed; and the advocates of this important and salutary measure were for the present permitted to continue their peaceful and charitable course without farther interruption or disturbance.

CHAP. II.

While the controversy, of which a brief view has been given, was thus carrying on, the person, whose zeal and activity had principally given occasion to it, was quietly pursuing his voyage from India to his native country. Of the incidents which occurred during the five months which intervened between Dr. Buchanan's departure from Point de Galle in Ceylon to his arrival in England about the middle of August, no memorial appears to have been preserved. The following extracts from letters to several of his friends, though they fail in expressing his emotions on revisiting his native shores, after an absence of twelve years, during which he had been employed in so important and honourable a manner, and had experienced such vicissitudes of joy and sorrow, of repose and toil, of gratification and trial, will yet afford some notices of his proceedings. They will serve also to shew his filial affection, his wish for retirement, yet his desire of usefulness as a minister of the Gospel, and his lively interest in the progress of true religion in this country.

His first visit, on his arrival in London, was to the house of Mr. Newton; "but judge," said he, to one of his correspondents, "what were my '' feelings, when I was informed that my venerable "friend had entered into rest some months before. "I next proceeded to Cadell's, expecting to have "had the 'Christian Institution' put into my "hands; but here also I was disappointed."

Thus deprived of two of the principal objects of his immediate attention, Dr. Buchanan turned to others of a more private and domestic nature.

"London, 20th August, 1808.

"I arrived here two days ago, and was happy to "hear that you and your family were well. I go "down to Northwold in a day or two, whence I shall "proceed to Scotland to see my aged mother; and "on my return I hope to pay you a visit in Corn"wall.

"I have enjoyed good health on board ship. I "have no thoughts of ever returning to India again. "My wish is, to take a cure of souls, and to grow "old preaching the Gospel; and I look out for re"tirement. The chairman and his deputy were de"sirous that I should conciliate the Directors, by "waiting on them individually in the usual manner. "I have accordingly paid my respects to them all. "It seems, that on Wednesday next there is to be a "grand discussion on Indian missions. Lord Minto "has sent home my letter to him, to the Court, and "this is the subject which calls for its attention on "Wednesday.

"In the mean time I dismiss it from my mind "altogether, being careless of the result, as it affects myself. I read no pamphlets, and scarcely know "what has been doing. Nor do I wish to know any "thing, till I have seen my family in England and "Scotland, and have enjoyed for a time their tranquil "society."

"Northwold, Norfolk, 30th Aug. 1808. "I received your letter as I was leaving London. "Your affectionate expressions well accord with your "long proved kindness to me and my family. It "would indeed give me a sincere delight to visit you "at this time with my two little girls; but I have "not lived with my mother these twenty years, a "fortnight excepted. I have a long arrear of filial "affection and personal attention to bring up, and "must first fulfil this duty. . "I shall probably stay over the winter in Scotland. "There is an Episcopal Church in the vicinity of my "mother's house, where I may exercise my ministry, "and where I may possibly remain, if I should find "my labours useful. "Charlotte and Augusta are so much grown, that "I should scarcely have known them. The natural "feelings of children to a father, and of a father to "his children, have been. displayed in a remarkable "manner in many instances, and with such powerful "sympathy, as has been delightful even to the be"holders."

"Stamford, 12th Sept. 1808.

"Much more good has been done by the pro"position of the literary prizes than I ever ex"pected.

"Wherever I go, some commotion prevails;

"a conflict between light and darkness, which was "not known when I left England twelve years "ago."

"Glasgow, 28th Sept. 1808.

"We arrived here on the 20th instant, and found "my mother and family in fine health, both in body "and spirit. We stopped on Sunday at Stamford, "on Wednesday at York, and on Sunday at Carlisle. "The Dean of Carlisle, with whom we dined, "lifted up his voice against the races for the first "time. He had long been oppressed in spirit on "the subject; and he devoted his last day of preach"ing this season to the consideration of it. The "cathedral was crowded, and he preached the word "with great energy and eloquence.

"Mr. S has written to me, hoping I am not

"offended at his interfering with the publication of "the book. I have answered, that on the contrary

"I consider his and Mr. G 's interference as

"the act of Christian friends; that I doubt not "they acted for the best, according to their judg"ment; but that I can form no opinion on the sub"ject myself, as I have not yet read the publications "of the controversy."

When the attachment of Dr. Buchanan to the plan developed in the work just alluded to is considered, his acquiescence in the judgment of his friends affords a striking proof of his diffidence and humility.

"On Sunday last," Dr. Buchanan again writes from Glasgow, " I preached in the English church "here to a crowded auditory. The Presbyterians "come to hear, notwithstanding *the organ.* Both "in England and Scotland a more tolerant spirit "seems to pervade the different sects than for"merly.

"In a few days I propose to leave Scotland, and "to proceed with my little girls to Bristol. If I "stay any longer at Glasgow, I fear I shall never get "away. "

Dr. Buchanan arrived at Bristol on the 21st of November, and on the 25th gave the following account of his journey from the North.

"I returned from Scotland by the way of New"castle and Durham, after passing a week at

"Edinburgh. I was frequently with Professor,

'-' with whom I discussed the Edinburgh Review, "which I told him was denominated in the middle "counties of England, The Northern Blast.' He "assured me that he had now nothing to do with that "work, directly or indirectly; and seemed to lament "that it was conducted with so little judgment. I "asked him whether it was too late to retrieve its "character; I was anxious for the fame of my coun

"trymen; the Bishop of Durham had already re"nounced it, and his example would soon be fol"lowed by others. The Reviewers observed in de"fence, that most of the obnoxious articles have

"come from England. told me that it

was "with the greatest reluctance the editor admitted "the Review on Indian Missions, and that he wrote "a long note in qualification of the text.

"I passed two days at Bishop's Auckland. Tha "Bishop entered into various subjects of religion "and literature with great spirit. He told me it "was true he had forbidden the Edinburgh Review "to lie on his table. He did not think it right to "sanction a work which had so grossly insulted re"ligion. Some other gentlemen had expelled it on "the same ground.

"I took an opportunity of mentioning to his "Lordship, when he was asking what appeared "strange to me after a twelve years' absence, that "I thought the Bishops seemed to have too little "correspondence with each other on the interests "of religion; that they were like twenty-four in"sulated kings or barons in their castles, while the "enemy Were scouring the plains, and did not suf"ficiently encourage men of learning and piety to "come near them, and offer their counsel on subjects connected with the Church at home and "abroad.

"I visited Mr. Cecil yesterday, who is close "by me here. He is much better; and is very "anxious that I should write the Life of Swartz. "I was happy to hear him talk with such spirit."

For the various excellencies of the eminent minister of Christ whose name occurs in the preceding sentence, and who was then near the close of his earthly career, the author of these Memoirs gladly seizes the opportunity of testifying his affectionate veneration. In a subsequent letter, Dr. Buchanan adds another brief notice of this admirable man.

"Notwithstanding his weakness, he seems to feel "a singular pleasure in hearing me talk on oriental "subjects, and the diffusion of the Gospel generally. "It seems he once preached a sermon" which led "him to some enquiry on these subjects; for most "people, I perceive, know little about them.

"You notice the spirit so hostile to you among "your relations. If it be merely on account of "the Gospel, there is nothing more to be said or "thought of it than this, 'That the reproach "of Christ is great riches; and that to you it is "given not only to believe, but to suffer for his "sake/ j

"I have been called to preach a charity sermon "for the Bristol Infirmary. Arid they now wish "me to preach the annual sermon at Mr. Bid"dulph's church, for 'Missions to Africa and the "East.' They think more highly of me than they This was Mr. Cecil's ablffancl impressiye sermon before the Church Missionary Society, in the year 1603.

Vol. ir. o

"ought to think; hut being now somewhat of a "public character, my testimony is acceptable. But "my chief employment is at St. Mary Redcliffe.

"I have no thoughts of going to India. There is no peculiar sphere of usefulness for me there; "nor is it probable that any will offer. As for my "place of residence for the remaining years of my "life, I have no partiality. I care not where I live "or go. It sufficeth that I am employed for the ' present."

In the course of the autumn in this year, Dr. Buchanan, received two letters from his friend Mr. Brown, dated about two months after his own departure from India; the following extracts from which are strongly expressive of that excellent man's esteem for his late valuable colleague.

"I begin," he says, "with acknowledging the "receipt of all your letters from Columbo, Cochin, "Tellicherry, Goa, Bombay, and lastly from Point "de Galle. The news all good. Your journey "prosperous, and promising the best fruits.

"Well! You have fought your fight, and finished with the Archbishop of Goa, and are gone; May "peace and safety attend all your paths; and may "the providence of God preserve you to embrace "your children, and to clo good in the world!

"I have the best accounts of Martyn, Sabat, and "Mirza. The Persian and Hindostanee are both "ready. You will see we want a press for Martyn.

"I send you a copy of the Archbishop's letter. ' No name was upon it. The inscription on the "Cover was 'The Vice-Provost,' and it was brought "to me.

"Since you left me, war has been in all my "gates. But I have nothing to lose; neither fame "nor money. Let them burn me if they please. "I shall make as good a fire as Brahmin women; "two of whom were burnt last week near us; one "before my eyes. I get disgusted and indignant "on these occasions, and am always weighed down "for some days after witnessing such horrible sa"crifices to Moloch. Surely the 'Christian Institution' will demolish this most diabolical religion.

"I now send you two copies of Lord Minto's "college speech. Mr. Harington, to whom I had "sent the report of the Chinese examination, took "it to his Lordship. He doubted at first whether "all this was real. To be certain, he sent Dr. Ley den to me; to whom the whole was rehearsed, "and who gave ' confirmation strong' to the report. "Lord M. made several enquiries of me, and "seemed pleased with what had been done.

"While I am writing, I have received a long "account of the particulars of 's death, from "his son. His end was most blessed. The victory "was complete. He was surprised to be told he "was dying, but it did not discompose him for a "moment. His language was, ' Whom have I in "heaven but thee?' He broke out in Dr. Watts's "translation of these words, which were his last. "I shall find, a week or two hence, some interesting "things to say in a funeral sermon, which I am "requested to preach, and should have preached if "not requested; for these are our hest occasions "for working on the dead mass; and you were al"ways diligent to improve them.

"I used to think you would make some improve"ment of my death. It must now be left to Lim"rick. Let him say, Alas! my brother, and I shall "be satisfied. I have been a brother to him, and "am yet; and shall be when I die, if I die before "him. I shall have something to add, perhaps, but "I say here,

"Yours affectionately,
"D. Brown."

The letter to which Mr. Brown refers in the preceding extract was from the Archbishop of Canterbury; and it is here added, as a proof of his Grace's approbation of the important measure which it was the great object of Dr. Buchanan's Ecclesiastical Memoir to recommend, and of his anxiety to promote its accomplishment.

"Lambeth Palace, Oct. 3d, 1807.

"Reverend Sir, "When I look back on the date which the manuscript transmitted through your means, from the college of Fort William, to the archiepiscopal library at Lambeth, bears upon its earliest pages, I am fearful lest I should appear to yourself, and to those with whom you are connected, insensible to the value of this splendid gift, or strangely negligent of common courtesy. At the time it arrived, I was anxiously employed in communicating with those, as well in office, as out of office, who were best acquainted with the wants of the Protestant Church in British India, and best able to supply them. If in my answer to your letter, written in the first pages of the Koran, I could have reported some progress in the great work of regulating the Church in India, I should have felt that in fulfilling my duty I had made the best return in my power for the munificence I had experienced from you. Under this expectation, I have been led imperceptibly to a longer silence than ought to have been permitted; and I am now obliged to break it, without making that report, which would have been its best apology. Nevertheless, Sir, I will not despair of ultimate success. The object we have in view is a reasonable object, and must not be lightly abandoned. It is not the spirit of making proselytes by which we are actuated, but the sober wish to maintain, in its pu-rity and strength, Christianity among Christians. If it shall please God through these means, the best, I had almost said the only means, in the hands of man, to spread the blessings of Christianity, it is a result devoutly to be wished, but not impatiently pursued. Experience may have taught us that they are blessings that will not bear to be crudely and prematurely obtruded; they must be left to grow at their ease, and to ripen out of the character, and discipline, and doctrine of that Church which is planted in India, and which is necessarily the object of daily and curious observation.

"I have the honour to be,--
Reverend Sir,
Your faithful humble Servant,
C. Cantuar."

The speech of Lord Minto, copies of which Mr. Brown mentions that he had transmitted to Dr. Buchanan, was that which his Lordship delivered on the 21st of February, 1808, after the annual disputations in the college of Fort William; and in which, amidst his testimony to the progress of oriental literature in that institution, he took occasion to advert in terms of high praise to the proficiency in the Chinese language of the missionaries at Serampore, which must have been peculiarly gratifying to Dr. Buchanan, as the early friend of that most important pursuit.

"I must not," said his Lordship, " omit to com"mend the zealous and persevering labours of Mr. "Lassar, and of those learned and pious persons "associated with him, who have accomplished, for "the future benefit, we may hope, of that immense "and populous region, Chinese versions, in the "Chinese character, of the Gospels of Matthew, "Mark, and Luke; throwing open that precious "mine, with all its religious and moral treasures, to "the largest associated population in the world."

To this liberal and enlightened tribute of applause to the importance of the Chinese translation of the Scriptures, Mr. Brown in the second of his letters to Dr. Buchanan added the gratifying and unexpected intelligence, that Lord Minto supported the translations generally, and had subscribed to some of the works then carrying on at the Seram'pore press.

The following extract from one of Dr. Buchanan's letters to a friend, in January 1809, on the dangerous illness of a near relative, as well as the tenor of the concluding remarks, shew the prevailing piety of his mind.

"I sincerely sympathize with you on this afflic"tion; but the excellent accounts you give of her "spiritual state must be your chief consolation. "Happy for her that her affliction hath been sanc"tified! Whatever be the event, there is great room for praise and thanksgiving. I feel this "the more from having just heard that a beautiful "young lady, of good family and great fortune, has "finished her course at the Wells here, and died "without a ray of hope. Blessed then is your "family, which hath ' this hope,' in the midst of a ' perverse generation. May it be your hope unto "the end!

"All is well in India; only Buonaparte is ex"pected. And if the news of this day be true, he "*may* be expected. But ' the Lord reigneth, be "the earth never so unquiet.' I behold the tumult "of the present scene with much tranquillity. But "we must be in the circumstances in which

"Miss now is, to be able to view it aright; "and to see the utter insignificance of things tem"" poral, when weighed in the scale with things "eternal."

In a letter to Mr. Brown about the same time, the following passages occur.

"People imagine that I am meditating war. "Nothing is farther from my thoughts. I am at "present reading the Bible, and studying some "subjects for sermons to poor people.

"I stand remote from the world. I do not even "know whether the Court of Directors pays my "furlough allowance. But on this, and other sub"jects, I shall be able to say more after I have "been a year in the country.

"The Chinese printing" (which had been sent to him by Mr. Brown) " is very admirable. You "are cheaper too than I was, when *l* gave four "annas for every character.

"The arrival of Mr. Thomason will brighten "your prospects. I told Mrs. M. her prayers "would bring good men.

"Mr. B. here is a most useful evangelist. I "shall enclose to you an account of the death of "his daughter, aged fourteen. He lost four chil"dren in one year, and preached nobly to the hearts "of his large congregation during the whole pe "riod. So you see good men have their trials on "the banks of the Severn, as well as on the "Ganges.

"You will regret to hear that Henry Kirke White "was first proposed to Mr. Thornton," (meaning for his own benefaction to some student at the University,) " and," for reasons which do not appear, " was rejected."

On the 26th of February Dr. Buchanan preached his sermon, entitled " The Star in the East," at the parish church of St. James, Bristol, for the benefit of the Church Missionary Society. This was the first of that series of able and well-directed efforts by which its excellent Author, in pursuance of the resolution he had formed in India, endeavoured to cherish and extend the interest he had already excited for the promotion of Christianity in the East. The object of this sermon was to detail some of the more prominent proofs, that " the day" had at length begun to " dawn," and " the day-star to "arise" on the benighted inhabitants of Asia; and its peculiar excellence consisted in the strength and simplicity with which these evidences were exhibited.

After stating the labours and the success of the Church of Rome, and of the Protestant missionaries, more particularly of the venerable Swartz, Dr. Buchanan introduced the highly interesting account of the martyrdom of Abdallah, and the conversion of Sabat, which can never be read without the deepest emotions of admiration and pity.

The subsequent apostasy of Sabat from the faith which he once appeared to have so cordially embraced, while it affords a lamentable proof of the depravity of the human heart, does not in the slightest degree affect either the truth of the narrative, or the object to which it was applied, of illustrating the divine efficacy of the Gospel. That will still remain the same, whether the unhappy apostate should, as there seems to be some faint reason to hope% again be " renewed to repentance," or become the final victim of impenitence and unbelief. Nor ought the deplorable defection of this once promising convert to be adduced as any proof of the want of judgment or penetration in Dr. Buchanan, and others', who, in common with him, trusted to the fair appearance and the striking evidences of sincerity, which this learned but deluded Arabian manifested during several years; though it may, and undoubtedly ought to teach a lesson, both of caution to the Christian minister, and of humility and self-distrust to the professed convert, not only in the East, but in every quarter of the world.

In a letter published in the Asiatic Journal for January last, from a Prince of Wales's Island Gazette, this wretched man refers to Dr. Buchanan's account of him in the " Star in "the East," and affirms, that he has never ceased to believe the truth of the Christian religion. Particularly the late Rev. Henry Martyn. The conclusion, however, which was drawn by Dr. Buchanan from the various facts he had enumerated, and which he afterwards strengthened by some other encouraging considerations, was sufficiently established, that the time for diffusing Christianity in the East was come. The remainder, therefore, of this interesting discourse was occupied with an earnest and persuasive appeal to his hearers on the duty of cordially supporting this important measure; which is so appropriate to every period, and contains so valuable a testimony to the nature and necessity of spiritual religion, that it can scarcely be deemed irrelevant to introduce a part of it in this place.

"Behold then, my brethren, the great undertake "ing, for the promotion of which you are now assembled. If it were in the power of this assem"bly to diffuse the blessings of religion over the "whole world, would it not be done? Would not "all nations be blessed? You perceive that some "take a lively interest in this subject, while others "are less concerned. What is the reason of this "difference? It is this: every man who hath felt "the influence of religion on his own heart will "desire to extend the blessing to the rest of raan"kind: whereas he who hath lived without concern "about the Gospel of Christ will not be solicitous "to communicate to others a gift which he values "not himself. At the same time, perhaps, he is not "willing to be thought hostile to the work. But "there is no *neutrality* here. 'He that is not with "Christ in maintaining his kingdom on earth,-' is "against him.' Every one of us is now acting a part in regard to this matter, for which he must "give an account hereafter. There is no one, how"ever peculiar he may reckon his situation or cir"cumstances, who is exempted from this respon"sibility.

Begin then at this time the solemn enquiry, "not merely into the general truth of Christ's re"ligion, but into its divine and converting power. "You observe that in this discourse I have distin"guished between the *name* of Christianity and "the *thing*. For it seems there are some persons "in this country, who having departed from the "principles of our Reformation, admit the *existence* "of the Spirit of God, yet deny his *influence;* and "who agree not with the Apostle Paul, that the "' Gospel cometh not in *word* only,' but ' in *power,* "and in the Holy Ghost, and in much assurance.'

"The great Author of our religion hath himself "delivered the doctrine in the most solemn manner "to the world. 'Verily, verily, I say unto you, (' Except a man be born again, he cannot see the "kingdom of God.' *Verily, verily;* it is an un"doubted truth, an unchangeable principle of the "heavenly dispensation, that, except a man be re"newed in his mind *by* the Spirit of God, he shall "not have power even to *see* or behold the kingdom "of God. If our Saviour hath delivered any one

"doctrine of the Gospel more clearly than another, "it is this of a spiritual conversion; and the de"monstration of its truth is found in all lands, "where the true Gospel is known. Christians, dif"fering in almost every thing else, yet agree in the "doctrine of a change of heart, through faith in "Christ. This is, in fact, that which distinguishes "the religion of God in Asia, from the religions of "*men.* In every part of the earth, where I my"self have been, this doctrine has been proclaimed "as the hope of the sinner, and the glory of the "Saviour."

The sermon from which the preceding extract has been taken was immediately published, and was not only universally circulated, but generally productive of a corresponding feeling in the minds of its numerous readers.

The services of Dr. Buchanan not being permanently required at Bristol, he was desirous of obtaining some settled employment; and, with the humility and anxiety to be actively engaged in his Master's service, which had ever distinguished him, would gladly have retired to some country curacy. "I "wish, too," he observed to a friend, " to be fixed "for a time, if it were but to organize a library;" having brought scarcely any books with him from India, except the Bible.

In the mean time he projected a journey to the University of Oxford, where he arrived at the beginning of April, and remained about ten days. His object in this visit was to look into the libraries, and to compare and collate certain oriental manuscripts. He appears to have been received with much civility by the Heads of Houses, and to have been gratified by the society of several members of the University. During his stay, he preached at the parish churches of St. Martin and St. Giles.

It might perhaps have been expected that the University would have conferred some mark of its respect on Dr. Buchanan, as the munificent patron and promoter of oriental literature and religion. The University of Cambridge had not, indeed, as yet set the example of such a step, though it took the first appropriate opportunity of so doing. It may, however, be regretted, that no proposal of any similar honour should have been subsequently made at this place; though Dr. Buchanan himself was so far from any feeling of this nature, that in a letter to one of his friends shortly after his visit to both Universities, he observed that they had been very kind to him, and had done every thing that he wished.

A few extracts from several letters written from Oxford, and its neighbourhood, will not be unacceptable. The first, it will be perceived, is to one of the sisters of the late Mrs. Buchanan.

'' Oxford, April 3, 1809. "This is the day on which I was united in mar"riage to your sister Mary. I rejoice when I think "that you and M. are following her steps. She is "now in the enjoyment of scenes of bliss, while "we are afflicted by contests below. But she had "her day of affliction also, and when she was suf"ficiently purified by the refiner, she ascended on "high.

' I hope you and I shall be carried through in "like manner, and leave some testimony that we "were not of this world. How great is the change "made by grace on a young person! May you be more and more conformed to his image, and learn "to know (what St. Paul saith passeth knowledge) "the length, and breadth, and height, and depth of "the love of Christ to usward.

"My love to your husband; and believe me to be very affectionately yours,
"C. Buchanan."

"Woodstock, 4th April, 1809.

"I spent yesterday in the Bodleian Library, and I am to-day looking over the Duke of Marlborough's "at Blenheim. He has a noble collection of ori"ental Bibles. I want to compare some Biblical MSS. from the East, with the Bodleian this week, "with the aid of Drs. White and Ford. Dr. Ford "is a well-informed vigorous scholar; but Dr. "White seems nearly worn out. There is nothing "that wears well in old age but heavenly learning: "a proof this, that there *is* a wisdom which "cometh from *above.*' It is only the Christian who "can say,,

"The soul's dark cottage, batter'd arid decay'd,-.
"Lets in new light thro' chinks that time has made:"

"Oxford, 13th April, 1809.

"In my last I asked you to aid me in doing a "service to the *English* church in India Will "you now grant a boon to the *Arabian* and *Per*"*sian* church? I want to send out immediately to "Calcutta a fount of Arabic and Persian types for "printing the Scriptures and other works in these "languages. The Persian is most urgent. I shall "want to see a specimen of the type before the "agreement be concluded.

"I have been at Blenheim two days, looking into the "Duke of Marlborough's library, where I found my

"old fellow collegian,, author of, domestic

"chaplain. I had not known it was my own friend "who was the author of that work. 'What,' said "I, ' have you spent the last twelve years in writing "*verses,* and to be mangled by the Edinburgh Re"view after all?' I urged him to run off imme"diately. He possesses noble talents; and looks "forward, though not with much ardour, to the "opportunity of making a better use of them than "he has hitherto done.". a This was respecting an organ, which Dr. Buchanan had been requested to procure for the mission church at Calcutta.

From Oxford Dr. Buchanan proceeded to London, from whence he wrote to Colonel Sandys as follows.

"London, 28th April, 1809.

"I received your last while I was at Oxford. I "stayed there about ten days; and left a manuscript "of the Gospel of St. John in the Ethiopic lan"guage, which I found in the East, with the Ori"ental Professor, Dr. Ford, who is going to collate "it. Other MSS. of the Hebrew and Chaldaic "Scriptures I propose to deposit in the public li"brary of the University of Cambridge. I proceed "thither to-morrow, to preach on Sunday in Mr. "Simeon's church.

"My friends here wish me to take Welbeck cha"pel, while Mr. White, the present preacher, goes "to his living in the country. If I find that my "endeavours are blessed, I shall probably remain in "it. But it is rather my wish to retire to a parish "in the country.

"The 'Star in the East,' I find, has excited a "general interest. I breakfasted yesterday with the "Bishop of London, who said he was sure it would "do a great deal of good."

The valuable Oriental manuscripts which, according to the intention expressed in the preceding letter, Dr. Buchanan presented to the public library, on his first visit to the University of Cambridge VOT. IX. P after his return to this country, were those which he had procured during his journey to the coast of Malabar. They were twenty-five in number, chiefly Biblical, and written in the Hebrew, Syriac, and Ethiopic languages. The most curious and important of these manuscripts are a copy of the Hebrew Pentateach, written on goatskins, and found in one of the Black Jews' synagogues at Cochin; a copy of the Bible, containing the books of the Old and New Testament with the Apocrypha, written on large folio vellum, and in the ancient or Estrangelo character, which was a present to Dr. Buchanan from the venerable Bishop of the Syrian churches; and a version of the New Testament into Hebrew, executed by a learned Rabbi in Travancore, about one hundred and fifty years since. This version was transcribed by Mr. Yeates, at Cambridge, by the appointment and at the expense of Dr. Buchanan, chiefly with a view to promote the production of a translation of the New Testament in the pure-style of the Hebrew of the Old, for the benefit of the Jews, and in aid of he laudable design for this purpose of the London Society for the conversion of that ancient people. The same laborious scholar afterwards published a collation of the Indian copy of the Pentateuch, which had been also made at the expense of the munificent donor, and was printed by the Syndics of the University Press for the benefit of Mr. Yeates.

A few extracts from various letters to his friends will serve as a brief journal of Dr. Buchanan's proceedings at this period.

"Terrace, High Street, 12th May, 1809.

"I returned yesterday from Hertford college, "with which I was much pleased. Of course it "owes its present efficiency chiefly to a wise selec"tion of professors. Dealtry alone would do honour "to any institution.

"My friends have found me out here, and my "engagements multiply; but after a short time I "hope to be at large. I find a great body of In"dian families in these streets, who appear to have "really less religion here than they had in the East. "In the great multitude with whom they are now "mixed, their conduct is not so easily recognized "as in India; and being less conspicuous, they "think themselves less responsible. It is difficult "to know what or how to preach to such. I must "pray for divine direction. 'The Ethiopic Gospel is now at Cambridge; "and one of the professors is about to examine and "collate it, as soon as he has improved himself a "little more in the language. Other persons will.." be appointed to examine the other MSS.

"A few Sundays ago I preached the annual cha"rity sermon at the Lock Hospital, where I found "a great body of the religious world of London of "the higher cast. Instead of entertaining them "with news from India, which, perhaps, some ex"pected, I gave them an account of the spiritual "resurrection."

In the letter which next follows, Dr. Buchanan notices the distinguished honour which had been just conferred upon him by the University of Cambridge, and adds some interesting particulars respecting his ministry at Welbeck chapel.

"Cambridge has conferred on me the highest "honour in her gjft. She petitioned his Majesty "to grant me the degree of Doctor in Divinity. "The mandate was issued, and I received the de"gree on the commencement day last week. Dr. "Ramsden, as Regius Professor of Divinity, deli"vered a speech on the occasion, in the name of "the University, in which he referred to the evan"gelization of the East, and to my endeavours. "The Duke of Gloucester and many of the nobility "were present. I waited on the Bishop of Bristol "after my degree, and received from his Lordship " an assurance, that he would ever support the "cause in which I had been so long engaged. "He subscribed at the same time to the Bible So"ciety. All the Heads of Houses whom I saw "professed their gratification at the public notice "the University had taken of the subject. I shall "be shortly called to preach before the University.

"I live very retired at present; preaching regu"larly to my congregation, and attend"" Uttle to "public affairs. The nobility have mostly left town; "but their seats at my chapel are filled generally "by the poorer sort. The Duke of Gordon, Lord "R. Seymour, and others, yet remain. I pray to "be enabled to persevere to the end of my time "with them, next November; and after that, to "the end of my race, wherever I shall be called to "run.

"The Christians in Travancore are suffering per"secution, which may do them good. I foresee "another conflict on missions: may we all be found "faithful and prudent, wise and harmless!

"Before the nobility left town, I delivered to "some of them at Welbeck chapel my views of the "pious and useful life of the late Bishop of London. "I noticed his exertions to preserve the purity of "public morals; and gave them an account of my "last interview with the Bishop, a few days before "his death, and of his testimony to serious piety. "Speaking of a public trial then pending, in which "some allusion had been made to the religious cha"racter of one of his friends, he observed, that the "character of public men professing religion was "severely tried, and often greatly misrepresented "in the present age. And, addressing himself to "the Master of a college in one of our Univer"sities, then in company, he added these words: "'The man who shall at this day conduct himself "in a strictly religious manner, and make a pro"fession of serious piety, must be content to be "misunderstood by some, and called by a name of "reproach.'"

The following is a somewhat fuller account of the effect of Dr. Buchanan's ministry at Welbeck chapel, from a letter to a friend soon after he had left it.

"The power of religion which I witnessed in "Marybone was more among the lower than the "higher classes; though even among them I have "reason to believe that good has been done. A "general spirit of conciliation was manifest. Lady retains an abiding impression, and does the

"works of righteousness. I visited her frequently.

"Lady also has evinced a just sense of true

"religion, and others of rank. But the glory of the "Gospel was chiefly manifested in Mrs. B. who "died last month. She was but in humble life; "but many of the nobility visited her, and benefited "by her example."

In the month of August Dr. Buchanan left London on a journey into Yorkshire; the object of which will be perceived by the following extract from a letter to Colonel Sandys.

"London, 31st Aug. 1809.

"I have been absent from London the last ten "days. My friends wished to know if I should like "to fix at Scarborough, if the advowson of the "Kvirag were purchased; and I went down to see the "place and the people. There is but one church, "and seven thousand inhabitants, besides the vi"sitors. I found the Rev. Mr. Robinson of Lei"cester there; and we both preached last Sunday, "he in the morning, and I in the evening. It was "calculated that three thousand persons were in "church. I do not think that I shall settle there; "but I leave the event to Him whose providence "governs all things.

"While at Scarborough, I was hospitably en"tertained by a family I have long heard of, and "wished much to see, Mr. Thompson's of Kirby "Hall.

ƒ I am glad you are reading Milner's Church "History. He has combined more real piety and "sound sense in these volumes than are to be found "in half the books of the day.

"I am engaged by Mr. Burn to preach two "sermons at Birmingham on the 8th of October "next, on some annual occasion. My journey has "refreshed me, I think, after some months residence "in London, though it was rapid, and chiefly in the "mail. I am glad that William has such an awful "sense of the importance of the ministry. That "is more likely *in time* to lead him to it, than to "drive him from it."

About the first week in October Dr. Buchanan took a second journey into Yorkshire, and returned at the end of a fortnight, for the purpose of preaching a series of sermons on the interesting occasion afforded by the fiftieth anniversary of the reign of our venerable Sovereign; and with the last of these discourses he closed his engagement at Welbeck chapel.

CHAP. III.

Early in the ensuing month Dr. Buchanan communicated to the friend to whom the preceding letter was addressed his intention of again entering into the marriage state. The lady with whom he formed this second engagement, was the daughter of Henry Thompson, Esq. of Kirby Hall, near Boroughbridge, in Yorkshire. Dr. Buchanan, as we-have already seen, became acquainted with this respectable family during his first visit to Scarborough, and was attracted towards Miss Thompson by her piety, her active benevolence, and her filial duty and affection. This connection was particularly agreeable to Mr. and Mrs. Thompson, and was universally approved by the friends of Dr. Buchanan. The marriage accordingly took place in the month of February following; from which period he fixed his residence in Yorkshire.

A few extracts from his letters will describe the plan of life upon which he now entered, and shew with how much promptitude and diligence he engaged in the duties of the ministry.

' Kirby Hall, March 1810. "We live at Moat Hall, or Parsonage, within a "quarter of a mile of the mansion. I have under"taken the whole charge of the parish of Ouseburn. "On the Thursday and Sunday evenings I have a "meeting of my parishioners in my own house. I "read a portion of Scripture to them, and expound "it; and generally incorporate the subject of the "lecture in a prayer. I ought to be thankful for "the attentive ear of the people.

"Mrs. Buchanan enters into these plans, with "much ardour and affection,

"After staying here some months, I shall probably return to London; at least my friends urge me "to resume Welbeck. I published three Jubilee "Sermons, as a record that I was once there. "They are passing through av second edition, to "which is to be annexed ' the Star in the East.'"

The friend who originally introduced Dr. Buchanan to Welbeck chapel was anxious that he should be permanently fixed in that or in some similar station, which he had shewn that he was so well qualified to fill. He therefore proposed the building of a chapel in one of the western parishes of London, and wrote to Dr. Buchanan for his approbation of the plan. To this he replied as follows.

"Accept my sincere thanks for your kind con"gratulations. I was about to write to you, that "our correspondence might not cease on account "of distance.

"I have next to thank you, in the name of "the Church in India, for your zeal in relation to "the organ.

"I much approve your proposal for building a "chapel; and I trust it will please Providence to "bring the work to a conclusion. I take it for "granted that you mean a building which will con"tain two thousand people, with all the latest im"provements in church accommodation, and pro priety of decoration.

"I know not how it may please God to dispose "of my life and services in the revolution of years, "but I consider the situation you propose as highly important; and I beg you will proceed with your "plan of building the chapel, under the presumption "that I shall be its minister.

' Great simplicity, I think, ought to be observed in the construction and finishing; approaching "nearer to the Gothic than the Grecian taste, but "not to be wholly in either style; for there is no "such thing, I allege, as *truth* in architecture. An "oval or oblong octagon is by far the best general "plan of an edifice, having the pulpit in the phonic "centre. But I shall submit to your judgment in "all things."

Notwithstanding the apparently promising nature of this, and of a similar plan, which was supported by many opulent inhabitants of Marybone, various difficulties, well known to those who embark in such engagements, prevented the accomplishment of either; and circumstances in the life of Dr. Buchanan not long afterwards occurred, which proved that the expectations of his friends upon this point would, as far as *his* ministry was concerned, have been but too soon disappointed. In the mean time the idea was mutually cherished.

The Jubilee Sermons, to which reference has more than once been made, were published early in the year 1810, and were very generally read and admired. The threefold view Dr. Buchanan took of a subject, which the well-known circumstances of the occasion rendered peculiarly interesting, gave him an opportunity of embracing a variety of topics, which a more limited plan would scarcely have allowed. The first of these sermons exhibits a view of the Mosaic jubilee, as a religious, moral, and political institution; together with its analogy to "the acceptable year of the Lord," proclaimed by the Saviour of the world. The second was devoted to the British jubilee, and contained an animated review of the political and religious blessings which had been bestowed upon this favoured country during the lengthened reign of his present Majesty; amongst the latter of which he particularly dwells on the preservation of our national Church in her faith and polity, the increase of true religion throughout the empire, the general instruction of the poor, and the universal diffusion of the Holy Scriptures. The last of these excellent discourses, which is perhaps the most generally useful and important of the three, leads us forward to the closing scene of all, the heavenly jubilee. The employment and felicity of heaven, and the character of those who shall be admitted to the celestial jubilee, are here considered; and the whole is concluded by a copious application of the subject, which includes the most important practical topics, adapted to the circumstances of the higher classes of society. Amongst these Dr. Buchanan introduced a powerful appeal as to the duty of propagating the Gospel in heathen nations. Though the subject of these sermons partook of an occasional character, the general views they display will doubtless preserve them from oblivion, and render them more than temporary proofs of the various knowledge, the fervent yet rational piety, and the warm yet enlightened benevolence, which distinguish the writings of their author.

Of the second edition of his Jubilee Sermons,

Dr. Buchanan sent a copy to his eldest daughter, accompanied by the following note. "My dear Charlotte, "I have the pleasure to send you a book, which

"I hope you will receive as a mark of my affection.

"My chief desire in regard to you and Augusta is

"that you may be prepared on earth for the *heavenly "jubilee;* and in regard to myself, that I may meet

"you there.

"I hear from some, that you are not inattentive "to religious subjects. This gives me real pleasure. "It is a noble thing to see the young daughter follow "the steps of her departed mother. That mothej now rejoices in the heavenly jubilee, and looks for "the time when her two children shall join her in "singing the song of the Lamb."

In the spring of this year, Dr. Buchanan received letters from Mr. Brown, which announced to him the tranquil and even prosperous state of things in India, as to the promotion of Christian knowledge, and the active labours of many learned and excellent persons in forwarding the designs of his Christian Institution, under the fostering care of the Corresponding Committee of the British and Foreign Bible Society. Mr. Brown dwelt with peculiar energy and delight on the exertions of Mr. Martyn and his associates, and pleaded strongly in behalf of the new Arabic translation of the Scriptures, then recently undertaken by Sabat.

Another Indian letter which Dr. Buchanan received at this time was from the Rev. Mr. Kolhoff, the pious and excellent missionary in Tanjore. It is dated October 21, 1809, and is as follows. "Rev. and very worthy Sir,

"Your very kind letter of the 4 th of January di' rected to the Rev. Mr. Horst and myself, we had "the pleasure to receive on the 8th of July last, and "beg you to accept of our hearty and sincere thanks "for your kind remembrance of us, and for the affec"donate regard and attention you have shown to"wards the mission committed to our care.

"Upon the receipt of your favours, Mr. Horst "has, agreeably to your request, without delay, set "about collecting materials for publishing the life of "our much respected and beloved predecessor, the "late Rev. Mr. Swartz, and has now ready about ten "sheets closely written, which will give nearly the "same number in print, and which he would have "despatched ere this, if he had not found out that "he had unfortunately omitted several material "points in the very beginning of Mr. Swartz's life.

"It gives us great pleasure to acquaint you, that "the Honourable the Court of Directors have taken "into their benevolent consideration our humble pe"'tition addressed by us to the government of Ma"dras, at the end of the year 1806, and have been "kindly pleased to grant an addition of seven hun. " dred to their former donation of five hundred pa"godas on account of the Protestant schools of this "mission.

"The resolution of government came to our "hands on the 13th of this month, at a time when "we were ready to despond and sink under the bur"den which oppressed us, and has given us a fresh "motive for thankfulness to God for his fatherly "care towards us. To you also, my dear Sir, our "warmest acknowledgments are due, for having sug"gested that measure to us, and we beg you to '' accept the assurance of our most lively gratitude "for your friendly advice, which has had such a be"neficial effect on the cause of the mission, and of "the Gospel of Jesus Christ."

The life of that eminent missionary, the venerable Swartz, which is thus alluded to in his worthy successor's letter, was a favourite subject with Dr. Buchanan. He had proceeded so far with it as to be intending to publish it a year or two before his own death; but was prevented from exe, curing his plan by the information he received of the same work having been undertaken by another person. The papers which he had collected for this purpose are now in the hands of his family.

The following extracts from Dr. Buchanan's correspondence, in the spring of this year, will illustrate his piety and Christian sympathy, as well as the habitual activity and ardour of his mind with reference to the great object of his life.

"Kirby Hall, 1st May, 1810.

"My dear Sister, "Your letter gave me great pleasure. You have a hope of being restored to your family and to active service a little while longer. I say a little while; for you must not look to long life, unless it should please God to restore you soon to strong and confirmed health. But let us not talk of life, but of how we are to live. I admire your expression, and the spirit which animates it, ' I trust I have an encreasing desire to devote myself to the Lord.' May this desire, my dear Sister, live in your heart till you die. It will be like ' a well of water springing up into everlasting life;' for this desire of which you speak has been imparted to you by the Holy Spirit, which our Lord compares to the water of life. 'If any man thirst, let him come to me and '-drink;' and then it is added, ' This spake he of the Spirit, which they that believe on him should receive.' John vii. 37. Blessed are they in whose hearts this desire has been awakened! It is more to be valued than crowns and diadems. How beautiful is this desire in a female, and in a young person, and in the mother of children! For who led your steps to ' the waters' when you first heard the invitation, ' Ho every one that thirsteth? Behold the world around you, how few thirst-for the waters!-'--, -

"I now behold in you, your dear sister Mary thirsting after righteousness. The promise will be fulfilled to you, as it was to her. 'They shall be filled.' I have no admonition to give you. You are under heavenly guidance. One thing I will notice;-this is your season of prayer. Let your prayers be offered up incessantly at this time for your husband and children; first, that he also may be a well of water, nourishing the souls x)f others unto, eternal life; that he may ' increase,' if you are to decrease-; and that new strength may be given him as he approaches the vigour of life and understanding. You know that by the divine command the persons appointed to the 'service of the tabernacle'-were confined to the period between thirty and fifty; and that is-certainly the period of the most effective service.

Vol. 11. a

And it will cost him and me many a sigh, if, when that period has elapsed, any thing should have interrupted our zeal and labour in the heavenly ministration. Secondly, that your dear children may grow up in the nurture and admonition of the Lord. For now is the time to lay up a treasury of prayers for them, which may be answering when your spirit is on high, and your body is in the dust. And pray for me also, that I may be found faithful. If I should survive you in life, it will be a great satisfaction to me, to reflect that I once had your prayers. And pray for your brother in the ministry, and for your father and mother, and all your family. For when ' the spirit of grace and supplication is poured out,' (Zech. xii. 0.) its objects are indefinite. When we 'look upon Him whom we have pierced,' we shall be anxious to bring all we love to behold the same glorious Redeemer. Then do we understand for the first time what is meant by charity that charity whose boundless praises are set forth in the 13th of the 1st of Corinthians, and which the world understands not.

"My love to your brother, and to my little girls. Adieu..

C. Buchanan."

"Kirby Hall, 16th April, 1810. "I rejoice to hear that C. is alive and well, and "that the Malayalim version of St. Matthew's Gos"pel has been *printed.* There are upwards of two "hundred thousand Christians, Catholic and Syrian, "who can read it.

"I should gladly aid the, if I could; but

"the truth is, I have no papers by me, not even of "a year's standing. When in India, I emptied my "bureau every year regularly, and committed papers "and letters to the flames. But I shall think of "something for you now and then.

"I am looking out with some solicitude to see "what may be done, both in regard to England "and India; and I think Providence will soon open a way. In the mean time, the Gospel is preached "both at home and abroad, and 'the kingdom' "advances. It is ours to work to-day.' To *(rfoegov "j«iA.si ful.* Christ will see to his own church 'to"morrow.' I pray that I may do in the right spirit "the portion of work assigned me, whatever it be; "if indeed I belong to the family of Christ, and "have found mercy to be faithful.

"I am not qualified to meet the public eye often. "I am neither copious nor ready j and I can truly "say, I never write what pleases myself. But I "will give you bones now and then, if you will give "them flesh. And I pray that you and I may en"crease in *zeal* in the great work. There is no "zeal without *intemperance,* as the world defines it. "For what is temperance? Ask first at the equi"noctial line, and then at Nova Zembla. For so "extensive are the latitudes of thinking among the "servants of the Gospel; even amongst those who *P* are promoting most successfully the interests of "Christ's kingdom."

« Kirby Hall, 23d April. "The ship Charlton, in which I returned from "India, has been carried into the Mauritius by two "French frigates. Poor Limrick went down in the "Calcutta, together with L—— and his heaps of "paper.

"The organ for the mission church has been "shipped. It is a noble one.

Hebetude and illiberality are apt "to creep on our minds after a long retirement in "a nook of the vineyard. We need to be 'with"stood to the face,' like St. Peter, and to reeeive "the bastinado on the soles of our feet once a month at least, to keep us active and operative, "according to 'the gift that is in us.' Men who "walk in and about a house for a whole life are at "last afraid of people who walk abroad, and begin "to criticise and to despise them; for they really "do not understand what they are doing. And "we must bear with such. For we should have "been just the same had we vegetated in a corner."

On the 12th of June, Dr. Buchanan

preached the annual sermon before the Church Missionary Society, at St. Anne's, Blackfriars. It was a grand occasion, and a collection of nearly four hundred pounds proved the interest excited by the preacher on behalf of the great objects of that important Society. From the text, "Ye are the light of "the world," Dr. Buchanan forcibly addressed his Christian audience on the solemn duty attached to their profession of giving light to a benighted world. After some excellent observations on the sermon upon the mount, for the purpose of pointingout the moral character of the "children of the "light," the preacher observed, that if Christianswished to be "the light of the world," they would draw their light from Christ, and send forth preachers bearing the character which he hath delineated; and that if they were instruments of the "true light," they would be zealous in adopting the most effectual means of diffusing it. In discussing these two propositions, Dr. Buchanan recurred to a subject he was so well qualified to describe, the moral darkness of the Pagan world, gave much interesting information, and suggested many valuable hints relative to missions to the heathen.

The following observations on the Society before which this discourse was delivered, and on the British and Foreign Bible Society, are added for the purpose of recording some express testimony to his warm approbation and support of both those ad mirable institutions.

"Your object and that of the Bible Society is "the same. It is—to give the Bible to the world. "But, as that sacred volume cannot be given to "men of different nations until it be translated "into their respective languages, it is the province "of your institution to send forth proper instru"ments for this purpose. Your Society is confined "to members of the Established Church. You do "not interfere with the 'Society for the Propaga"tion of the Gospel in Foreign Parts/ nor with "that 'for promoting Christian Knowledgefor "neither of these professes the precise objects to "which you would confine yourselves. It does not "seem to be possible to frame an objection to your "establishment. When the design and the proceed"ings of your institution shall have been fully made "known, you may expect the support of the epis"copal body, of the two Universities, and of every "zealous member of the Church of England.

"It has been objected to that noble institution "to which we have alluded, the British and Fo"reign Bible Society, that it is in its character "*itniversal;* that it embraces *all,* and acknow"ledges no *cast* in the Christian religion: and it "has been insinuated, that we ought not to be "zealous for Christ's kingdom, if we must asso"ciate, in any degree, with men of all denominations. "But, surely, there is an error in this judgment. "We seek the aid of all descriptions of men in de"fending our country against the enemy. We "love to see men of all descriptions shewing their allegiance to the King. Was it ever said to a "poor man, You are not qualified to shew your "allegiance to the King? You must not cast your "mite into the treasury of your King? My bre"thren, let every man who opposes these institu tions examine his own heart, whether lie be true "in his allegiance to the King of kings..

"For myself, I hail the present unanimity of "hitherto discordant bands as a great event in the "Church; and as marking a grand character of "Christ's promised kingdom; when ' the 'leopard "shall lie down with the kid; and the calf, and the young lion, and the fatling together, and a little "child shall lead them.' Isaiah xi. 6. *I* consider "the extension and unity of "the Bible Society as "the best pledge of the continuance of the Divine mercy to-this land: and I doubt not, the time "will come when the nation wrH reckon that So"ciety a greater honour to her, as a Christian "people, than any other institution of which she "can boast."

One scene of exertion in the life of Dr. Buchanan was followed by another. On the 23d of June he thus wrote to a friend.

"I am appointed by the University of Cambridge to preach before them two sermons on Conamence"ment Sunday, the 1st of July next. I am rather "weak in spirit at present, and not strong in bodily "health: but I pray for strength, and I trust the "Lordwill sustain me. My sermons will be pub"lished.". 7 '-'..-,

Of Dr. Buchanan's Commencement Sermons we.shall have occasion to speak more fully when wenotice their publication. In the mean time, the. following brief account of them by himself to one of his friends soon after they were delivered may not be unacceptable to the reader.. -..

"London, July 11th, 1810.

"Your letter of the 30th ult. followed me to. "London; for I only stayed at Cambridge two days. "after I preached.

"I addressed the students on the importance of "the sacred office, in conclusion; and intimated,"that the time was now come, when every ma% "who. stood on the' side of religion, must be con"tent to bear a name of reproach; for it was a "necessary evidence of his character.

"I preached for three quarters of an hour in the "morning, and above an hour in the afternoon.i "There was the most solemn stillness. The church "was crowded....

"On the Tuesday following, the Bishop of Bristol "came up to me in the Senate House, and thanked "me for the discourses, and expressed a hope that "they would be published. Others did the same.. "Dean Milner,. who is Vice-Chancellor, informed "me soon afterwards, that he thought-himself au"thorized to grant the imprimatur of the University"for their publication; and I am' preparing them 7 for the press accordingly-. I mean to publish "important matter as an Appendix. Adieu;.-.

':.. c:.. ... . " *To Colonel Sandys..* '. ." "Scarborough, 24th Aug. IS 10, -" I thank you for-your excellent letter of the,. 27th July. A letter from you is always worth "something. Continue to pray for me, and to, "exhort me... '. .

"Since my arrival here, I have been engaged in. "preaching regularly on Sundays and Wednesdays., "at the great church, to the strangers and residents at the Spa.

"I should have published my University Sjer mons, and many other things by this time; but, the truth is that the congregations at Scarborough,, and the hope of some utility, have put Cambridge, an.d its scenes, almost out,of my head. I preach "here a fortnight longer, and then return to Kirby. "Hall.. After my return, I shall sit down to the, "Cambridge lucubrations." "

In the autumn of this year Colonel Macaulay, one, of the most valued friends of Dr. Buchanan, returned to this country. It is to this circumstance,, and to the intimate association between the name of that gentleman and the Malayalim version of the New Testament, that the following extracts, from letters to him,.and to his brother, Z. Macaulay Esq.. refer.

"Kirby Hall, 2Sth Sept, 181-0.

"I rejoice to hear that your brother is soon ex"pected, and that he comes by land. That will be "a proper *finale* to his pilgrim life. I am happy "to hear that two Gospels are finished in Malayalim, "I had been informed that St, Matthew only had "been printed, and that it had been distributed j "and I said so in my sermon. But it is better now "that the four Gospels should be distributed, bound "up together. I shall write to Mr. Woodhouse on "the subject. How many copies has he sent you? "If he has sent many, I shall forward them to Cal"cutta, the fountain-head of distribution, with in"structions to Mr. Brown.

"Will you have the goodness to send a copy "neatly bound to the Rev. Mr. Kerrich, Librarian "of the University of Cambridge, for the public "Library?

"You may also send bound copies to the Bible "Society, Bartjett's Buildings Society,.and to the "University of Oxford; also to the Universities "of Edinburgh, Glasgow, St. Andrew's, and Aber"deen. To save you trouble, if you will put them into the hands of your bookseller, he will transmit "them; arid I will pay bis bill, with thanks to "you."

"9th October. "This is great news. And so C. is thus far "through the wilderness; once more in his aative "land' May he pass through the Jordan flood at "last with the voice of triumph and thanksgiv"ing!

"Will you have the goodness to forward the "trunk to me as soon as it ean be rescued from "the India House? It contains some papers, I be"lieve, which I wish to see before what I am now "preparing goes to press.

"There is no person in this country who can "improve the Malayalim translation, because it is '' performed by men to whom the language is ver"nacular. It is not like the versions executed by "Europeans.

"The Bible Society may assume great credit to "itself by patronizing this version, for the demand

'' for copies will be perpetual and inexhaustible;

"even until ' the mountains shall be cast into the

"sea.'"

"*To Colonel Macaulay. "*7 th November.

"I am concerned to find that Cheltenham is ne"cessary for you. But I think you will not remain "there long. A little of the waters is enough. "Pray retreat as soon as the cold weather warns "you. The warm town is the place for you. I "have been at Bath, Clifton, Cheltenham, Scar"borough, since my return. But there is no place "like warm and busy London in the winter; unless, "like me, you had a fireside of your own, and a "wife and a hissing urn and a sofa to wheel round, "to read the book of four pages. Another argu"ment for an early *hejira* from Cheltenham is its unprofitable society. I have looked through all "these places, and would rather pass a month at "Chetwe or Trivandupuram with you, than be con"demned to mix daily with the visitors at a water"ing place in our own country..' ."I find the difference of *cast* greater here than "in India. I am thankful that I can aspire more, "day by day, to be of the high cast. I wish to be "a pure Namboory among Christians. And if the "Sooders will not go off the road for me, I must "go off the road for them. —'. is in this sense

"a. Brahmin of high cast. He is indeed ' a gift of "God' to his country; follow him, even as he fol".lows Christ.

"1 give you twelve months complete before you "settle; and if you settle then I shall be thankful; "though perhaps Providence has ordained that you "should ever continue, like Abraham, a pilgrim and a "sojourner in the land, in which you have no inherit"ance, ' but look forward to another country,' to a "city whieh hath foundations, whose builder and "maker is God.' Blessed is the man who wishes "not to build a city in this world. This is often a "ruling passion with Indians; they come home to

"build a city and a tower.-« is building a mansion with seven turrets on his estate.

"Adieu, my dear Sir,

"c.buchanan.

The following passage in a letter to another friend contains the first intimation of a tendency to serious indisposition which Dr. Buchanan appears to have felt since his return from India.

"Kirby Hall, 7th Nov. 1810.

"We returned lately from Scarborough, where "I passed two months, ministering twice a week in the large church there. Since my return, I have been visited with an indisposition, which the fa"culty do not seem to understand very well. It is "merely a great quickness of breathing, and great "lassitude from slight exercise, without any other "complaint whatever.-I desisted from preaching "for a fortnight; but mean to resume it. It is "probably some illness induced by a hot climate; ".and it becomes me to ' work while it is called "to-day.' '..-'-'- ';.' ".-'

"My letters from India state that tine Gospel "flourishes in almost every quarter. The seed sown "is producing fruit where there has been very little "cultivation; and now our attention is directed to "the Malay isles; for the whole Dutch'empire in the "eastern ocean will probably soon be ours. The "word of truth, I am happy to inform you, runs arid "is glorified in these parts" in Yorkshire) "also; "but the chief evil is, that it is rather *fashionable* "among the lower classes. I find the most useful "preaching is to draw aside the cloak of.profession, "and see what is under it.",'..

Dr. Buchanan was now employed in preparing his Cambridge Sermons for the press. To these he was intending to add as an Appendix a variety of new and interesting matter, connected with the great subject of his discourses, and illustrating the progress of the Gospel in the East. Distrusting, however, his own judgment upon a few points, amongst which was the name which this appendage should assume, or willing, at least, to submit it to that of others, he referred the whole to the revision and ultimate determination of two or three able and judicious friends. It is to them that the following extracts refer; and they will serve at once to evince the Christian simplicity and humility which adorned the writer's character.

"Kirby Hall, 22d October, 1810.

"Tell K. that the half of my Appendix is gone

"up. I requested and to expunge any "thing they thought wrong: and intimated to "them, that I wished not to give any unnecessary "offence in word or manner; but that it was my "purpose to pronounce a faithful and unequivocal "testimony to the truth of the Gospel. I pray that "God will overrule the evil of my work for good "to the souls of men. For it hath enough of evil, "although I trust the purpose is good.

"I do not want fame, (I mean, as a carnal ob"ject,) but I wish to glorify Christ on earth, as I "can, the few days that may remain to me. I "think with you, that W. had enthusiasm and "many infirmities. So had Luther. *"sit mea anima cum illo V*

The succeeding passages were addressed to Colonel Macaulay; whose long residence in the south of India, and intimate acquaintance with the principal scene of Dr. Buchanan's researches, peculiarly qualified him for the friendly office which he was requested to undertake.

"Kirby Hall, 20th December. "I shall be very thankful for your revision, par"ticularly of the 'Syrian Christians;' for I quote "much from memory and imperfect notes. Only "finish it in your own words for I am not very "strong for

study at present, and my church occu' pies my attention. What I say to you, I say to "your brother: for you are both friends of the truth in an evil day.

"I expect no particular effect from the Christian "Researches, farther than affording some gratifica"tion to the advocates for Christianity, and some "vigour, perhaps, to their hopes.

"If your alterations are important, you may just "mention what they are, but it will not be neces"sary to return the manuscript; for I can rely on "your just judgment. I have rather a rugged style. "Be pleased to add a word, and qualify my abrupt"ness when it offends you."

"31st December.

"I concur with you in every sentiment contained *Nihilominus*

"in your letter. My friends in India have long "urged me to notice the exertions of the Church of "England there, under the name of ' The Christian "Institution. in the East;' and I was preparing to "publish *A* list of its members at the conclusion of "the work. But the promotion of Christianity is "the grand object; and the expression of your ' feats is isufncient argument for me to suppress "the name of the 'Christian Institution' for the "present..-''.

"Be pleased, therefore,-to obliterate the name, '' and substitute that of 'Christian Researches in "Asia;' and retain as much of the introductory "pages as may comport with your view of utility. "I have no copy by me; and I am in poor heahhj and have Other avocations. I desire nothing but '' to promote the glory of the Christian dispensa"tion. I could wish to make my work as-Catholic as possible, so that *tll* may love its object. ' If you will make it such, you will make me happy. '" I want the work to be printed by the 10th of February, for transmission to India. India is "more in my view than England, in regard to its "utility. If you find any *sarcasm,* pray expunge '" it: but do not sacrifice a word oftruth.-"I should write to you more particularly, but "Mrs. Buchanan's confinement has been attended "with circumstances which endangered her life; and I think of little at present but what is mo"mentous and

eternal. She is.now better.'"

The conclusion of the preceding extract referred to a season of great trial which had taken place a few days before, and which after much suffering had terminated safely. Mrs. Buchanan recovered; but the child, who was named Claudius, survived only three days. "On the morning of the first day "of the new year," observed his pious father, " I "committed the little stranger to his parent earth. "Mrs. B. has more of joy than sorrow from these "events.'

Amidst the anxiety occasioned by the illness of Mrs. Buchanan, and the interruption of personal indisposition, Dr. Buchanan prepared for the press his University Sermons, and the " Christian Re"searches in Asia." The subject of these Sermons was similar to that of his discourse before the Church Mission Society,—the diffusion of Christian knowledge throughout the world. From the words of the divine *fiat,* " Let there be light," as applied to the course of the great '' Sun of Righte"ousness," Dr. Buchanan noticed three distinct eras of this heavenly illumination; that of the first promulgation of the Gospel, the Reformation from Popery, and the present period. After an able and interesting historic view of these three eras of light, he urged a series of arguments, to which a reference only can here be made, to convince the Church of England of her obligations to exert herself in the great work of evangelizing the world. Having led the way by patronizing about a century since the VOL. II. R

Protestant mission to India, it became her, he said, to resume her former station, and, " standing as "she does like a Pharos among the nations, to be "herself the great instrument of giving light to the "world." It is, however, only doing justice to the subject of these Memoirs, to extract a few passages from the Sermons in question, which convey his sentiments on the fundamental truths of Christianity.

"That which constitutes a Christian is ' faith, "hope, and charity; these three. ' Much human "learning is not essentially necessary to constitute a Christian. Indeed a man may be a profound theologian, and not be a Christian at all. He "may be learned in the doctrines and history of "Christianity, and yet be a stranger to the fruits "of Christianity. He may be destitute of faith, "of hope, and of charity.

"Let us not then confound the fruits of religion, "namely, its influence on our moral conduct, its "peace of mind, and hope of heaven, with the cir"cumstances of religion.-True religion is that "which its great Author himself hath declared. "It is a practical knowledge of the love of God the "Father, ' who sent not his Son into the world, to "condemn the world; but that the world, through "him, might be saved;' of the atonement of God "the Son, by faith in whom we receive remission of "our sins, and are justified in the sight of the Father; and of the sanctification of God the Holy ' Ghost, by which we are made meet ' to become "partakers of the inheritance of the saints in light.' "—The preacher who can communicate this know"ledge to his hearers, (and it is true, that if he "possess a critical knowledge of the Bible, and of "the history of Christianity, he will be likely to do "it with the most success,) the same is ' a work"man that needeth not to be ashamed, and a good "minister of Jesus Christ.' 1 Tim. iv. 6.

"Let every student in theology enquire, whether "the religion he professes bear the true character. "Instead of shunning the reproach of Christ, his "anxiety ought to be, how he may prepare him-" self for that high and sacred office which he is "about to enter. Let him examine himself, whe"ther his views correspond, in any degree, with "the character of the ministers of Christ, as re"corded in the New Testament. 'Woe is unto "me, if I preach not the Gospel.' 1 Cor. ix. 16."

Dr. Buchanan thought it to be his duty to conclude his discourses before the University, with again delivering his testimony to that divine change which constitutes the essence of real Christianity.

This change of heart," he observes, " ever car"ries with it its own witness; and it alone exhibits "the same character among men of every clime. "It bears the fruit of righteousness; it affords the "highest enjoyment of life which was intended by "God,.or is attainable by man; it inspires the "soul with a sense of pardon, and of acceptance "through the Redeemer; it gives peace in death, "and a ' sure and certain hope of the resurrection "unto eternal life.'"

The substantial truth and honest freedom of these remarks were no less honourable to the Preacher, than was " the candid attention," with which he gratefully acknowledged they were heard, to the learned body to whom they were addressed. It is scarcely necessary to add, that the repetition of such sentiments is far from being unseasonable. —May they be universally prevalent!

It has already sufficiently appeared, in the course of these Memoirs, that Dr. Buchanan was far from being a mere declaimer, either as to the evils which he lamented, or the remedy which he proposed. With respect to the former, he did not content himself with the representations of others, but exhibited the result of his own personal observations, and revealed the gloomy recesses of Asiatic superstition, the "thick darkness" which "covers the people" of that widely extended region. Splendid too, and unlimited, as were the prospects which he unfolded of their illumination and relief, and sanguine as were the hopes which he indulged of their accomplishment, both were founded upon the vigorous and persevering adoption of the ordinary means within our power, and particularly of the universal circulation of the Holy Scriptures.

Dr. Buchanan's Eight Sermons, pp. 255, 289, 291.

It was to the development of both parts of this picture, of the light as well as of the shade, that Dr. Buchanan devoted his Christian Researches. He accordingly introduced them by an account of his own endeavours and those of Mr. Brown to promote the translation of the Scriptures, and of his two journeys to the coast of Malabar, which have been before detailed. He then proceeded to notice, in a series of distinct articles, the Chinese, the Hindoos, with a particular reference to the relative influence of Paganism and Christianity, the Ceylonese, and the Malays. The Syrian and Romish Christians, and the Inquisition at Goa, form the next objects of attention in this interesting work; which are followed by notices of the Persians Arabians, and Jews, and of the versions of the Scriptures which were then preparing, or the preparation of which was suggested, for the use of those various nations. The Bibliotheca Biblica, or repository for Bibles in the oriental languages, comprising a library for the use of translators of the Scriptures, founded by the late Rev. D. Brown, is next adverted to; and finally, the Armenian Christians. Before Dr. Buchanan concluded his Researches, he recurred to the subject of his first Memoir, and advanced some new and forcible arguments in support of an Ecclesiastical Establishment for British India.

Though it has been thought necessary to give the preceding brief analysis of this important and valuable work, it will be obvious, that more was not required; not only on account of its great notoriety and extensive circulation, but because many of tbe topics which it embraced have been already noticed in this narrative. The conclusion, however, of the Christian Researches demands more particular attention, because it comprises what may be called the practical application of the whole. Dr. Buchanan, like Lord Bacon himself, aimed not so much at inculcating new principles, as at exciting a new spirit; and though he did, indeed, make some important discoveries, as to the moral necessities of an immense portion of the human race, it was one of his main objects to teach others to follow him in his course, and to point out the way to its successful pursuit. In this view, the concluding observations of his work deserve the most serious consideration.

"In the progress of these Researches, the author "has found his mind frequently drawn to consider "the extraordinary difference of opinion which exists "among men of learning, in regard to the import"ance and obligation of communicating religious "knowledge to our fellow-creatures. And he has "often heard the question asked by others, What "can be the cause of this discrepancy of opinion? "For that such a difference does exist is most evi"dent; and is exemplified at this moment in some "of the most illustrious characters for rank and "learning in the nation. This is a problem of a "very interesting character at this day, and worthy "of a distinct and ample discussion, particularly at "the seats of learning. The problem may be thus "expressed: 'What power is that, which produces "in the minds of some persons a real interest and "concern in the welfare of their fellow-creatures; "extending not only to the comfort of their exist"ence in this world, but to their felicity hereafter; "while other men, who are apparently in similar "circumstances as to learning and information, do "not feel inclined to move one step for the promo'' tion of such objects?' The latter, it may be, can "speculate on the philosophy of the human mind, "on its great powers and high dignity, on the "sublime virtue of universal benevolence, on the *f.* tyranny of superstition, and the slavery of igno"ranee; and will sometimes quote the verse of the "poet;

"'Homo sum: humani nil a me alienum puto:'

"but they leave it to others, and generally to the "Christian in humble life, to exercise the spirit of "that noble verse. This is a very difficult pro"blem; and it has been alleged by some, that it "cannot be solved on any known principles of phi"losophy. The following relation will probably "lead to principles by which we may arrive at a "solution."' The solution of the problem thus proposed is derived by the author from the penitent humiliation of the great Babylonian conqueror; who, when "brought to himself," expressed the sincerity of his conversion to the knowledge of the true God, by proclaiming his greatness, asserting his glory, and inviting all nations to magnify him, and bow to his dominion.

-"Such a proclamation," says Dr. Buchanan, to "the nations of the earth was a noble act of a king, "and ought to be had in perpetual remembrance. "It reminds us of the last charge of Him 'who "ascended up on high; Go, teach all nations.' "It discovers to us the new and extended benevo"lence, greatness of mind, and pure and heavenly "charity, which distinguish that man whose heart "has been impressed by the grace of God. How solemn his sense of duty. How ardent to declare "the glory of his Saviour! His views for the good "of men, how disinterested and enlarged! It is "but too evident, that all our speculations con"cerning a Divine revelation, and the obligation ' imposed on us to study it ourselves, or to com"municate it to others, are cold and uninteresting, "and excite not to action, until, through the "tender compassion of God, the day-spring from "on high visit u», to give light to them that sit "in darknessto humble our hearts at the re"membrance of our sins against God, and to affect "them with a just admiration of his pardoning "mercy.

» Daniel, chap. iv.

"Let Great Britain imitate the example of the "Chaldean king; and send forth to all the world "her 'testimony' concerning the true God. She "also reigns over many nations, which 'worship "idols of wood and stone;' and she ought, in like "manner, to declare to them 'the signs and won"ders of the Almighty.' And in this design every "individual will concur, of every church, family, and "name, whose heart has been penetrated with just "apprehensions of the Most High God; who have "known his judgments, and experienced his mercy."

The circulation of the Christian Researches was immense. The first edition of seventeen hundred copies was soon exhausted; and before the end of the year three others had been printed. The labour, however, which their excellent Author had undergone in preparing this interesting volume for the press, probably led to a painful, though apparently unimportant seizure, which was evidently the prelude to one of a more serious nature. It occurred whilst Dr. Buchanan was leading the morning family devotions at Kirby Hall. He suddenly lost his speech, and to the great alarm of the affectionate circle around him, was unable to proceed with the prayer. It is to this attack that he refers in writing thus to a friend.

"Kirby Hall, 19th Feb. 1811. "I have had an illness of a peculiar kind; a "slight debilitating stroke, affecting the voice and "right hand, of the paralytic kind. My hand is "not itself yet, as you may see; nor is my voice "perfectly restored. The faculty ascribe the im"mediate cause to study, a sedentary habit, and "anxiety of mind on Mrs. B's illness. But what"ever the cause may be, it is a *memento* from the "Lord, that this is not my rest. Nor do I wish it "to be so. # # # # "The town of Leeds have sent me an "invitation to succeed the late Mr. Atkinson, their "worthy minister, who died last week. I have "not yet answered them; but my late repeated "attacks of illness will determine me to decline it. "My constitution is evidently not settled suffi"ciently for laborious study. But the Lord is "my shepherd. He will lead me in green pas"tures, and make darkness light before me. The "people of Leeds deserve a better pastor than "I am, and the Lord will be their shepherd "also." 26th March.

"I am now well enough to be able to write a few "lines. I have been gaining strength with the re"turning spring; for I love the sun, and to look at "it in this cold climate. It is a fine object in this "evil world. But I like the sun chiefly, as it is an "emblem of ' the Sun of Righteousness.' It gives "light and heat. I love your letters, for they have "light and heat, reflected from the same glorious "luminary.

"You will be happy to hear that Mrs. L. has "become a most serious and intelligent Christian. "Her only desire is to live to the glory of her Sa'' viour. She weeps at the recollection of her ob"durate heart in India, loves Mr.. Brown, and thinks "him ' a man to be wondered at.' I mean to send "two of her letters to Calcutta, and to ask whether "they can shew such things in India! Perhaps they "will answer ' Yes we can: behold S.'

"My love to Mrs. S. and the sufferer.

Surely she "must be all pure gold by this time. The dross and "tin, a miner would say, must now be at the bottom "of the furnace.

'' I have received letters from India so late as Oc tober. Mr. Martyn was expected in Calcutta in "fine health and spirits, with his Hindostanee and Arabic translations."

As the spring advanced, Dr. Buchanan's physicians having agreed that his complaint was chiefly a nervous debility, for the removal of which cessation from study was desirable, he formed a plan with a view to an object which he had long cherished, and which might, he hoped, prove beneficial to his health. This was no less an undertaking than a voyage to Palestine, with the view of investigating subjects connected with the translation of the Scriptures, and the extension of Christianity. We have already noticed his proposal of returning from India overland, for the purpose of visiting the churches in Mesopotamia and Syria, the names of upwards of one hundred of which he had received from the Syrian Christians, and also of enquiring into the present circumstances of the Jews in those regions and in Palestine. This was the design to which he was now anxious to render an intermission from sedentary occupation subservient. Another object of Dr. Buchanan's enquiry in his proposed visit to the Holy Land, was to be the state of the Syriac printing-press of Mount Lebanon, from which various works have issued; and to ascertain whether it might be practicable to establish presses in Jerusalem or Aleppo, for the Hebrew, Arabic, and Syriac languages; and to open a correspondence with England for their encouragement and support. He wished also to learn, what language (with a view to the translation of the Scripture) is most generally used at this time in the Holy Land.

It was Dr. Buchanan's intention to touch at Alexandria, in his voyage to Palestine, and to return from his tour by Lesser Asia, through the region of the seven primitive-churches. He proposed to pass over from thence to Athens and Corinth, to visit the principal Christian churches in Greece, and afterwards those of the larger islands in the Archipelago. A chief object here was to ascertain, whether a translation of the Scriptures in one dialect of modern Greek would suffice for the continent of Achaia and the Archipelago, (which he did not think to be likely,) or whether some principal dialects had not been already cultivated.

In order to give publicity to his proposed voyage, Dr. Buchanan transmitted a notice of the preceding particulars to the Christian Observer, adding a request, that the queries of the learned concerning the present state of the countries he intended to visit, in connection with the promotion of Christianity, might be communicated to him, and intimating that he would take charge of Bibles for distribution in his way in Portugal, Spain, and Malta, and would endeavour to establish a channel of correspondence in those countries with England, for the supply of the authorized version of each country respectively, as far as the existing governments might be pleased to countenance the design.

Such was the intention of Dr. Buchanan with respect to this distant and laborious undertaking. Greatly, however, as we must admire the ardour of his piety which could prompt him to form such a plan, it was, perhaps, originally of too extensive and difficult a nature for the already debilitated state of his constitution. He seems, in some measure, to have felt this in announcing it to a friend, to whom he sent a notice of his design, adding, "I cannot tell the purposes of Providence. Per"haps I may lay my bones in the Holy Land."

Towards the end of May, Dr. Buchanan paid a short visit to Buxton; where, intent as usual on For May 1811, p. *31t.* doing good, he embraced the opportunity of preaching a sermon, the occasion of which may be explained in his own words.

"Buxton, 3d June, 1811.

"Having had some revival of spirits these three "last days, I was not willing to allow the Day of "Pentecost to pass without notice, particularly as "the company here were desirous that I should "preach. Viewing them from my window all day "drinking at the medicinal waters, I composed a "discourse from John v. 2, 3, 4% which I deli"vered yesterday (Whitsunday) in the great dining"room here; Captain Payne, aide-de-camp to Lord "Wellington, who returned wounded from Busaco, "acting as my clerk. This sermon I mean to pub"lish immediately, for the benefit of the company "during the gay season. I shall not, however, "send it to the press till my return to Kirby "Hall, (whither we go on the 5th or 6th inst.) "for I have no Concordance here, nor indeed "any »ther book but the Bible."

The sermon thus hastily but benevolently composed was published in the course of the summer, a "Now there is at Jerusalem by the sheep-market a pool, "which is called in the Hebrew tongue Bethesda, having five "porches. In these lay a great multitude of impotent folk, of "blind, halt, withered, waiting for the moving of the water. "For an angel went down at a certain season into the pool, "and troubled the water: whosoever then first after the trou"bling of the water stepped in was made whole of whatsoever "disease he had." under the title of "The Healing Waters of Beth"esda." It was, as might be expected, altogether of a practical nature. But though devoid of that peculiar attraction which his preceding publications derived from their connection with oriental objects, it abounded with sound Scriptural instruction, and was well calculated to awaken in the minds of those to whom it was originally addressed a salutary train of feeling and reflection, and to lead them to associate with the spring to which they were resorting for bodily health, the thought of that heavenly fountain which can alone purify and refresh the soul, and strengthen it unto life everlasting.

In the month of June, Dr. Buchanan wrote to Colonel Sandys as follows.

« Kirby Hall, 24th June, 1811.

' I have lately returned from Buxton, whither I "was sent to drink the medicinal waters. I have not found much benefit from them; but we now "proceed to Scarborough, and I doubt not I shall "be refreshed by the sea air.

"I shall probably leave England in autumn, and "be absent about a year. Had any important spi "ritual charge been assigned to me, I should "not have thought of leaving England again; but "circumstances at present are very favourable to a "temporary absence. I mean to go down to Scot"land in a few weeks hence to take leave of my "mother, who is in a declining state, and does not "expect (or perhaps hope) to pass through this next "winter.

"I have a good appetite generally, and sleep "well; but when I speak, my spirits are easily "hurried; and the slightest exercise fatigues me.

"I hope that you and your family continue well, "and more particularly that' your soul prospereth.' "I make a little progress perhaps, but it is scarcely "sensible. *TVhen I stand on Calvary, if it be "given me to see it,)* I hope my spirits will be re"freshed, and my affections enlivened to love and "serve *the Lord who suffered there—May* I have "a single eye to his glory!"

'' Scarborough, 20th July.

"The Bethesda Sermon arrived yesterday. One "hundred copies have been sent here, and sell "rapidly. I seldom see any Review; for I wish "to be hid from the strife of tongues.

"I am willing to go ' through evil report' unto "the end. That is not my cross.

"We set off to-morrow for Scotland. I have "acquired but little strength at Scarborough. The "change of air in the North may possibly be more "beneficial to me."

"Greenock, 5th August. "I have found my mother in tolerable health of "body, and in high spiritual health at seventy-five. "She astonishes Mrs. Buchanan by her eloquence "on the prophecies, which she utters in hard words, "without affecting at all the English language. "She can read the Bethesda without spectacles, "and likes it better than the Star in the East.

"We have seen and entertained almost all the "Greenock clergy, and have visited some of the "best religious families. In a few days we return "to Glasgow. Your future communications must "be addressed to Kirby Hall, for I know not where "we shall be in ten days hence.

"I find the sea air more refreshing here than at "Scarborough. Somewhere in Bute is now rec"koned the Montpelier of Scotland. It boasts, it "seems, many recoveries from consumptions. I "consulted the Edinburgh faculty in passing. Dr. "Gregory delivered to me five quarto pages com"posed oracularly on the subject of my complaint, "which he seems to understand well. The length "of this letter will intimate I am rather stronger "than before."

"Glasgow, 18th September.

"I have been favoured with your letter of the "10th inst. inclosing Mr. H's Dedication. He "seems animated by a noble spirit. I have had a "letter from himself, and have recommended him "to enlist under the banners of the Society for pro"moting Christian Knowledge, and to think no"thing of the Syrians, till he have passed a tran"quil year in the bosom of his family in Coroman

Vol. u. s

"del. Thence he may proceed where he likes. "He asked me what would be his principal diffi"culty. I told him it would be learning Malay"alim (which is more useful than the Syriac) in his old age!

"The companion of my tour to Syria is already "engaged; a Fellow of a college in Oxford, whom "I met at Scarborough, the son of a family inti"mate with that at Kirby Hall; a young man of "strong health, good learning, good sense, and "good fortune; of sound theology, and one who is." likely to become an author.

"As to Rothley Temple, if it be practicable, we "shall visit it; but the season advances, and we "have not got through Ireland yet.

"We proceed on Monday next to Lainshaw, the "abode of Mr. Cunninghame, late of India, and "thence, by Ayr, to Port Patrick. Letters addressed "to me, at the Post Office, Dublin, will find me "till the 20th of October."

Early in November Dr. Buchanan returned from his tour to Kirby Hall, from whence he gave his friends a sketch of that part of it which has not been yet mentioned.

"Kirby Hall, November 20. "We arrived at this place about ten days since, "and found all our family well. We spent a month "in Ireland, and about a fortnight in Wales. Mrs. "B. liked the tour very well, for we found friends "every where. I am glad that I have had an op"portunity of surveying the state of religion in "Ireland. I had much intercourse with the mem"bers of Dublin college, and hope to engage them "in the support of evangelizing plans. They seem "in general animated by a good spirit.

"I visited Maynooth college, and investigated "the Catholic question. I could consult the best "authorities on both sides. My opinion is, that "Maynooth college may be extended with safety. "It has already added to the number of Protes"tants; and the Roman Catholic bishops begin to "be alarmed at the light and knowledge which "proceed from it. I saw Messrs. C. and C-, the priests who have recanted. They preach in Dub"lin; but when I arrived they had not received "any cure or support from Church or State. I ex"pressed my astonishment at the delay and marked "indifference which seemed to pervade the Protes"tant church on the subject. Government has "now espoused the cause of the young men, and "ordained them immediate provision and a Cure in "the church. They both appear to me to be con"verts on conviction.

"I passed a day with the Bishop of Bangor, in "my way through Wales. We had much confer"ence on the state of religion. He is candid, and "earnest to do good in the church.

"The Scotch Kirk have almost wholly ceased to "read the Scriptures as a part of divine service. "I have noticed the subject in the fourth edition of "the Christian Researches now printing.

"I have proposed to the University of Cambridge "to print an edition of the Syriac Scriptures; and "have offered a considerable sum to commence; "but I have not yet had their answer. I promised "to send the Scriptures to the Syrian Christians, "and am ashamed at the delay.

"I have gained a little strength by the journey, '' but I am easily exhausted."

In the autumn of this year arrived Mr. Martyn's eloquent and successful Appeal, in a sermon at Calcutta, on the 1st of January, in behalf of nine hundred thousand Christians in India, who were in want of the Bible; together with the gratifying intelligence of the formation of an Auxiliary Bible Society at that Presidency, at the head of which appeared some of the chief members of the supreme government. The letters which announced this auspicious event brought information also of the revival of the college of Fort William as a fountain of Scriptural translation, and a communication from Mr. Brown to Dr. Buchanan; the following extract from which, considering the circumstances of his departure from Calcutta, could not but afford him the liveliest satisfaction. "Pagoda, Serampore, 5 th March, 1811. "You are truly the root of our Bible Society. "I have had long and full discussions with Lord "Minto on all subjects of religion, missions, Scrip"tures, &c.; and he is very desirous to tread back "his steps, and to atone for the mistake which he "made at the beginning of his government.

"Your letter prepared the way for this reflux of "sentiment. Neither that, nor the Chinese, nor "any part of your labours, has fallen to the ground. "Therefore go forward; and obtain the crown of "righteousness which is before you."

On the 6th of December, Dr. Buchanan wrote to his friend Mr. Macaulay respecting new editions of his publications; desiring it to be observed in the dedication of his Memoir to the present Archbishop, that although he had " deemed it right to make a few "verbal alterations, he had seen no cause to change "any one material sentiment of the work." In the same letter he intimated his intention of proceeding on his proposed voyage early in the month of February following. A few days, however, only had elapsed before a second and more alarming attack suspended, and ultimately dissipated, all thoughts of accomplishing that extensive and interesting undertaking. His letter upon this trying occasion exhibits his characteristic piety and submission, and is as follows; "Kirby Hall, 17th December, 1811.

"My dear Sir,

"I must use the hand of another to inform you, that I was visited last week by an illness of the same nature with that in the beginning of the year. I have had a second paralytic stroke, affecting the half of my head and body, and forming a complete hemiplegia. My voice is not much affected, and the numbness is slight. But yet I consider that this may be the precursor of a third and last call to quit my earthly mansion. I view it, therefore, as a most merciful dispensation, and hope I shall ever retain my present thankful sense of the Lord's gracious mode of bidding me prepare for my journey, and of calling me gradually to himself. Whether this event will hasten me to a warmer climate, or whether I shall wait the Lord's will at home, I have not yet determined.

"I had just finished the revision of my sermons when I was attacked; and I suppose they are now in the hands of the printers. If you should recollect any thing faulty in them, I hope you will send for the proof sheets.

"I remain, my dear Sir,
Very sincerely yours,
C. Buchanan."

On the 2d of January, 1812, Dr. Buchanan had recovered sufficiently from his late attack to resume with a faint and trembling hand his correspondence with his friends.

"My hand is recovering from the paralysis, and "I can just hold the pen to inform you, that scarcely any thing remains of my indisposition but extreme "weakness. The faculty think they have at last "discovered the source of my complaints, and have "taken away about five pounds of blood. This has "afforded a most sensible relief to my breathing, "and has given rest during sleep, which before I "had not. In addition, they have lowered and at"tenuated the body during the last month; so that "all things are new. If when the body is thus re"generated, the soul could also be renewed, it "would be a salutary illness. I can indeed say, and "with great thankfulness, that my soul has had "more spiritual communion with God than for"merly. It would be a blessed thing were it always "to remain as it has been. ". I wondered at the peace I felt in the prospect of departing this life. It was perhaps greater "than it will be when the time comes. 'Whoso "endureth unto the end shall be saved.'

"Yesterday Cadell published the second edition "of my Memoir in octavo. Two editions of it were "printed in America this last year. On the I st of "February I hope all my sermons revised will be "published in one volume...'

"The University of Cambridge has done valor"Qiisly, as you have seen. What fine youths these "will be to preach to the people when you and I "have winged our flight!"

Notwithstanding the severe shock which the constitution of Dr. Buchanan had received by his late paralytic seizure, the powers of his mind were evidently unimpaired, and amidst great debility and languor, he retained all his ardour in promoting the cause of Christianity in the world. This was very shortly evinced by the following communication to a friend, who had apprized him of an. incorrect and injurious statement, which, on the authority of the Danish missionaries in India, had been inserted in the Report of the Society for promoting Christian Knowledge for the year 1811, respecting the Syrian Christians in Travancore. The substance of this communication was afterwards introduced into an able article in the Christian Observer.% forming a most satisfactory vindication of that interesting body of Christians. The original observations, however, of Dr. Buchanan may still be acceptable to those who may retain any doubts upon the subject to which they relate.

"Kirby Hall, 18th January, 1812. "All my books and MSS. concerning the Syri"an "Christians I deposited in the University Library, "Cambridge; but I shall desire Mr. Yeates to look "over the Liturgy of the Syrians, and if he can find "the passage in which they abjure the errors of the "Nestorians, to send it to you. When I passed "through the Danish missionaries on the coast of "Coromande), on my way to Malabar, they told me "the same things concerning the Syrians, which "they have now stated to the Society; but when "I arrived in Malayala, I found.they knew no more "of the Syrian Christians in that region, than people "in England know of the Syrian Christians in *Cy"prus*. I suppose the missionaries have written "thus by way of offering some apology for not ad"vising the Society to assist the Syrian Christians.

"In regard to an *official* union, it is scarcely "practicable in present circumstances, and need "not be thought of; but there is nothing to pre"vent a friendly connection, or, as the Bishop ex"pressed it, ' such a connection as should appear to both Churches practicable and expedient.' The "Romish church long solicited such an union, but "could not attain it; nor did they regard their "formerly having had (if indeed they ever had) Nes"torian bishops, provided they would now qualify "their system a little. They might even say mass "in another tongue than Latin. But the mission"aries cannot yield so much as this!

"The truth concerning the Syrians will be found, "I allege, in my more full account of them, pub"lished by the Bishop of London 'Their Li Ih 1807. See the Christian Observer for that year.

"turgy is derived from that of the early church of "Antioch, called *Liturgia Jacob'i Apostoli*. They "are usually denominated *Jacobites;* but they dif"fer in ceremonial from the church of that name '' in Syria, and indeed from any existing church in the world.'

"That they worship the Virgin Mary is a flagrant "error of speech. The practice might as well be "charged on the Church of England ".

A very different statement respecting the Syrian Christians has been lately published in a letter from the Abbe" Dubois, a Romish missionary in Mysore, inserted in the second Report of the Bombay Auxiliary Bible Society. The respectability of the quarter from which this document lias proceeded may naturally seem to claim for it a considerable degree of credit. But whatever may be its value, as to points within the writer's own knowledge, it is undoubtedly erroneous as to the Syrian Christians. Nor can this be a matter of surprise when it is considered, that all his information concerning them is confessedly derived from other persons, who may very probably, like himself, have never visited them, and be members of a church whose tyranny and oppression the Syrian Christians in Travancore have for ages nobly resisted. "This sect," observes the Abbe, " still "obstinately adheres to the religious tenets held by the here siarch Nestorius. " It is, however, somewhat extraordinary, that the late venerable metropolitan of the Syrian church, in an official communication to General Macaulay, then Resident at the court of Travancore, distinctly disclaimed the errors of Nestorius, as well as those of other heretics; and that Dr. Buchanan and Dr. Kerr agree in representing their creed as not materially differing from that of our own Church. It may be added, that their account of them is substantially the same as that of La Croze, Assemannus, and Mosheim..' For farther in

"In regard to their morals, learning, and civil "state, I have merely recounted ths conversations "I had with their most learned members, and no"ticed that ' I perceived all around symptoms of ' poverty and political depression that they were "in a degenerate state, yet ' like a people who had "known better days.' I also notice, that 'they "have some ceremonies nearly allied to those of "the Greek Church;' and I intimated to the Bi"shop, ' that there were some rites and practices "in the Syrian Church, which our Church might "consider objectionable or nugatory.' If I have "not filled my page with these particulars, it was "because I had no pleasure in describing them. "Finding a Church in their peculiar situation, pos"sessing the Bible, and abjuring the Romish cofc"ruptions, what more was required to make them "an useful people in evangelizing that dark region? "And it is not decorous in the Church of England "to seem to take pleasure in holding up to a kind "of opprobrium an ancient people, found in such "interesting circumstances; possessing too an or"dination, with which ours is scarcely to be com"pared. A former President of the Bartlett's "Buildings Society, (Archbishop Wake,) negotiated "for an union with Rome herself!
formation upon this subject, the reader is referred to Dr. Buchanan's Christian Researches, and to the Christian Observer for December 1816.

"As to the moral and civil state of the Syrians, "Dr. Kerr has given them a higher character than "I have, in hi6 official document to the Madras "government, which on this subject may now be "quoted as a proper authority. All that he has "said also concerning the facility and expediency "of an union, may now be pressed with much ad"vantage; for Dr. K. was sent from the very place where the Danish missionaries dwell, to obtain "information for government.

'' But on this subject, Colonel Macaulay is the "highest authority in the world. If he will address "the Society in a respectful, conciliating manner, "and urge the incontrovertible facts founded on his "own knowledge and Dr. Kerr's official report, it will have immense effect.

"He may observe that an union is not to be "thought of at present, on account of political con"siderations; but that such an interesting people "deserve our countenance and every aid for mental "improvement, by assisting them in the translation "of the Scriptures, and encouraging them to hold "out against the Romish Church. They are also "proper subjects of occasional pecuniary assistance: "for the oppression of the Hindoo government "has of late been very great: but for the future "they will, perhaps, be able to retain what they "acquire.

"It would be proper that Colonel Macaulay shoujd "mention his own political transactions with the "Travancore and the English governments on their "behalf, and on behalf of the Romish-Syrians. "For *they* also want the Bible.

"My hand, you see, is a little better; but I am by no means strong. I can only sit up half an "hour at a time."

It is surely to be lamented, that no application was made on the part of the Society to the two persons best qualified to afford information upon this subject, Dr. Buchanan and General Macaulay; and that no steps appear to have been taken to communicate that encouragement and support, which the Church of England is plainly bound to extend to a community of Christians thus brought into such immediate contact with the British government.

In the mean time, Dr. Buchanan continued his own exertions with a view to supply the Syrian Christians with a translation of the Scriptures. Thus he wrote in February and March to Mr. Macaulay.

"I enclose a letter, which I wish to go by this "fleet. It is to give money to Timapah Pulle, *f* who superintends the Malayalim version at "Bombay.

"I have received a copy of the second edition of the Memoir, and immediately discovered improve"ments. Many thanks to you for this service. "And yet I have little satisfaction in looking at the "book. I wish now to flee away to regions of peace "with the wings of a dove—and be at rest."

"Kirby Hall, 7th March.." The day after I wrote to you last, I was obliged "to leave the writing table entirely, and have not re"sumed it since. The sensation of paralysis is but "slight, but it appears to be now permanent; at "least during the cold season."

"26th March.

"La Croze and Geddes are the principal authors for 's purpose, and I have neither.

"Gouvea, and Bartolomeo's India Christiana, and "other curious works, I deposited, together with the "MSS. at Cambridge.

"If you could call on Mr. Yeates, he could possi"bly furnish you with La Croze, or Simon, or Asse

"mannus. It is a fine subject for 's contem

"plation, and one which would greatly interest the "public mind. A few pages only, however, will suffice for the Society. But after he has done that, "he may possibly meditate a larger work. These "are times when *every thing a man has,* which "may be in any way for the advantage of Chris"tianity, ought to be given to the world. For we "shall soon die, and then shall ' all our thoughts "perish.'

"Mr. Yeates writes thus in a late letter. 'Si"mon, in his Critical History of the Religion 'and I

"Customs of the Eastern Nations, has ably vin"dicated the Syrian Christians against the Catho"lies, and exposed their rage and persecution as the "result of papal tyranny. I have read so much in "Assemannus and other authors, as to know that "the Syrian Christians are the Protestants of the "East. The Church of England, as a National "Church, cannot extend her assistance to greater "advantage, than in restoring and building up the "ruins of the Syrian communion in Antioch, Meso"potamia, and India, by the immediate dispersion "of copies of the Scriptures. And when this is "done, they will supply missionaries for the exten"sion of the Christian faith among the Mahome"dans and Pagans.'

"I rejoice to hear that ' Ethiopia does not stretch "out her hands' in vain. This will be a great ac"cession of fame to the Bible Society. The Uni." versity will not lend out my Ethiopic Gospel. "You must send a person to transcribe it in the." public library. If you should find any diffieultyin . " the access, I will give you a note to the Vice"Chancellor."

The next subject to which the attention of Dr. Buchanan was directed was that to which he had devoted his Memoir, and which he had ever considered as of primary and fundamental importance. This was the organization of a more extensive Ecclesiastical Establishment for British India. The time was now approaching for the renewal of the Charter of the East India Company; and the friends of religion were anxious to improve this opportunity of pressing the consideration of the measure in question upon the attention of government and of the legislature. It was evident that no man was better qualified to suggest the best method of proceeding upon this occasion than Dr. Buchanan. Some distinguished persons, who took a lively interest in this weighty subject, accordingly applied to him to prepare a sketch of what he might deem advisable with respect to the proposed Establishment, for the purpose of submitting it to the consideration of his Majesty's ministers, and of others particularly concerned in the determination of this question.

It was with this important point that the correspondence of Dr. Buchanan was occupied during the spring and summer of this year. The following extracts from his letters to Mr. Macaulay will exhibit not only his zeal, but his piety and judgment respecting the accomplishment of the great measure which he had so long advocated.

"Kirby Hall, March 1812. "India has scarcely crossed my mind since I "wrote to you last; I mean in regard to legislative "measures. I do not expect to be able to do any "thing till the warm weather approach. Mr. Wil"berforce writes to me, that the Anglo-Indians "question the fact of the burning of women stated "in my Memoir; and I read in the British Review, "that they doubt that of the self-devotement of a "man at Ishera, stated in my Researches under "the article 'Juggernaut in Bengal.' I shall pen "two sentences below on each of these subjects, "which you may use as occasion may serve.

"Short as the above letter is, I have been nearly "two days in writing it; and I do not now find "myself able to finish my two sentences. I hope "to recruit in a day or two, when I shall send "them."

The two sentences thus meditated, branched out into two sheets; the substance of which afterwards appeared in the Christian Observer.

Dr. Buchanan's next letter is as follows.

"Kirby Hall, 13th April, 1812.

"My dear Sir, ' I send to you and Mr. Wilberforce by this day's mail a Prospectus of an Ecclesiastical Establishment *Fot* April, 1812. In this paper it is stated, that the calculation in question as to the number of women burned in the vicinity of Calcutta during a given period, was inserted in Dr. Buchanan's Memoir on the authority of an official report to the College of Fort William, when the officers of that institution were collecting information to serve as an authentic record upon the subject of this female sacrifice. The truth of the fact respecting the self-devotement at Ishera was declared to rest upon the authority of the late Rev. D. Brown, whose country-house was near the spot referred to. VOL. II. T for India. I will thank you to submit it to Mr. Grant and Lord Teignmouth; and I shall be obliged to them to make such alterations in it as they shall think proper. If they suggest any thing which you and Mr. W. approve, be pleased to incorporate it, and to revise the whole according to your judgment.

"I then wish you to send one copy to Mr. Perceval, and another to the Archbishop of Canterbury.

"When you are ready let me know, and I will send a note to accompany each copy. From Mr. Perceval I have lately received a very kind letter, in which he professes to have 'a respect for my character and exertions.'

"If after you have sent in the copies, you should think that any part of the Prospectus might be useful to Parliament, you may publish it in such form, and with such addition as you please, with my name or without it.

"I am much obliged to you for offering to do me service, if I can move southward; but now that you have the Prospectus, you will not want me. I certainly should not have written it, if you had not pressed the subject. I can scarcely at present walk down stairs without help. As soon as the season opens a little, I propose to go to Scarborough for the benefit of the warm baths at that place. I am now seeking the comfort of the holy Scriptures, and their promises; and love to contemplate Augustine and Luther. I look forward to nothing in this life but these two things, repentance, with bitter tears for past sins; and joy in the Holy Ghost. These two blessings I am encouraged to look for, for they are promised to sinners; they are ' the gifts to the rebellious.' In the mean time I pray to do the will of God, and to use my voice, my pen, or my feet, as he wishes me, while these members have any strength for his service.

"My dear Sir,
Very sincerely yours,
C. Buchanan."
"*Z. Macaulay, Esq.*"

The Sketch of an Ecclesiastical Establishment, mentioned in the preceding letter, was not only transmitted to his Majesty's ministers, and to other distinguished individuals, but communicated to the East India Mission Committee of the Society for promoting Christian Knowledge, through Mr. Wilberforce, on the 1st of June. It was received by them with expressions of approbation, and of entire concurrence in the views of its author; and an abstract of it having been reported by that Committee to a general meeting of the Society, held on the 23d of that month, a series of important resolutions, in support of the measure thus proposed, as well as in favour of the general duty of promoting Christianity amongst our Indian fellow-subjects, European and native, were moved and adopted.

The following passage from a letter to a friend, who had suggested an alteration in a part of his "Sketch," will shew, amongst other instances of a similar nature, how far Dr. Buchanan was from an unbending or disputatious temper.

"I am just? favoured with Vout letter, and am "greatly obliged to you for writing it. I consent "to the section being omitted, and to the word "' colonization' not appearing in the whole book.

"I am only anxious that the eause of God should "have due honour, and that ' exclusion of Christian "teachers in Asia' should be plainly represented as "repugnant to God's will and revealed word. These "are days of great measures. When we stand "upon the *Rock,* we need not fear the conflicting "currents of public opinion. But it is right to "avoid obnoxious terms if we ean; and if an object "is likely to be attained without fighting for it, it "is best."

Dr. Buchanan was, however, at this time by no means sanguine as to the success of the proposed Establishment, though he rejoiced in the progress of Christianity in other quarters. The following is from a letter to Colonel Sandys in April.

"I had very little pleasure in writing further on the "subject; but as I had given a beginning, I thought "I would give the end. It is not probable that any "thing of importance will be done. We ought to "be satisfied with the great doings of the present "day. Indeed the Bible Society's triumphs have "been so great of late, that it is time (according to "the usual dispensations in relation to the Gospel) "we should look for a *check,* to humble us a little, "and keep us in our proper place.

"Since my return from Ireland, I have been "much engaged with correspondence from that "kingdom. There is a fine evangelical spirit, even "amongst the nobility. I had urged Trinity Col"lege, Dublin, to organize a Bible Society. The "students were for it; the elder members against "it. Matters, at this moment, are very interesting. "The Irish want the Bible almost as much as the "Hindoos.

"My affectionate remembrance to Mrs. S. and Miss J., not forgetting Claudius, (look into Mil"ner's History, for the life of Claudius, of Turin. "I have just discovered in a volume of Arch-bishop "Usher's, that there is a manuscript Commentary "on St. Matthew in the library of Pembroke Hall, "Cambridge, by this very Claudius: a fact which "Mr. Milner does not seem to have known,) who, "for the reason stated in the parenthesis, must go "to Pembroke Hall, as a student of divinity. My "namesakes must not go about with *flint and steel.* "There is a higher warfare for them; in which I "hope you are all fighting, and are more than con"querors through Him who hath loved us.

"I am, affectionately yours,
"C. Buchanan."

The beginning of the following

month was marked by the appearance of some symptoms favourable to the intended measure respecting India, but clouded by the melancholy intelligence of the assassination of Mr. Perceval. Dr. Buchanan's observations on that lamentable event will be read with interest.

"Kirby Hall, 15th May, 1812. "I had a note from Lord Buckinghamshire thank"ing me for the Prospectus, and acknowledging its "importance; concluding with—' You may be as"sured, that it will receive from me all the attention "to which it is entitled.' Another note from Mr. "Perceval to the same effect. Happy Perceval! "if he have died in the faith, as I have long believed "he lived. In my last letter to him (about a month "ago) there is the following sentence. 'One thing "is certain,' (I had been alluding to his difficulties, "and the state of public affairs,) ' and it must be a "subject of permanent comfort to your own mind, "that however the course of affairs may lead you "in future life, good has already been done under "your administration, which cannot be undone; "and *even if life itself should not be long vouch"safed,* you would depart with the consciousness,' "&c. &c.

"I have been trying to move the general as"sembly to notice the extension of religion in "India. I have also urged Cambridge to petition "Parliament on the subject. If an University, "which has permitted its members to pourtray so "often the blessing of giving Christianity to India, "should hesitate to recommend the measure, who "can be expected to support it?

"I continue in an equable state of health. I "can walk for about ten minutes at a time, but my "weakness is very great, particularly in my limbs, "which start and throb very much in bed, some"times during the whole night. Last night an "experiment was made of applying leeches to "one foot. The consequence was, the throbbing "ceased in that foot, and was more severe in the "other.

"I am happy to hear that is better, and "with you. He may probably be offered a com"mand in Asia, in the course of a year or two. In "the mean while, time flies, assassins fire shots, "and we hear the voice, ' Be ye also ready.' I "doubt not but the death of Mr. Perceval will give "life to the religion of many a man in England. "Some men will feel it as sensibly as if he had "been a member of their own family."

In the month of June Dr. Buchanan proceeded to Scarborough, from whence he proposed a visit to the Bishop of Durham, and then to the Bishop of LlandafT, and the lakes of Westmoreland. This latter plan, however, he was compelled to relinquish, on finding that the exercise of a carriage was as yet too much for him. From Scarborough he wrote the following excellent letter to his daughters; ending with a confirmation of his hopes respecting India.

"Scarborough, 18th July, 1812. "I had the pleasure to receive your letter, Au"gusta, by Dr. B., and was much gratified by the "perusal; and I have seen Charlotte's letter to her "mamma, which is equally pleasing to me; for in "both letters I think I perceive a love of piety, or at "least a wish that you *could* love it. It is indeed "so amiable a quality in young persons, that I "cannot contemplate them with any pleasure, if "they be destitute of it. For what are all other "acquirements or possessions compared with this! "Nothing. I wish you both to possess that which "will give you hope, and me comfort, in the pros"pect of your dissolution. I wish to see you smile, "and have inward peace, when you are shutting "your eyes on the glories of life. But they are not "glories. They are vanities. *I* cannot make you believe this. The grace of God alone can teach "you this truth. And this grace is given often"times to children as young as you. When Christ "said, ' Suffer little children to come unto me,' and "when he quoted the Psalms to the Jews, where it "is said, Out of the mouths of babes and sucklings "thou hast perfected praise,' he meant to intimate, "that the grace of God is communicated to young children as well as to old persons; and that chil"dren may adorn the Gospel by the beauty and "piety of their conduct as well as the aged Chris

"tian. But how is this grace to be attained? It "will not be given to you unless you intreat God "to bestow it. That is an ordinance or rule of "God. And it will not do to ask in words only, in "a formal way; but you must lift up your voice' "in your closet, and expect it earnestly, as if you "expected ' a treasure.'

"Be so good as to tell «-and that

"I have received a letter from Colonel Macaulay "this morning, informing me that a deputation of "Messrs. Wilberforce, Grant, Babington, &c. had "waited on Lord Liverpool on the subject of evan"gelizing India, and that his Lordship surprised them "by offering almost more than they wished. He "intimated his intention to carry the three following "important measures; 1st, To establish a seminary "at each Presidency in India for instructing natives "for the ministry. 2nd, To grant licenses for mis"sionaries, not from the Court of Directors, but "from the Board of Controul. 3d, To consecrate ' bishops for India.

"Your mamma joins me in love to you both; "and I remain, my dear girls,

"Your affectionate Father, "C. Buchanan."

The following extracts from letters to several of his friends will shew the general state of Dr. Buchanan's health, feelings, and employments, during the remainder oPthis eventful year.

"Kirby Hall, 17th August. "I am just returned from Scarborough, where "I have been for the last six weeks trying the "efficacy of the warm baths at that place. I "have been strengthened a little, but am still very "weak.

"I have hardly any news but what I find in the "Bible; and that book is always new. I keep "far aloof from the world; at least I wish to do so "and my present indisposition favours my wishes. "But even in this evil world every week produces "joyful events. The city of London has formed "itself into a Bible Society; and the Chancellor of "the Exchequer has stood forth boldly as the ad"vocate and supporter of the religion of Christ. "But if I were to recount all the blessings of God "to this unworthy land, I should need a quire of "paper: a quire! If all the blessings to this unworthy land were written, the world itself (to use the bold hyperbole of St. John) 'would not contain the books that should be written.'

I rejoice to hear that you find yourself fully employed from day to day, feeling the weight of the labour, and yet obtaining strength for the day. For this, believe me, is the happiest state of your existence. The exertion of mind, under parochial, domestic, and scholastic cares, is like the budding ' and blossoming of trees which promise plenty of fruit. By and by it will be the autumn for you and Mrs. K.; labour and sin and sorrow will cease, and a glorious state of felicity will begin: of which I pray, that all your children and all your pupils may partake!"

"14th November. Thanks to you for your kind letter. I am in much the same state I have been, but I cannot write a page without difficulty. The paralytic affection remains without sensible abatement in my right hand, foot, and side. I can however walk and ride a little: and I have preached regularly this last month. There is no hope of my acquiring *strength* soon, for I do not take sufficient *food*. I am therefore content to do a little, not knowing whether I shall obtain strength to do more..

"I have just had a letter from Mr. Owen, (to whom I had occasion to send sixty pounds for the Bible Society, and ten pounds for Serampore to Mr. Macaulay, from the family here,) in which he manifests great alarm about Mr. Brown. Mr. Thomason's letter stated, that he was not expected to live a week. But my letter is the latest I presume. You would hear of the Serampore conflagration. The missionaries will soon recruit their money; but the work will be somewhat *retarded*."

"Dec. 17.

"I thought I was going on very well, but I was suddenly threatened with a return of illness. It has hitherto been mercifully prevented; but I am obliged to desist entirely from my labour in the ministry; and am forbidden to engage in severe study.

"I rejoice to see you working with so much alacrity and content while strength is afforded you. "'Be thou faithful unto death, and I will give thee "a crown of life.'

"What a terrible retribution is the modern Sennacherib experiencing on the wolds of Russia! What an event for the use and edification of the Christian! I fear both nations and individuals will suffer morally from their exultation. May you and I live to God, whether Buonaparte live or die!" "Dec. 19.

"What a loss will Mr. Robinson be to the Christian world! How many has he blessed in various ways, by preaching, writing, and family exhortation! What a shining example to all the midland ministers! I esteemed him the greatest preacher in England; as Mr..Scott is the greatest divine.

I rejoice to see you continue in a spiritual frame.

"It is the balm of life. If Mr. has seen and

"tasted that ' Christ is precious, he will ' set his face like a flint.' If his convictions have only been general, he will not be very useful in a higher sphere."

"Dec. 29.

"I received your welcome note, and desire the best blessings may be your portion in return. I suffer at present from the effects of a blister on the neck, which has taken a strong hold of my constitution, and can only write a few lines. If I could write, I have only to say, that I join with you in your hallelujah to Him who came at this season to redeem lost man, and to make us kings and priests unto God. May our song which begins now, last for ever!"

"I had not heard that H. Martyn was about to return. God, who ordereth all things well, will shew us perhaps that all these events are conducive to his glory."

At the close of this year, and the commencement of the following, Dr. Buchanan was occupied, at the suggestion of some of his friends, in preparing a new work, in the prospect of the approaching parliamentary discussions on the renewal of the charter of the East India Company, with reference to some more direct and effectual provision for the promotion of Christianity in our Asiatic empire. Before we proceed, however, with this important subject, we must advert to some events which deeply affected the domestic happiness of Dr. Buchanan during the first three months of the year 1813. These will be best related in his own words. In a note to Mr. and Mrs. Thompson on the 27th of February he wrote thus.

"I dare say your hearts will be filled with joy on the event of dear Mary having been so safely delivered. As for the little one, who would only stay half an hour in this evil world, there is no reason that we should grieve for him. I am happy to say, that his dear mother is perfectly composed and resigned to the dispensation.

"May the God of this family, even the God of Abraham, Isaac, and of Jacob, who surroundeth us with his comforts, administer to you also the consolation and support you respectively stand in need of, and shine on your path till you become partakers of his glory!"

On the same day, Dr. Buchanan communicated this event to one of his friends, and accompanied it with the following notice of the afflicting intelligence which had been lately received from India, and of the dubious state of his own health.

"I presume you have heard of the death of the Rev. Mr. Brown, of Calcutta, and of Mr. Martyn. And so these good men have ascended up on high in the vigour of age and life. Let us aspire to ' follow them, and join the assembly of the firstborn!

"I have no news for you, being, like yourself, much retired from the world. I continue in my former state, as to health; that is, I can make little progress in acquiring strength, while the danger of a third attack of paralysis (which is imminent) obliges me to take little nourishment, and yet to lose much blood."

On the 13th of March, Dr. Buchanan, in writing to another of his friends, added;

Mrs. B. recovers well, and has been applying to herself St. Paul's reasoning on the advantages "of being without the cares of a family. I tell "her St. Paul's is a wonderful book—it suits *every* "*state.*"

This favourable appearance, however, of recovery was but of short duration. The following brief narrative, drawn up by Dr. Buchanan for the consolation of Mr. and Mrs. Thompson, describes in simple but affecting language the sudden extinction of his hopes, and the repetition of the stroke which had once before laid low his expectations of earthly happiness.

"Long before her last illness, my dear Mary "haa frequently contemplated the probability of "her dying in early life. Her delight was to talk "of things heavenly and spiritual, and her studies "were almost entirely religious. Her spirits seem"ed to have been much chastened by personal and "by domestic suffering; and her affections were "gradually losing their hold of this world. After "her last confinement, her heart appeared to be de"voted to God in a particular manner. On the "third day she wrote the following note to her "dear mother.

"' You will rejoice to hear I am as well as can be expected, and that I feel a wonderful *serenity* "*of mind.* I feel a want for my poor little babe. "Yet I do not repine, for I have great need of all "the Lord's chastisements; and if I gain one step "towards heaven, I am abundantly repaid, and "would joyfully go through all over again to-mor"row to gain one step more. I have great need of "correction; but why my dear husband should be a "sufferer in these losses I cannot conceive, who is ' so much farther advanced in his heavenly course *H,* and experience in every way. Pray for me, that "I may so run as to obtain the heavenly prize.

"' My kind love to my poor little girls. Tell "them I hope, in the course of a day or two, to be "able to see them. I have great cause for thank"fulness in every way. Adieu, adieu.'

"Notwithstanding her continued indisposition, "accompanied by a high fever, she greatly enjoyed '' my prayers and religious converse. Having lost "her child, she frequently alluded to the pleasure "she anticipated in forming the minds of Charlotte "and Augusta, and preparing them for the heavenly "state. We mutually expressed the hope of devoting ourselves to the service of God for the time to "come, more affectionately and actively than we had "done in time past. She looked forward, certainly, "to the comfort of enjoying more the life of a saint "on earth; but I do not think she expected so "early to be a saint in heaven. The expectations "and assurances of all her medical attendants were "very flattering in regard to her recovery. A rapid "recovery was prognosticated; but she more than "once intimated that they did not understand her "case.

"On the night previous to her death, while she "sat on the couch in my study, she begged I would "give her the Bible, and a little table, and a candle. "She read one of the Psalms very attentively, the "46th I believe, beginning with these words, ' God "is our refuge and strength, a very present help in "trouble.' And when I took the Bible out of her "hands, finding it open at that Psalm, I read it to "her as a portion of our evening religious exercise.

"On the morning of the day on which she died, "after I had kneeled by her bedside, as usual, and "prayed with her, and had left her, she desired her "maid to read a hymn to her. She began one, but "immediately said it was a funeral hymn; to which "she replied, 'a funeral hymn will suit me very "well.'

"About an hour afterwards she was brought into "my study, and took her seat in the arm-chair. "About one o'clock her dear father and mother "came to visit her. After her father had stayed "some time, he and I went out in the carriage for an hour, while her mother remained with her. On VOL. II. U "our return, her mother took her leave, and I ac"companied her down stairs to the carriage. On "my coming up, my dear Mary had just got up "from her chair, and walked over to the couch with "a quick step assisted by her nurse, from an appre' hension that she was about to faint. I immediately "supported her in my arms. Slight faintings suc"ceeded, but they were momentary. She complained "of a pain near her heart. On my saying, I hoped "it would soon be over, she replied, O no, it is not "over yet; what is this that is come upon me?— "send for mamma.' After a few minutes' struggle, "she sat up in the couch with much strength; and "looking towards the window, she uttered a loud "cry, which might have been heard at a considerable "distance. She then drank a little water; and im"mediately after drinking, without a groan or sigh, "her head fell upon my breast. I thought she had "only fainted; but her spirit at that moment had "taken its flight. It was just three o'clock in the "day.

"Thus died my beloved wife. She was ready for "the summons. She had long lived as one who "waited for the coming of her Lord. Her loins "were girded, her lamp was burning, and the staff "was in her hand. She had nothing to do but to "depart.

"' Blessed are those servants whom the Lord "when he cometh shall find watching; and if he "shall come in the second watch, or come in the "third watch, and find them so, blessed are those "servants.' Luke xii. 37." "Moat Hall, 1813."

A few days after this afflicting event, Dr. Buchanan expressed his personal feelings more fully, and detailed, in his *"*Private Thoughts," with genuine Christian humility, those " peaceable fruits of "righteousness," which he was chiefly anxious to derive from his loss. The notice of some of them will, doubtless, interest many readers.

"My first emotions of thankfulness (when I could "seek subjects of thankfulness) were, ' that her last "trial was so short.' It was given me to witness for "my soul's health, I trust; and it was awful indeed, "but it was short."

"Monday Evening, 29th March. "I have passed this week in a mourning and dis"consolate state. I have lost appetite for food, and "dwell almost constantly on the circumstances of "my loss.

"I suffer chiefly from the reflection, that I did "not commune with her more frequently and di"rectly on the state of her soul. God or"dained her personal and domestic sufferings to "mature her for her approaching change. "Mature in my heart, blessed Saviour, this afflic The inscription on Mrs. Buchanan's tomb, written by her affectionate husband, will be found at the end of the volume.

"tion, and enable me to obey the new command"ment, 'that ye love one another.'

"This love exercised towards a wife or children "acquires a double force; natural affection coope"rating with spiritual love.

"Teach me, O Lord, to love my children as I "ought to do, both in a natural and spiritual sense." « April 2,1813.

"My grief has been growing more and more "faint and languid; but blessed be the God and "Father of our Lord Jesus Christ, my sense of "things heavenly and my penitence for past sins "have rather increased. I am enabled to pray three "times a day, and am not as usual driven hastily "from my knees. O that this may continue! I "have long prayed for a spirit of grace and supplica"tion, and now the Lord hath been pleased to give "it by means that I did not expect. However it "comes, it is a long lost blessing.

"The chief petitions in my prayers have been "these:

"1. That God would strike the rock of my af"fections with his rod, and cause the waters to "flow; that I might become tender hearted, truly "humble and solicitous about the spiritual state of "men.

"2. That I might open my mouth in the cause "of God. Hitherto my lips have been locked in a "torpid silence. There is, indeed, much that is con"stitutional in this taciturnity; and my late ner".vans indisposition has greatly increased it. Like "Hooker, I can scarcely look my children or ser"vants in the face.

"I have prayed that this unaccountable weakness "may be removed; that I may become vocal for "God at all times and in all places; that I may look "earnestly into the eyes and countenances of men, "and seek anxiously their salvation; that I may "never forget the agonizing looks and powerful "voice of my dear wife in the struggle of death; and "that I may call forth some animation of soul in *my* "looks and *ivords* during my *life.* "3. That I may learn to seek the glory of God as '' the first objeet in my conversation in the world, "and to pray earnestly for the conversion of all men.

"4. Let me look on every person whom my eyes "survey with benevolence, loving my neighbour as "myself, and utter a mental prayer for that person, "' May this be a vessel of mercy prepared unto "glory!'

"5. That the spirit of grace and supplication may "never depart from me; and that God may hear my morning, noontide, and evening supplication "during every day of my pilgrimage.

"6. That I may fix my love, hopes, and "affections on God; and obtain that fellowship "which I learn from Scripture is attainable by man "in his present state. Amen."

Dr. Buchanan's communications to his friends upon this melancholy occasion breathe the same spirit as his more private meditations, and will still, it is presumed, be thought interesting and instructive. The following are extracts from some of them.

"Kirby Hall, 2d April, 1813.

After replying to one or two points respecting public events, he adds;

"But I do not know what is passing in these days. "The death of Mrs. Buchanan has removed to a vast "distance from my mind subjects which were fami"liar to it.... I could not have believed that I "should have been so much moved by the event as "I am, or that my affections would have been so "powerfully awakened.—May the spiritual impress "sion I have received never be obliterated from my "soul!

"Offer my Christian love to your wife who is yet "alive. And may you and she enjoy much spiritual "communion with each other, before the hour of se"paration arrives!"

"4th April.

"My dear Sister,

"Charlotte has shewn me your kind letter. I thank you most sincerely for your tender sympathy on my late loss. The summons came suddenly for Mrs. Buchanan, but she was evidently matured for her new state of existence; and I believe she in some degree anticipated it. Her death has, I trust, been blessed to myself, and, I would hope, to my children.

"While your dear husband is spared to you, and you are spared to him, enjoy as much spiritual converse together as is possible. For when the separation comes, you will reproach yourselves bitterly, if you have not been tenderly communicative on this subject.

"I remain,

My dear Sister,

Very affectionately yours,

C. Buchanan."

"*To Colonel Sandys.* "15th April.

"Accept my sincere thanks for your kind letter "of condolence. Your topics of consolation are all "excellent; and you point to the right source, the "heavenly Paraclete.

"I shall not be able to make a journey into Corn"wall. I return you thanks for your most obliging "offer, which is a true mark of your personal friend"ship, and of Christian regard. My infirm state "forbids my moving from home for some time, ex"cept in a case of urgent necessity.

"I can write but little. My pen refuses to say "much since Mrs. Buchanan's death. But I hope "I have been affected by it chiefly in a spiritual "manner."

"*To Colonel Macaulay.* "April 16.

"I thank you most sincerely for your kind let"ter. The mournful event has, I trust, been sanc"tified to me. Some, such affliction appears to "have been necessary to soften a hard and proud "heart. I pray that the salutary effects may never "pass away.

"I am happy to hear you speak so favourably "of the disposition of government in regard to the '' extension of Christianity in the East. Mr. Wil"berforce has urged me to go up and give evidence "at the bar of the House of Lords. I told him I "am willing to appear; the only question is, whe"ther it be physically practicable. The physicians oppose my going. I do not know what will be the "event."

The latter sentence in the preceding extract leads back our attention to the great subject which occupied the minds of religious men during the former part of this, year, and with reference to which, it has been already seen, that Dr. Buchanan was employed, when his thoughts were for a time diverted from it by the late afflicting event in his family. To this important' subject, therefore, we will now return.

CHAP. IV. THE light which had been thrown a few years since, chiefly by means of Dr. Buchanan's writings, on the state of religion in India, and the interest which had been in consequence excited upon that subject throughout the nation, produced a very general impression as to the duty of urging upon the attention of Parliament the necessity of making some more effectual provision for the religious instruction of British India, and of encreasing the facilities of imparting the blessings of Christian knowledge to the unenlightened millions of our native subjects. To promote these most important objects, several valuable tracts were published by the friends of religion; amongst which may be particularly mentioned an admirable "Letter to a Friend "on the duty of Great Britain to disseminate Chris"tianity in India, occasioned by the proposed re"newal of the Charter of the East India Com"panyV and a masterly " Address to the Public-," on the same momentous topic, by the Rev. Robert Hall.

The subject was also briefly but powerfully touched by an able and eloquent defender of the general system of our East Indian administration; See the Christian Observer, vol; xi. p. 261. Robert Grant, Esq.

who, in combating an insinuation of a valuable writer on the south of India, thus expresses his own views upon the subject of promoting Christianity in the East.

"The question respecting the introduction of "Christianity into Hindostan does not, it must be "owned, fall precisely within the subject of the pre"sent work; but its high importance will justify a "few words upon it, even at the expense of what "may seem a digression.

"The idea of *coercive* proselytism, however mild "the compulsory means employed, merits all the "epithets which the language of reprobation can "attach to it; and even that of proselytism by the "simple exertion of state influence, seems, in Hin"dostan, to say the best of it, highly objectionable. "But surely the idea of proselytism by the bare "effect of conviction,—by the effect of an unforced, "unbribed, and unbiassed acquiescence in truth "and reason,—however visionary it may appear to "some persons, can only by a very singular rule of "arrangement be classed with unmanly, ungenerous, "and unchristian deception. To such a pitch of "refinement would this valuable author have us "carry our reverence for the superstitions of Hin"dooism! Their sanctity seems to be like what is "said of the priestly character, indelible. Their "sovereignty is so essential and inherent, that they "not only cannot be deposed, but cannot even vo"luntarily abdicate.

"A few years ago this subject was debated with ' great heat; but at present will surely receive a "calm attention. The accomplished Sir William "Jones, who was equally distinguished for his acute"ness, his philanthropy, and his candour, has given "his sanction to attempts, cautiously and fairly con"ducted, for the introduction of the Christian re"ligion among the natives of Hindostan. If, in"deed, as Colonel Wilks justly affirms, 'it never "can be a question, whether the English or the "Hindoo code of religion be entitled to the prefer ence,' the wish must naturally suggest itself to "every humane and unprejudiced mind, that the "better system should have every chance of the "wider diffusion. Only the distinction is ever to be "carefully observed between making it a matter of "*option* and a matter of *authority;* a distinction "which, even as applied to this particular case, the "experience of many years has now shewn that the "natives are perfectly able to comprehend. The "uncompelled and tranquil circulation of the Chris"tian Scriptures (the method peculiarly recom"mended by Sir William Jones) appears so free "from all possibility of exception, that it ought to "receive the fullest and most willing toleration from "the Indo-British Presidencies. Otherwise they "would indeed ' forcibly stand between' the Hindoo "population and the highest and deepest hopes "that can be infused into the human heart. And surely no government calling itself Christian can, "without incurring a fearful responsibility, refuse "to a Christian missionary, so long as he shall "demean himself with strict loyalty, steady discre"tion, and unimpeachable virtue, the opportunity "of exerting his unbought and honourable labour "among the natives of Hindostan."

It was natural, however, to look to him who had first awakened the public mind to the imperious duty of regarding the religious concerns of our oriental empire, to lead the way in an appeal to the legislature upon this subject. Accordingly, amidst the pressure of domestic sorrow and of personal debility, Dr. Buchanan composed and published, early in the spring, a work entitled, " Co"lonial Ecclesiastical establishment: being a brief "View of the state of the Colonies of Great Britain, "and of her Asiatic Empire, in respect to religious instruction: prefaced by some considerations on ' the national duty of affording it."

Though the state of the question relative to the promotion of Christianity in India was very materially and happily changed since the year 1807", when it was so fully discussed, and thoughtful and religious-men were in general persuaded «f the necessity and importance of that measure, Dr. Buchanan still deemed it expedient to commence his work by briefly but pointedly urging this duty upon a Christian nation, and by arguing from various considerations, that the voice of Providence was evidently calling upon Great Britain to under take it. He next entered upon an examination of the means of thus diffusing Christianity; and under the head of one of them, " the extension of the "National Church," gave a sketch of a general colonial establishment, and of the state of religion in the West Indies. Dr.

Buchanan then argued the question as to the policy of promoting Christianity in India.

On the subject, however, of parliamentary interference, he stated, that it was-not his intention to urge the legislature to adopt any direct means in the way of expensive establishments for proselyting the natives. All, he said, that was expected at present in regard to them was, that the governing power would not shew itself hostile to the measure of instructing them. Great Britain, he alleged, owed her primary obligations to her own children. The work, therefore, is closed by a powerful appeal to Parliament as to its duty and responsibility upon the approaching decision of this momentous question, and with the sketch of an Ecclesiastical Establishment for British India, which has been already mentioned.

Such is a brief outline of the contents of this volume, which was very extensively circulated, particularly among the members of both Houses of Parliament, and made a strong and general impression throughout the country.

» See the preceding chapter.

But it was not merely by the press that the friends of religion endeavoured to instruct and awaken the public upon this critical and momentous occasion. They resorted to the legitimate and constitutional measure of petitioning Parliament upon the subject, and nine hundred addresses from the cities, towns, and even villages of the United Kingdom, crowded the tables of both Houses, imploring the interference of the legislature in behalf of the moral and religious interests of India. The contest was long and arduous; but the voice of Christian duty and of sound policy, which must ever be inseparable, at length prevailed. A resolution to the following effect was introduced by his Majesty's ministers into both Houses; and after very full and lengthened discussions, in which Mr. Wilberforce, Mr. W. Smith, and Mr. Stephen particularly distinguished themselves by their able and eloquent efforts in its support, it was in the House of Commons carried by a great majority, and in the House of Lords without debate and without a division.

"That it is the duty of this country to promote "the interest and happiness of the native inhabit"ants of the British dominions in India; and that "such measures ought to be adopted as may tend "to the introduction among them of useful know"ledge, and of religious and moral improvement. "That in the furtherance of the above objects, suf"ficient facilities shall be afforded by law to persons "desirous of going to and remaining in India, for "the purpose of accomplishing these benevolent "designs."

A previous resolution had already passed, by which a bishop and three archdeacons were to be appointed to superintend the clergy of the Established Church in India; thus accomplishing, though not to the extent which he deemed necessary, the two great objects which Dr. Buchanan had so ably and so perseveringly pursued.

It is to these important and interesting transactions that the following extracts principally refer. With the exception of the first, the letters from which they are taken were addressed to a friend, to whose judicious and zealous exertions much of the success which ultimately attended the cause must be ascribed.

"Kirby Hall, Feb. 4, 1813.

"You go up, you say, to witness the battle

"between the Government and the India Company. "It rages very furiously at present. It is a fine "trial of the honesty of religious men. It is true, "indeed, good men often live and die the slaves of "particular prejudices; but, generally speaking, con"science will take the alarm, if we are not honest "in our vote in a cause between *God and man.*

"God will direct the event according "to his counsel. There may be no remarkable tri"umph at this time: but other parts of the great "catastrophe (the revelation of Christ's kingdom) "are approximating, and you may live to see its "advance. The expiration of twenty years more is "likely to be a grander period in the Church than "the present.

"I have just submitted to the insertion of a large "seton in the integuments of my neck. So you "see the constitutional propensity to paralysis con"tinues. But this is the best state for me. I "could not have *chosen* a better; and it does me "a great deal of good. I need slow fires to purge "away my dross. But the Refiner is merciful, and "gives me strength to bear the heat of the fur"nace."

"Kirby Hall, April, 181S. 'The circumstances of my health render it im"practicable for me at present to move to London. "But I shall probably afford you any information as "satisfactorily by correspondence, as if I were on "the spot.

"Your accomplishing the object of a numerous "meeting at the London Tavern was a grand mea"sure, and the whole Christian world is'indebted "to you for it. The resistance to your purposes "wilt be most resolute. The public voice alone "promises something. If every city and town in "England and Scotland were to petition, (which is "practicable,) the business would acquire a new "complexion before the end of May.

"The duty, however, of a Christian is to be obe"dient to the powers that be. To claim as matter "of *right* the permission of preaching Christianity "to the Hindoos is highly absurd; and the assertion "of the *right* ought to meet with a rebuke.

"Mr. Wilberforce's speech in the committee on "Catholic claims will produce some sensation among "religious men in England. I am of opinion that "he has judged rightly. Liberal concession to the "Catholics and Dissenters will be good medicine "to some; and will favour measures for enlarging "the spiritual Church of Christ. We may be sure, "that the country will make no concession to the "Catholics which will *materially* injure her. If ' she does, she can retrace her steps, as she has "done before."

"May 15.

"Many thanks to you for Christianity in India,' 'It is drawn up in the manner I entirely approve, "which I could not say of the former summaries. It comes in well after the petitions; and its per"spicuity and brevity will fix and fascinate the care"less eye. I begin almost to *sympathize* with your "Indian opponents, the battering of religious Britain has been so tremendous.

"Like you, I am not anxious as to the terms of "concession in regard to the question. The deed "is done. Britain has lifted her voice in her "Christian character, and the effect will be per"manent and blessed. By this concussion religion "rises at least two degrees in a scale of twenty, "both in its character and interests. The Bible "Society too shares in the triumph.

VOL. II. X

"Mr. Dealtry's sermon was well timed; and "would be, I doubt not, a *coup de grace* to the '' dying prejudices of some.

"I have just read Dr. Milner's Strictures; and "have praised God, who hath given such under"standing to men. He is a host in himself; and "the Church will begin henceforth to view him in "a new light. They will dread his principles less, "and reverence his abilities more. I trust it will "please God to spare his life for some years.

"The publication of the Society's India Reports "is just what we want. It identifies them with us, "and confirms the truth of facts.

"Spare your health, and take repose; for you "know not but you may have as much to do next "year." "Kirby Hall, June 2d.

"I congratulate you on your great "triumph. Such a resolution proposed under such "circumstances! The moment it actually passes, '' the petitioners ought to unite in one national "hallelujah.

.... " What does... think of *civilization* now? "Lord Castlereagh has put the question to rest. "He says, the fear of it is a chimera."

"11th June.

"I am charmed with Whitbread, when he sounds "the right note. Before the Church Missionary Society. ."I continue stationary at present. I have had "blood abstracted twice by cupping within the last "month."

"5th July.

. "And so Mr. Venn is dead! What a varied "scene has he passed through in the evening of "life! permitted, no doubt, for his soul's health and eternal good. The Church may mourn in"deed for Venn and Robinson. Let us be followers of them, who through faith and patience "have inherited the promises!" July 7th. "I enclose an additional paragraph for the Re"marks. Mr. Lushington having declared so gravely, "that I had recommended the Hindoos to be con"verted *by force,* perhaps it would be right to ad vert to a matter, which I had never thought it worth my while to notice before.

"I hope now to give you no further trouble. "It must be a great relief to you when Parliament "and their India questions break up for good; and "I should be glad to hear that you had gone for a "while to the Isle of Wight; whence, as from a "safe haven, you might look back on the tumul"tuous sea you have navigated."

"July 24.

"I congratulate you sincerely on the issue of "your campaign; far more interesting to thousands, "than that of Lord Wellington.

"And now we are likely to be all disgraced"Parliament has opened the door, and who is there "to go in? From the Church not one man! "Lord C. anticipated this *denoument* in a very "pleasant vein. We may hope that the Church "Missionary Society will excite a new spirit in "various places. And we must believe, that the "late great national movement, in behalf of Christ' "and his kingdom, will have a reward in the fruits"of righteousness within the year."

The labours, however, of Dr. Buchanan in this great cause were not yet completed. In the course of the debates in the House of Commons, upon the question of allowing efforts to be made by pious and benevolent persons to promote Christianity in India, his name and his writings were introduced by several of the Anglo-Indian opposers of that measure, in terms which can scarcely be excused even on the ground of their own sincere, though mistaken, apprehensions of the subject. He was represented by these gentlemen as the calumniator of the Hindoos, and as having given to the world a false, or at least an exaggerated, statement of their cruel and immoral superstitions. They, on the contrary, wished the House and the public to believe, upon the authority of their alleged local knowledge, that the Hindoos, though idolaters, Particularly by Sir Henry Montgomery and Mr. Lushington; the latter of whom did not, however, vote against the retulwtion.

and enslaved by a blind and corrupt superstition, were still a very harmless and moral race of people; and, in support of the excellence of the Brahminical system, quoted a variety of passages from the Heetopades, and other Hindoo books, to prove what pure and exalted sentiments they entertained of the Supreme Being, and of the great duties of morality. Witnesses, however, without end, possessing more than all the boasted local information of these gentlemen, from Mr. Holwell to Sir William Jones, Lord Teignmouth, and Sir James Mackintosh, had already convinced every calm and unprejudiced enquirer, that, whatever may be the speculative merit of their sacred books, or the social virtues of individuals, both the religious system and the moral practice of the Hindoos in general were, what we might be certain, from abstract principles as well as universal experience, the heathen ever must be, "corrupt, abominable, and unto every" really "good "work reprobate." And it would, in fact, be quite as practicable and as just, to charge the sacred writers themselves in their descriptions of the idolaters of Greece and Rome, however distinguished for their advancement in learning and the arts, with exaggeration and uncharitableness, as the representations of Dr. Buchanan on a similar painful and deplorable subject.

It happened, in the course of the examination of evidence upon the India question before the House of Commons, that Dr. Buchanan's Memorial to Lord Minto in the year 1807, together with the reply of the Bengal government to that paper, and the observations of the Court of Directors on both, were exhibited, and afterwards printed by order of the House. The account given by Dr. Buchanan of the atrocities of the idol-worship at Juggernaut was also opposed and attempted to be invalidated by Mr. C. Buller, M. P. for West Looe, in a way which will shortly be stated.

The unfounded allegations of the gentlemen first named were generously repelled by Mr. Wilberforce, in one of his admirable speeches in the House, in the following terms.

"It is unwillingly that I bring in the name of "one other person; I mean Dr. Buchanan: but I, "should be extremely wanting in the office and feel"ings of friendship, did I not take this opportunity "of vindicating the character of that excellent "man. The other night, the House will remember, "it was stated by a friend near me, (Mr. W. Smith,) "that I had not mentioned a single fact or propo"sition on the authority of Dr. Buchanan. This, "however, was not because Dr. Buchanan was no "authority with me; but because I knew there was "a great, but most unjust outcry raised against "him: as, indeed, it was natural to expect there would be against any man who had endeavoured, "with his zeal, to draw the public attention to this "great cause. Thinking, therefore, that my facts "would be more readily admitted, if I supported "them by other less obnoxious names, I did not mention the name of Dr. Buchanan, although his "testimony would have corroborated all I said. "But I should not do justice to my sentiments, if I "did not say, that I feel Dr. Buchanan to be a marf "who deserves to be spoken of in a very different "way from that in which some gentlemen have "chosen to mention his name. Lord Wellesley ' selected Dr. Buchanan to be Vice-Provost of the "college of Calcutta; and he says of him—' I have "formed the highest expectations from his abilities, "learning, temper, and morals;' if, therefore, I "think most highly of Dr. Buchanan, as I certainly "do, I am not alone in thinking well of him. And "let me here remind the honourable member, that "Dr. Buchanan did not, at least, act like a man who "wished to deceive the public, and to obtain their "assent to a false proposition; for Dr. Buchanan "published that very work, which states roost fully "and particularly all the great circumstances of "Hindoo enormity, while he yet resided in Bengal, "and the book was in circulation there a year or "two before he quitted that country. He himself "presented to the supreme government of India a "copy of this work; I mean his Memoir in favour "of an Ecclesiastical Establishment for India; by "which he drew as much attention to the subject as "he could, and, at least, manifested his desire that "the real truth should be ascertained. And in jus"tice to Dr. Buchanan, I must observe, that, not "withstanding the unjust and illiberal aspersions "which have been thrown out in a general way "against him, I have never yet heard him distinctly "charged with any specific mistatement of any fact "which he has brought forward."

To Mr. Lushington and Sir Henry Montgomery, Dr. Buchanan wrote privately in vindication of his sentiments respecting the Hindoos. A copy of his letter to the former gentleman is here introduced, not merely for the purpose of defence and explanation, for this is by no means necessary, but to shew his exemplary mildness and forbearance under violent and undeserved reproach.

"Kirby Hall, Borobridge, 29th June 1813.. " Sir,

"I do myself the honour to address you for a moment, in consequence of my having been informed that, on a late occasion in the House of Commons, you censured my statements concerning India as being unchristian and unjust; or in terms to that effect. Had such a stricture been made by a person who was hostile to the introduction of Christianity into India, I should have paid no attention to it; but coming from respectable authority, and from one who is friendly to that measure, I think it due to him and to myself to offer some explanation.

"As you are an advocate for instructing the natives of India, I must think that you approve in general of my endeavour to give some account of the state of the people, and of the nature of their superstition; for, without some account of this kind, how should our nation ever be excited to interest itself humanely in their behalf? I must believe, then, that you do not object to the giving such account, but only that you disapprove of the *manner* in which it is done. I am not conscious that there is any thing intemperate in my manner of writing. Had I been intemperate, the nation would not have listened to me. It remains, then, for me to believe, that you advert to some insulated facts stated by me, which you consider untrue. If you will have the goodness to refer me to any book, or other respectable authority, which plainly invalidates any particular fact, I shall be happy to publish the authority in the next edition of my work, and to confess my mistake. I assure you, it will cost me no more to retract an error publicly than to write this letter. My only object is to promote the cause of truth in the world, by legitimate means. My own fame (since all men possess not the same information and principles, and cannot be equally pleased) ought to be of little moment, and is, I hope, a secondary consideration. But I beg you will do me the justice to remember, that on these subjects there is great diversity of opinion, even among those who are adverse to my general views. Scarcely two persons from two different parts of India will be found, who will give the same account of what they have seen and heard. Nor is agreement to be expected in describing the various nations extending over three thousand miles of territory. But as to those passages in my own work which you characterize as unchristian or unjust, I am at as great a loss to know which they are, as if you had charged them with high treason.

"I understood some time ago, that the statement in my publications which chiefly provoked animadversion, was that which referred to the burning of women. But you are aware on what authority I published that account; and, I presume, you are informed, that subsequent indubitable statements veiy far exceed it, and set this question entirely at rest.

"Probably you may have not heard,

that a work has been recently published in Bengal, in four volumes quarto, entitled a History of the Religion, Manners, and Literature of the Hindoos, which has been bought up with avidity in India, has already passed through two editions in that country, and is now publishing at home. It was printed under the immediate eye of the Bengal government, (as you know it necessarily must be,) and possesses an unquestionable authenticity on the various subjects concerning which it treats. It takes the high ground of literal translations from the Hindoo books, recent facts, and living witnesses. Now this work not only confirms my statements in almost every case which was controverted, but goes far beyond them. In describing the atrocities connected with the burning of women, self-devotement, and the impurity of the Hindoo worship, I find I have scarcely entered the vestibule. Will those, then, who pause at my statements, be able to assail this authority?

"There is another consideration, to which I would request you would advert. Speculative strictures on the character of the Hindoos constitute a very inconsiderable portion of my writings. In three publications concerning India, I do not think that criminatory reflections on the Hindoo character in the abstract would occupy three pages. I treat, in general, of entirely different subjects. It was not till the other day that I was induced to give an exposition of a radical principle of an impure character in the Hindoo worship; and that exposition would certainly never have been given, but for the statement of Mr. Buller, From his representation the nation would have been left to conclude, that the indecent emblems on the temples of the Hindoos have no evil effect on the morals of the people. Now if I was entirely convinced that the contrary was the truth, would it have been right in me to aid, by my silence, the promulgation of such an error?

"I would flatter myself, that when you have read this letter, you will be disposed to consider the object of my writings more favourably. There is a particular reason why I wish to obtain from you an expression of approbation."

Here Dr. Buchanan introduced a reference to the charge which he had received from the late Sir Stephen Lushington, on his going out to India, which has been already mentioned in these Memoirs. He then continues as follows.

"If you will do me the honour at your leisure to look through my writings, I think you will approve the motives and general design; and I hope you will pardon.particular aberrations. If you do not, I shall regret it; but I bear no resentments; and shall trust that time, which produces great revolutions in sentiment, will abate, and not en crease, your unfavourable opinion.

"I have the honour to be, Sh,

Your most obedient and humble Servant,

C. Buchanan."

"*To S. R. Lushington, Esq. M. P.*"

Such was Dr. Buchanan's temperate and satisfactory address to Mr. Lushington. To Mr. Buller's allegations, he thought it necessary to reply more publicly.

This gentleman perceiving in the course of the examinations which took place in the House of Commons, that the enormities practised at Juggernaut had made a deep impression on the minds of many members, deemed it his duty, from his personal and intimate knowledge of the subject, with a view of effacing that impression, to address a letter to the Court of Directors of the East India Company, intending that it should be laid on the table of the House; where it accordingly soon afterwards made its appearance. Mr. Buller's letter contained a plausible defence of the tax on pilgrims resorting to the temple of the idol in question, and an attempt to palliate the atrocities alleged by Dr. Buchanan to be customarily committed during the celebration of the Rutt Jattra. Of the indecencies said to be exhibited there, he professed his total ignorance. This. vindication of Juggernaut was probably intended, together with the defence of the Indian government, to discredit the testimony of Dr. Buchanan on that particular point, and thus to produce a general distrust of his statements. The failure of this scheme shall be given in the words of a writer in a valuable periodical publication before alluded to; which nobly redeemed its pledge given some years since, never to abandon the sacred cause of promoting Christianity in India and throughout the world; and to whose pages in the year 1813 the author gladly refers, for a complete and masterly view of this whole subject.

"Had it pleased Providence," said the Christian Observer, " that the severe illness with which Dr.

If Dr. Buchanan's representations of this point needed any, support, we might resort to the coincident and unconscious testimony of the Danish missionaries, particularly that of Mr. Ilutteman, which is contained in the Report of the Society for promoting Christian Knowledge for the year 1762. Review of Buchanan's Apology for Christianity in India, vol. xii. p. 0'48.

"Buchanan has recently been visited had either "deprived the Church of his valuable life, or re"duced him to an incapacity of employing his pen "in her service, it would obviously have been diffi"cult, if not impossible, to have effectually defended "him from this assault. But while the pressure of "disease confined him to his couch, and almost ' denied his tongue its office, the use of a hand was "spared to him, and his mind retained its more "than youthful vigour. In a few days his reply to "Mr. Buller was in the hands of every member of "the House of Commons; and it may be consi"dered as no unfair presumption that the reply was "complete and satisfactory, that in the parlia"mentary discussions which afterwards took place, "not the most distant allusion was made to the "letter of Mr. Buller, by any of his friends, al"though it cannot be doubted that, when first pro"duced, it was intended to serve important pur"poses in debate. We do not deny that we may "be fairly suspected of feelings of partiality towards "Dr. Buchanan. Our cordial respect for his cha"racter, and our gratitude for the important ser"vices he has rendered to the Christian cause, may "very possibly give a bias to our sentiments in his favour. We think, however, that had we been mistaken in attributing to his reply correctness of statement and solidity of reasoning, we should ere this have heard, that either in Parliament or out of it, some one of those Anglo-Indians, who have been accustomed never to pronounce his name without some expression of vituperation, would have accepted the challenge of his friends, and have descended from the convenient but impotent generality of hard names, to the specification of some particular mistatements of fact.

As soon as Dr. Buchanan's reply to Mr. Buller's letter had thus produced its intended effect in the House of Commons, he prepared to publish it, together with some other documents, to the world. It accordingly appeared in the course of the summer under the following title; "An Apology for promoting Christianity in India: containing two Letters, addressed to the Honourable East India Company, concerning the Idol Juggernaut; and a Memorial presented to the Bengal Government in 1807, in defence of the Christian Missions in India. Printed by Order of the Honourable House of Commons. To which are now added, Remarks on the Letter addressed by the Bengal Government to the Court of Directors in reply to the Memorial. With an Appendix, containing various official papers, chiefly extracted from the Parliamentary Records relating to the Promulgation of Christianity in India."

This valuable and interesting volume is so well known, and is still so accessible, that it would be unnecessary to do more in this place than refer those who may be desirous of investigating the important subjects of which it treats, to the perusal of its various contents. Two passages, however, deserve to be extracted. One is from the close of the first letter to the Court of Directors; and is worthy, as it has been justly observed, of so distinguished a combatant in this field of sacred warfare.

"The annual waste of human life, from the causes that have been mentioned, in the territories under the dominion of the Honourable the "East India Company, is a subject of appalling contemplation. Every friend of humanity must be often putting the question, Is this scene to continue for ever? Can there be no melioration of human existence in India? Are there no means of mitigating the anguish of reflection in England, when we consider that the desolations of Juggernaut exist under our government? Yes, we answer, there are means. We have seen with what avidity the holy Scriptures are received by the pilgrims. These pilgrims come from every part of India; some from Cabul, a distance of sixteen hundred miles, and some from Samarchand. They are the representatives of a population, amounting, as we have seen, to 'two hundred millions.' They are of every caste, and many of them of no caste at all. The Bible is, by the inscrutable providence of God, at hand: it has been translated into the languages of India. Would it not, then, be worthy of the East

"India Company fo order ten thousand copies to be distributed annually at Juggernauts in any manner that prudence would justify and expedience direct, as a sacred return for the revenue we derive from it, if it should be thought right that that revenue should still be continued? The Scriptures would thus be carried to the extremities of India and the East. Is it possible that the shadow of an objection should arise against such a measure, innoxious, as it is humane and heavenly, ih its tendency? Are we afraid that ' the wretches who' come to lay their bones within the precincts of Juggernaut' would mutiny and take away our dominion? Would not the conse'' quence be rather, that ' the blessing of Him that was ready to perish' would rest upon you?"

The other passage which it may be right to quote from the volume in question, is the following general defence by Dr. Buchanan of his Memorial to Lord Minto, with which the Bengal Government was so much offended, and which did not escape the more gentle reprehension of the Court of Directors.

"Of the accuracy of the facts stated in the Memorial, I think there can be little doubt. I challenged enquiry before I left Calcutta; but the government did not think it necessary to investigate them. They wrote their Letter to the Court of Directors while I was yet on the spot, without communicating their sentiments to me VOL. II. Y

"in any manner, although I was on terms of personal civility with every member of the administration; and they sent the letter home without my knowledge by the same fleet which conveyed myself. Nor did I ever see it, until it was recently printed by order of the Honourable the House of Commons.

"The second remark I would make refers to the charge of disrespect' which is preferred against me, in the letter alluded to, for addressing government at all on the subject; and to which they frequently revert with lively sensibility. I am not at all anxious about self-justification in this matter, except as the honour of religion may be concerned: and I hope little personal feeling will be visible in these Remarks. But in regard to the charge in question, I only request that the Bengal government will look back to the transaction, and survey the *nature* of the subject and the circumstances in which I stood. Let them say whether I had any personal interest in the cause at issue. 'Did I address government foimy own advantage? Was it to recommend myself to the favour of the Court of Directors when I returned home? No. It was not my own cause, but that of Revealed Religion, which I maintained. Christianity had been dishonoured. Its teachers were oppressed and silenced; and there was nobody to appear for the truth. I stood for a moment the representative of ' Him who is higher than the highest.' And is this to be denominated disrespect; especially when the words of my Address are perfectly respectful? I think that in the judgment of candour and of enlightened minds, it will be thought that I barely did my duty. The public voice in the settlement of Calcutta was certainly in my favour; for the proceedings "against the missionaries were very generally con"demned."

It will now be necessary to return to the more private history of Dr. Buchanan, and for this purpose to recur to his letters to various friends. The following extracts are partly of a general nature, and partly refer to the subjects which have been lately discussed.

"*To Colonel Sandys.*

"Kirby Hall, July 29, 1813. "Many thanks to you for your letter. The last "eleven years have indeed been eventful to you "and me; and it is possible that the next eleven "(whether in heaven or earth) will be equally "marvellous. My health, concerning which you "enquire, continues, we hope, to amend; but it "will be long before I obtain much strength, even "if there should be no relapse of paralysis, which "can only be known to Him who 'said to the "sick of the palsy, Thy sins be forgiven thee.' If "I am able, I must go up to town about the end "of autumn or the year, to superintend the pub"lication of some Syriac works which I have com"menced, viz. New Testament, Grammar, and "Lexicon.

"Since Mrs. Buchanan's death I have enjoyed "more distinct views of the heavenly state than I "had before; and have attained to more emphasis "in prayer. So far that event has been blessed "to me. May the fruits of righteousness grow "and increase to the end, even as they do with "you and the faithful children of God in every "place!

"I rejoice to hear that you and your family are "well. As for the spiritual state of those you "love, that must be for the trial of your faith and "hope, even unto the end. 'Remember David and "all his trouble.' Children seldom shew signs of "grace until they grow up. David had one hope"ful son, Solomon; and he became an idolater. "What may have been his end is not well known. "But I think the Preacher became a monument of "grace."

"I am not surprised that was *sick* when

"you addressed a letter to him on Christian sub"jects. His is as remote from the right way as "poor and. And yet even these may be converted by Him who made the world before they "die." *To Z. Macaulay, Esq.* "Kirby Hall, August.

"I thank you for your letter of the 2d inst. and was much pleased with your favourable account "of Mr. G's exertions in the Christian cause. He "gave me the perusal of his admirable book a few "days before I went to India; and I know not whe"ther it did not lay some foundation in my mind "for future investigations.

"I approve most highly of your patronizing Dr. "John's plans of native schools. They are pro"perly Mr. Swartz's plans. See the defence of "them in the last Church Missionary Register. I "visited some of the schools, patronized by go"vernment, and witnessed their operation. They "may be justly termed Mediate Schools' for ehris"tianizing the Hindoos, though their effects be not "immediate. I had the same plan in view in pro"posing the numerous schools attached to the Ec"clesiastical Establishment in my last work." ." Kirby Hall, August 20.

"I only received copies of the Apology' yester"day. The editorial part reflects great credit on "your attention; and the various improvements "which I mark in many places demonstrate your "kindness to me, and affection for the cause in which I have been engaged.

"The battle is now, I hope, jover; and I would "gladly forget all that is past, and turn my face "Zionward, for the rest of my pilgrimage.

"Neither Sir Henry Montgomery nor Mr. L. "has condescended (as the Scotch say) on a single "instance of mistatement in my volumes. As to "what Mr. L. has alleged which Mr. Smith should "consider not *defensible,* I have not the smallest "idea; unless it be, as Home Tooke says, ' eating "little children alive without being roasted.'"

"Kirby Hall, 8th September.

"The strange circumstance of *your* being at "a watering-place, doing nothing but bathing, "mounting hills, and looking down on the tumult "below, induces me to write you a few lines in "the style of Pope, that is, about nothing. What "labours of mind that man Pope achieved in doing "nothing! And yet he thought he did something. "But Horace did as much as he. Johnson ftat"tered himself he did a little more for virtue and "the chief good than the other two. But, alas! "he, like they, 'knew not the way to the city; "and in vain attempted to shew it to others. But "I am likely to fail in writing a letter in the style "of Pope, and shall therefore approximate a little "to business.

"I had a letter from-lately, accompanying

'' a present of his book on India. He had been "reading my Apology, and says he thinks my two "letters to the Court of Directors, particularly the second, and my remarks on the letter of the Go"vernor General in Council, ' are the best of my 'controversial pieces.' He adds, I am the more "glad of this, because it is an evidence that your "long course of illness has not affected your mental "powers, whilst it may have invigorated qualities of "a still more important kind.' It is certain, how"ever, that I have suffered from my illness. *Man* "*sum qualis eram.* Would that this were true in "the other sense to which he alludes! He further "says, ' Something seems yet wanting to expose to "the public the irreligious spirit which has animated "the Anglo-Indians in the whole of this question of "introducing Christianity into the East.'

"I have answered, that I would not be an assailant "any more. I seek peace and an oblivion of past "scenes; and have suggested that he himself might "probably have leisure now to send forth a few pages "on that subject.

"mentions, that one of the Directors, 'who "is now removed to another world,' was a violent "enemy of mine. I do not know what is his "name; and so little have I been in the habit of "enquiring what is passing abroad, that I did not "know I had such a thing as a personal enemy in "the world."

The two next letters were addressed to Colonel Macaulay; and while they manifest the lively interest which the writer continued to feel in the great work of diffusing Christian knowledge, it will be a subject of regret that the voyage in question was not accomplished either by himself or his friend-.

"Kirby *Hall,* 24th August 1813.

"My dear Sir,

"I was not a little pleased to hear of your proposed voyage to the Mediterranean, both on account of your own health, and of the advantage which I doubt not will accrue to the Christian public. You will have opportunities of learning how far, and to what extent, the distribution of the Bible may be practicable, and what other steps we may take in regard to the translation of the Scriptures and of tracts, and to the disposition of missionaries in those regions. It is wonderful that the places consecrated by the travels and labours of the Apostle Paul, should be yet left in darkness, unexplored. If your health improve under that genial climate, I do not wish to see you home soon.

"My own health continues to amend. It is now seven weeks since I lost blood, the longest interval since my first illness.

"Lord and Lady L and family are now with me. They are zealous promoters of religious institutions in Ireland, and are returning provided with new books, tracts, and arguments. They consider five at least of their bishops as being enrolled in the cause. I have petitioned for two of them to countenance the Homily Society.

"If I should have no return of illness, I have thoughts of going up to town about the end of autumn, and propose in that case to call at Mr. Babington's and Mr. Kempthorne's in my way. But by that time I presume you will be upon the foamy deep. Wherever you are, I pray that a blessing may be upon you till the end of your pilgrimage; and remain,

"My dear Sir,

Very sincerely yours,

C. Buchanan." Kirby Hall, 2d September, 1813

"My dear Sir,

"I have been favoured with your letter, informing me that your voyage to the Mediterranean is just at hand. There are several important objects of research, which the course of your route will enable you probably to attend to; a few of which I shall mention, according to your desire.

"1. We hardly know any thing of the state of Christianity on the African coast, where it flourished in purity in the third and fourth centuries. Hippo, of which Augustine was Bishop, was the fountainhead. It is close to Carthage, (where the Christian Council was held,) and Utica, and Tunis; all which places are not much more than one hundred miles from the Sardinian and Sicilian coast. Your message to the Christians will be, that they may have copies of the Scriptures from Malta or England, if they choose to apply for them.

"2. The Jews inhabit almost every town on the African shore. The Hebrew Testament will be soon ready for them.

"3. The island of Cyprus is a grand field for Christian investigation at this era. 'The greater part of the inhabitants are Greek Christians. Be sides a multitude of Armenians, there are here a great many *Maronites,'* or Syrian Christians. This is the account of the Abbe Mariti. He adds, ' The Latins are far from being so numerous, and consist only of Europeans, and the brotherhood of St. Francis, known throughout the Levant under the name of the Fathers of the Holy Land.' —' There are very few English here; and it is doubtless for this reason that they have neither a church or chapel, nor a minister of their religion. Should they happen to multiply, they will probably endeavour to procure *all these things?* This is from an Italian priest! I trust you will be able to shew us how we may ' procure all these things.'

"You may tell the Greek Christians, that the Greek Testament is ready for them; and the Syrian Christians, that the Syriac Testament will be soon ready for *them.* I go up to London, God willing, to superintend the printing of it, and of a Syriac Grammar and Lexicon at the same time.

"4. It is said that *two-thirds* of the inhabitants of European Turkey are of the Greek, Syriac, Ar Mariti, vol. i. p. 8. menian, and Latin Church. A continual subject of enquiry will therefore be, how many of these denominations respectively live in any particular place, and how many copies of the Greek, Syriac, Armenian, (the Bible Society has not thought of the Armenian yet,) and Latin copies of the. Scriptures, including the French and Italian, may be required as a primary supply? Parcels may be sent at a venture.

"5. An accurate enumeration of the *churches* (buildings) is important, throughout every mile of your route, beginning with Lisbon, Cadiz, and Gibraltar. A church is an object of correspondence, if we know only how to address the priest in the language of his place.

"I consider you to be the fittest man in Great Britain to go upon a voyage of Christian discovery.

"I hope to avail myself of Mr. and Mrs. Babingtons kind invitation, and to stay with them two days in my journey up to London. I cannot say how soon I shall be able to set out. Again I follow you with my best wishes; and remain,

"My dear Sir,

Sincerely yours,

C. Buchanan."

Dr. Buchanan appears to have left Kirby Hall

» Armenian Bibles and Testaments have since been printed by the Theodosian Branch of the Russian Bible Society.

towards the end of October. One of his first visits was to his friend and relative the Rev. J. Kempthorne, at Claybrook, in Leicestershire; the following account of which by that gentleman cannot but be interesting to the reader.

"The last time," says Mr. Kempthorne, "that "he visited us, which was in his way to Cam"bridge, I thought him eminently dead to the "world, and, as it were, absorbed in heavenly "things. His deep domestic afflictions seemed to ' have been greatly sanctified to him. He appeared to watch for every opportunity of seasoning our "ordinary discourse with the salt of religion. "When we were speaking of Carey's Atlas, he took "occasion to refer, in a solemn and affecting man"ner, to the map of the heavenly city, which St. "John has given us in the Revelation. When I "spoke of Bonaparte's late astonishing overthrow, "he heard it with comparative indifference, and soon "adverted to the importance of the conversion of "the soul to God, as involving consequences of "greater moment than the fall of emperors and the "revolutions of the greatest states.

"After our family prayer, he with much kindness "and wisdom made some observations on my man"ner of expounding the Scripture; and after he "left me, he called on a common friend, and faith"fully expressed his fears respecting the safety of "his spiritual state.

"Yet I have heard a piously disposed person, "who saw more of his domestic habits, regret, that "his conversation, which was highly edifying when "he was called forth by pious visitors, was not more "frequently and decidedly spiritual in his own "family circle.

"With what exquisite sensibility of conscience "does he himself lament this in his private reflec"tions after his second wife's most distressing re"moval from him!"

On the 3d of November, Dr. Buchanan wrote to one of his friends from Cambridge as follows. The remark in this letter respecting a motto which he had assumed, shews his readiness to receive any suggestion respecting his conduct, even on slight and unimportant matters.

"I have been favoured with your kind letter. "I had heard of the ninth babe at Rothley. May "the dew of God's blessing descend on your in"creasing family, and make you all heirs of glory!

"As soon as I had read your observations on the "motto, I sent for a carriage-painter, and erased it. "We have had it nearly four years, and I never "heard a word concerning its peculiarity.

"I have experienced very general and more than "ordinary civilities from the members of the Uni"versity, particularly from the Bishop of Bristol. "His Lordship introduced me to his family, as the "man from whose books he and they had derived ' much instruction. He and Lord Hardwicke were "sitting together at Trinity Lodge when I called, "reading my letter to the Court of Directors re specting Mr. Buller, not knowing that the Apology "had been published since. It seems the book has "been so little advertised, that Dr. Jowett had not "heard of it till the review in the last Christian "Observer appeared. There is not a single copy of "it, or of the Colonial Establishment, at a book"seller's in Cambridge. The Bishop and his friends "partake of the spirit which animates you concern"ing Juggernaut.

"I expect to be in London soon, when I hope "to have the pleasure of seeing you. Your last "letter proves that you are as desirous I should be "without spot as yourself."

Dr. Buchanan appears to have stayed about ten days at Cambridge, and then to have proceeded to London, where he was chiefly occupied in his preparations for the Syriac New Testament. During his stay in town, he wrote the following pleasing letter to his daughters.

"22d Nov. 1813. -"My dear Charlotte and Augusta, I return you many thanks for your letter. I am happy to hear that you are both in good health; and I doubt not you are both making a due proficiency in your studies.

"I am very much pleased, Charlotte, with your proposal to give five shillings to the West Indian Mission, which I shall do when I find the treasurer of the Society.

"I sympathize with you, Augusta, on the death of the pretty bird, *Cherry*. But our grief is in vain. Its spirit will never return. But when Augusta's spirit takes the wing, it will live for ever; and those who loved her on earth will once more love her in heaven, if she and they prove worthy of eternal life. Cherry, it seems, was singing a few minutes before its death. So, oftentimes, does the Christian sing and exult in spirit at the thought of putting off the veil of flesh, and entering on the confines of immortality. May you and Charlotte, after you have accomplished God's will on earth, be enabled to sing your dying hymns!

"I may probably send your work-boxes, together with your Virgils, by the coach to Borobridge, before I return myself.

"Remember me kindly to Augusta; and believe me to be, my dear Charlotte,
"Your affectionate Father,
C. Buchanan."

In December, Dr. Buchanan returned to Cambridge, where he was diligently employed, not only in the learned work which he had undertaken, but in preparing an Address, the occasion of which will be shortly stated. Of this, as it proved, his last visit to the University, his friend Colonel Sandys, who came from Cornwall to meet him, gives the following brief but edifying account.

"I found my friend the most interesting

"Christian, while residing in the tower of Eras"mus, at Queen's college, the winter before last; where I passed my evenings with him while "busily employed on the Syriac version.

"Here the learned divine was, as it were, ab"sorbed in the humble follower of the Lord Jesus "Christ: and here he disclosed to me those views "of his faith, which I found beneficial to my own "soul. His whole dependence was upon Christ, "for wisdom, righteousness, sanctification, and re"demption!"'

The Dean of Carlisle speaking of the same period thus observes.

"I saw a good deal of him during the last "months of his residence at Queen's college; at "which time his constitution appeared to have "suffered exceedingly; yet not so much as to in"duce one to predict a speedy dissolution.

"He was to the very last most indefatigable in "his enquiries after eastern knowledge.

"You know how very entertaining and instruc"tive he has made the printed reports of his tra"vels and interviews with extraordinary persons: "I had the good fortune to hear many of the same "things from his own mouth."

From Cambridge Dr. Buchanan wrote to his eldest daughter as follows. Queen's College, 31st Dec. 1813. "My dear Charlotte, ' I am extremely concerned to hear of this accident to Mrs. Thompson, and accompanied with pain too. Tell her I truly sympathize with her. But, when we consider it in another point of view, we must not call it an *accident,* which you know means literally that which falls out by chance; for nothing comes from God by chance. We must view it as an evil permitted for some great good. I am pleased to see your assiduity during her confinement. I am also pleased, my dear Charlotte, that you have presented yourself at the table of the Lord. Your emotion on that occasion was very natural. I trust you will henceforward reap the spiritual fruits, and proceed in the way of the Lord rejoicing.

"I beg you will present to your grandpapa and grandmamma, Augusta, and all the family, my affectionate congratulations on the new year.

"I pray that it may be a year of temporal and spiritual blessing to you all. "I do not go forth to visits yet, as the Charge I am composing is not finished. I must send it to London on Tuesday next.

"I fully enter into your feelings on your first alarm, lest Mrs. T. should have been taken from VOL. II. z you. But you see she is yet spared to you; for although you are not her natural daughter, I hope you maintain and pray for a higher relation. There is.nothing durable and eternal but that union which is from Christ. Friendship, or relationship by blood, except growing on this foundation, will soon die.

"I remain,
My dear Charlotte,
Your affectionate Father,
C. Buchanan."

The employment which divided the time and attention of Dr. Buchanan with Syriac, during his residence at Cambridge, was the composition of a Charge, to be delivered, at the request of the Church Mission Society, to the Rev. Messrs. Greenwood and Norton, clergymen of the Established Church, proceeding as missionaries to the Island of Ceylon; and to the Rev. Messrs. Schnarre and Rhenius, ministers of the German Lutheran Church, proceeding in the same sacred character to the coast of Coromandel.

The readiness with which the Court of Directors of the East India Company granted the requisite license to these pious men to proceed to the objects of their destination, was a proof of the benefits resulting from the late solemn legislative recognition of the duty of Great Britain with respect to the diffusion of Christianity in its eastern empire; and the selection of Dr. Buchanan to address these oriental missionaries was equally judicious and appropriate.

The rapidity with which this admirable Charge was composed, and the various and important advice which it contained, proved the vigour of its author's understanding and judgment; while the pure and fervent piety which breathes in every page manifests the maturity of the advanced Christian.

The Charge itself comprises an exposition of that with which our Lord sent forth his Apostles to preach the Gospel. It forms, in fact, a manual of sound wisdom and instruction; and deserves to be frequently perused and thoroughly digested by every one who aspires to the character and office of a missionary. Like the former productions of Dr. Buchanan, this address contains much valuable and interesting information; and, though primarily intended for the missionary, may be read with much advantage by every minister of the Gospel, and by every private Christian. The following extracts will afford a brief specimen of the spirit and tendency of the whole.

Speaking of the periodical accounts which the missionaries would be expected to give of their labours, Dr. Buchanan introduced this important caution.

"Let every page which you write be consecrated "by sacred truth. Beware of that powerful self"deception, whose operation is sometimes commen"surate with a man's zeal for his object, which leads "him to deceive for God's sake, and to do partial "evil, under the hope and plea that great good may "come. If you would keep at a remote distance "from such a temptation, avoid amplification and "embellishment in what makes for the credit and ' honour of your personal labours, or of those of "your fellow-missionaries. Like great generals, "who recount their victories in few words, let a "modesty of description characterize your spiritual "trophies."

After pointing out in a faithful and striking manner the various ways in which a minister, whether at home or abroad, may deny Christ, Dr. Buchanan thus continued.

"My brethren, you may preach to the Hindoos, "and say, 'Repent, and be converted;' while, at the "same time, indolence, or avarice, or sensual pas"sion, seizes your own souls, and you are quite in"different about their repentance or conversion, ex "cept as it adds to your own interest, or the fame "of your mission.

"Some who have preceded you, and have been solemnly designated to the sacred work, have fallen away. They declined from sound doctrine, or they "were seduced from pureness of living; and, in"stead of doing the work of an Evangelist, they "have lived an useless burthen on the society which "supported them.

"I mention these things to warn you. But I "have more pleasure in directing your view to "other servants of Christ, whose bright example "has illumined the East,—who have been pat"terns of faith, diligence, prudence, and fortitude. "From the ministers of the two Churches to which "you respectively belong, I shall select two illus"trious characters, who have left a great example "for them that follow. I mean the venerable "Swartz, of the Lutheran Church, and the late Rev. "David Brown, of the Church of England. These men did not deny Christ. They did not love "father or mother more than Christ. They took "up their cross, and followed Christ. If you knew, "as well as I do, the conflicts which they were "called upon to sustain in the East, you would see "how fitly the words of our Lord might be ap"plied to them: 'Behold, I send you forth as lambs "among wolves. But, beware of men.' If you knew, again, the conjoined wisdom and innocence "which they manifested in these conflicts, you would ' acknowledge that they studied to obey our Lord's "admonition; - Be ye wise as serpents, and harm'' less as doves.' The character of both was marked '' by an extraordinary liberality of sentiment in "regard to the differences in religious profession; "a liberality which others, in a confined sphere, "could not well understand. In a word, they en"dured unto the end; and both of them were en"abled to glorify God in their deaths, by the mani"festation of a joyful hope in the view of their dis"solution.

". I have thought that this short record of these "good men would find a proper place in an ad"dress to young ministers who are in your cir"cumstances. 'Be ye also followers of them, who, "through faith and patience, have inherited the pro"mises.'

The Appendix to this excellent Charge contains some notices of the last hours of his late valued friend and colleague, Mr. Brown, which serve to illustrate the heavenly and devoted mind of that excellent man.

The health of Dr. Buchanan rendering it impracticable for him to deliver his Charge to the missionaries personally, that office was assigned to an eloquent friend, who did ample justice to the composition. On the 7th of January, it was accordingly addressed to them before a general meeting of the Church Mission Society, and was heard with a degree of attention and interest which appeared to promise the happiest effects from its author's exertions.

It is to the circumstances which have been just related, that some parts of the following extracts from letters to Colonel and Mr. Macaulay refer.

"Queen's College, 3d January, 1814.

"I have sent by to-night's mail to Mr. Pratt "thirty-three pages of a Charge to be delivered "to the missionaries on Friday next. As I am "quite unfit to go up myself, I have requested Mr. "Deartry to read the paper for me. He may se"lect such parts as he thinks best for the occa"sion.

"Dr. Milner approves of the passage upon ' de"nying Christ;' but I do not know what others "may think of it."

"Queen's College, 7th January.

"The Bishop of Chester has expressed his wish "that I would retain the curacy of Great Ouse"burn, which I was about to resign, under the im"pression that I could not conscientiously accept a "license (under the new act) as a resident curate, "when it was notorious that I am not resident. "But the Bishop is persuaded that the duties of the "parish will be performed to his entire satisfaction "by myself or by my direction. His diocese ex"tends to our parish.

"I inhabit Erasmus's rooms. They are chiefly "remarkable for an immense *corkscrew,* about a-,' third of a yard long, which tradition assigns to "that eminent scholar."

"Queen's College, 13th January.

"My dear Sir, "Many thanks for your letter. It is most satisfactory. I have constructed the note as you desired, without names or places. It is now round and smooth like a perfect chrysolite, and will excite many a smile and many a frown.

"I was smiling to think what a fine long letter I drew from you. I see you can work, if we will only tell you what to do,

"I entirely approve of your flitting to southern regions this severe weather. I cannot look out at the window on the dreary waste of snow, but I think I see Bonaparte and his squadrons, half covered, retreating towards Gogmagog hills. The thermometer is at 12.

"Wishing you good fires, and every blessing,

"I remain,

My dear Sir,

Very sincerely yours,

C. Buchanan." "Queen's College, 13th January. "It was indeed somewhat new to hear strains "of commendation from the lips of Mr. T. in pub"lic. The whole assembly seem to have been in "good humour. The view of the four missionaries "perhaps melted their hearts; and the news of "the allies crossing the Rhine had just arrived. "Mr. Farish says he enjoyed the occasion exceed"ingly.

"I consulted the college to-day concerning the "proposed admission of Mr. Lee, the Shrews"bury linguist. It was agreed to admit him at "Queen's."

"Queen's College, 7th February. "I see in the last Christian Observer, that "Schaaf's Lexicon is mentioned as preparing for "the press by subscription. Will you be so good "as to inform me who is publishing it? for I was "about commencing the work at my own expense, "and the printer had just sent me an estimate. "But I shall be most happy if the work has been "undertaken by another. Mr. Kelly, of Dublin, "wrote to me last week to say, that he was pro"jecting something in the way of a Syriac Lexi"con; but he wished me not to delay my work on "account of his, as he knew not when it would be "finished.

"I propose to leave Cambridge for Kirby Hall on "the 17th instant."

Dr. Buchanan returned into Yorkshire about the time just mentioned, and continued there till the month of July following. While there, he wrote thus to a friend—" I am stronger than I was; but "my defect in utterance and breath remains, and "also my want of memory; which shews that my "illness affected the mind a good deal."

The Committee of the British and Foreign Bible Society had now determined to print the edition of the Syriac New Testament, which Dr. Buchanan had been so anxiously endeavouring to obtain for the use of the Syrian Christians on the coast of Malabar. With his usual zeal and liberality, he engaged to prepare the text, and superintend the execution of the work, at his own expense. For this purpose he again left Yorkshire, and took up his residence, first at Cheshunt, and afterwards at Wormley, and Broxbourne, in Hertfordshire, at which latter place the printer lived who had undertaken the work. Soon after his arrival, he wrote to Mrs. Thompson as follows.

"Turnford Hall, Cheshunt, Herts, 23d July, 1814..

"My dear Mrs. T.

"I arrived here last Saturday, on which day I wrote you a few lines. Since that time I have been daily employed in superintending the press, and corresponding with the Bible Society, with the Syndics of the University Press, Cambridge, and with friends respecting tutors for the two noble families which I lately visited.

"I live with a widow lady and her daughters. They never had boarders before; but hearing that I wanted accommodation of this kind in the village, they received me. We have morning and evening prayers just as at Skelton Lodge. I have my meals by myself, being willing to husband my voice, in the hope that it will acquire some strength. I walk in the meadows by the side of the river Lee, and endeavour to meditate on things spiritual and eternal. There are few days in which I do not think of Mary, now among the blessed. I envy her happy lot, but yet I have just strength to pray that I may be enabled to serve God in my generation.

"Mr. Yeates is come from London to cooperate-with me. It is not decided yet whether one half of my work is to go on at Cambridge or not. They, however, expect me at Queen's college, and I think it probable I shall go there in about a month, if indeed I do not go nearer to London; for Mr. Watts, my printer, has just informed me, that he is about to remove his printing establishment to the metropolis.

"I hope to hear that your foot is almost well. Jacob, you know, ' halted' to the day of his death; but then every false step would remind him of his victory with God. And yet this 'prince with God' would not be comforted when he thought Joseph was dead! How encompassed with infirmity is man, even regenerated man; man, partaker of the divine nature!

"I hope that Charlotte and Augusta are happy and well. Jacob prayed, saying, God, which fed me all my life long unto this day, the angel which redeemed me from all evil, bless the lads.' That is a prayer whieh I would offer up for Charlotte and Augusta. *I* also have been ' redeemed from much evil' during an eventful life; and so have they hitherto. A boy about Augusta's age is dying near us here. He broke his leg by some imprudent exertion, and the fever induced is likely to prove fatal. His mother sits by him, and cannot eat. He belonged to a Sunday school, and desires those hymns to be read to him which speak of Christ's atoning for wicked children. My love to you all. Adieu. "C. B,"

The pensive tenor of a part of the preceding letter will appear peculiarly interesting, when it is considered that Dr. Buchanan was now fast approaching the confines of that world, whither so many of those who were dear to him had gone before. Amongst others, the son of his friend, Colonel Sandys, for whose welfare he had been affectionaCely concerned, was about this time departing in the faith and hope of the Gospel. He thus replied to the intelligence which had announced to him the delightful change in his views and feelings since the time when he had visited him in Yorkshire.

"What wonderful news you relate! Your dear "son William speaks of' the unsearchable riches "of Christ,' and magnifies his Saviour in the eyes "of men! This is certainly a great triumph of di"vine grace. However, I anticipated it, as I be"lieve you know; for I was persuaded he would "be given to your persevering prayers.

"Be pleased to give him my most affectionate '' remembrance; and tell him he is about to be ushered into a glory, which good men upon earth "have been contemplating for many years, but have "not yet enjoyed. He has obtained the victory "without the battle; for the Captain of his salvation "has fought for him. May his faith be firm and "ardent to the last, that he may persevere in and "complete his glorious testimony!"

The two following letters were addressed to the Rev. D. Wilson. The first was in reply to one requesting the advice of Dr. Buchanan as to the best mode of composing an elementary treatise on the Christian Prophecies, for the purpose of circulation among the Hindoos, on the plan suggested by Sir William Jones. The second may serve to shew the zeal and industry with which Dr. Buchanan was pursuing the intended edition of the Syriac New Testament.

"Wormley, Herts, 5th August, 1814. '; My dear Sir,

"I rejoice that you have taken up the prophecies for the Hindoos. Follow your own judgment and ruminate on your sofa, and you will possibly devise something new. The Hindoos want a short clear account, a striking picture, solemn assertion, and dogmatic theology.

"'The holy prophet Isaiah, who wrote in poetic strains, lived in such an era. Though ignorant and unlearned persons of India know it not, yet the learned of Europe, who are acquainted with the histories of the world, are as well assured that Isaiah wrote his prophecy in the times of King Ahaz, &c. as that such a man lived in the time of Gengis Khan, Tamerlane, or Akbar the Great.

"So of Matthew and his host of witnesses.' See the conclusion of his learned Dissertation on the Gods of Greece, Italy, and India, Asiatic Researches, vol. i.

"Short sentences, and no involved construction, will do best for oriental translation and capacity. Let your picture suit a Thames' street carman, and it will do for a Hindoo. A tract of ten octavo pages is a good size. But as you cannot easily confine within such small bounds all the fine things that may occur to you on the subject, proceed *ad libitum* to a pamphlet or book, which may be translated for the Brahmins and more learned. But the short tract is the book for use to the multitude. This you may express from the larger work when it is finished, as genuine spirit is drawn from the vat.

'' # # That the evidence of prophecy will convince the human mind is true: but that the leaves of the prophet quietly dispersed,' without concomitant illustration of historic argument and fact by preachers or writing, is not true.

"I hope you will not be in a hurry to deliver any thing to the Society. Short tracts on other parts of the Old and New Testaments are wanted, so as to embrace the whole code in different striking and simple forms. Nobody has told the Hindoos yet what our Shaster is. They have not got the *whole* book to read. If they had, epitomes are yet necessary for infant and ignorant minds, epitomes of one page, two, three, four, ten, twenty, and fifty pages. The whole Bible will occupy 1400 pages of their ordinary character of writing. t is but charity then to tell them what is in it, and invite their study.

"I am, dear Sir,
Very sincerely yours,
C. Buchanan."

"Wormley, Cheshunt, Aug. 17, 1814. "My dear Sir, "I have come to this place for a while, to superintend the printing of the Syriac works now in the press. I want the following books, which I cannot find in the public Library at Cambridge; viz.

"1. Reusch's Syrus Interpres cum fonte N. T. Grseci collatus. 1742.

"2. Michaelis's Curae in Actus Apostolorum Syriacos.

"3. Storrius, on the Syriac Language and Versions.

"4. Michaelis (the father) De Var. Lect. Nov. Test, caute colligendis.

"5. Gloster Ridley's Dissertatio de Syriacis Versionibus.

"6. Amira's Syriac Grammar; and "7. Professor Bode's Pseudocritica Millio-Bengeliana. 1767.

"Now if your own Library, or if the Oxford Libraries through your means, could supply me with these or some of them, you will confer on me a particular obligation. I have perused some of them at the British Museum,'but I cannot have them here.

"I rejoice to hear from time to time of your labours, and of the triumphs of the Gospel at the Church of St. John's. It is a theatre of grander events than the General Congress.

"My own health is slowly improving, but I am yet wholly incapable of vocal exertion. "I remain,
My dear Sir,
Very sincerely yours,
C. BUCHAKAN."

The succeeding extracts from letters to different friends describe the general state of Dr. Buchanan's health, feelings, and employment during the remainder of this year.

"*To Mrs. Thompson.* "Wormley, Herts, Aug. 1814. "I have been twice bled, I think, since I wrote, "and must, I fear, suffer further depletion. With "returning strength my constitution brought with "it what was to be apprehended, a tendency to "fulness. And possibly I must soon revert to ab"stemiousness and the painful seton. But the "Lord's disposal is the best for this world and for "the next. I seek to do his will."

"*To his Daughters.*
"August 22.

"I am not very sure that I shall be able to ex"ecute what I have undertaken by the time pro posed. There are three printing presses at work, "and I am obliged to read and correct every word "in Syriac, Latin, and English."

"*To Colonel Macaulay.*
"Wormley, 8th September.

"Two Cochin Jews, who recollect you very well, "are in distress for a passage back to India. I "would try. to aid them, if I knew to whom to ap' ply. But I fear the Company are not in the "habit of giving a passage to persons of their de"scription. You will know better than I what to "recommend them to do.

"Since the peace, you have been passing through "many countries, and doing good. I, on the other "hand, have been stationary, travelling slowly "through the regions of the New Testament. I "congratulate you on your equable health. My "own was well confirmed for a while; but it is "again in a critical state."

"*To Mrs. Thompson.*
"Wormley, September 14. "I know not God's will. I think less of seeing "another autumn than at any former time. If, "however, I live, I shall most probably go to Ire

VOL. II. A a

"land, r,v to the continent; I mean Paris and "Rome. I wish I could have visited both these "latter places before I had commenced my present "work."

"*To Miss Buchanan.*
"Broxbourne, 7th December. "My dear Charlotte,

"Many thanks to you for your letter. I am glad that Augusta's queries have afforded Mr. Graham so fair an opportunity of displaying his classical powers. But the true Virgilian model requires the first words to be *Sic vos non vobis.* Would, that poor Virgil could have understood the distich which Mr. G. has written. But, alas! that *divine* Poet, as he has been called, never heard of an atonement for the sins of men. He had, however, some confused idea of the coming of a Messiah, or Prince from heaven, who should regenerate an evil world. This you will see in his Pollio, one of the Bucolics; which I will thank you to read as soon as you have finished the sixth book of the Eneid.

"I am happy to hear that you read a little of the sacred language on Sunday. As there is no Italian teacher at present in York, you must postpone your acquaintance with the ' modern Roman' till an opportunity offers.

"I hope you will not leave thorough bass till you understand it *thoroughly.* "You ask me for Mr. Slater's drawing. I sat to him two mornings, but contrived to have a sheet of Syriac placed in the direction I was to look. He complained that I was thoughtful. I told him of the talent of Sir Joshua Reynolds; who by his fascinating discourse contrived to keep his *patients* (a proper term / think for persons subjected to this operation) in a state of high good humour, particularly with *themselves,* which shewed itself in their beaming and expanded countenance. When Mr. Slater had done, I looked in vain for the beaming and expanded look. Mr. S. accused the Syriac. I told him, I thought the picture was that of an ill-looking man. He said, he thought it was *a good likeness.* I only saw it for two minutes, after sitting to it two days. I told him he might send it down to Mrs. Thompson, and he should be at liberty to engrave it, if it obtained *her* approbation. I desired him to send with it, as a present to you and Augusta, a print of Mrs. Hannah More; that you may have before your eyes a lady who made so good an use of her opportunities for study between the fourteenth and seventeenth year of her age, that the world has been benefited by it ever since.

"Yesterday Mr B. and Mr. S. spent the whole day with me..Their object was to procure my name as secretary of the Jewish Society. But I had radical objections to the constitution of that society in its present form, and suggested renovation and improvement.

"I should like to be present at the famous duet for *three* voices. I hope I shall he with you shortly after Christmas. I must superintend the printers till the day they break up for their own holidays, which I suppose will be Christmas-day. Besides, I wish to see the four Gospels finished if possible before my long journey.

"I have not seen the Velvet Cushion. The ladies tell me it is a very amusing and instructive work.

"My love to Mrs. T. and Augusta, and "I remain,
My dear Charlotte,
Your affectionate Father,
C. Buchanan."

"Broxbourne, Herts, Dec. 17, 1814.
"My dear Sandys,

"I thank you for your letter of the 12th, which informs me that you and seven children are well. There are a great many blessings comprehended in that expression.

"I am glad that you have been enabled to write a narrative of the rise and progress of religion in the soul of William. Under whatever form it eventually appear, I doubt not but it will do good. Particularly among his young relatives in Cornwall, such a record must appear as a solemn witness.

"My health continues much the same. I take a little exercise on horseback, live low, go to bed early, and rise generally to read by candle light. By such means, under the blessing of God, I am enabled to carry on my present undertaking. But a slight return of indisposition would suspend the whole. I therefore would live a pensioner on God's mercy for the hour.

A letter from Mr. Udny informs me that Miss F. died lately, and had peace in death, ' her heart having been long previously weaned from the world.' He speaks with satisfaction of the effect of a work I published two years ago, entitled ' Colonial Ecclesiastical Establishment.'

"I beg to be affectionately remembered to Mrs. S. and to Allan. The purpose of the latter to cultivate his mind by classical knowledge is very gratifying to me.

"I am very affectionately yours, C. Buchanan." *To Mrs. Thompson.*

"Broxbourne, Dec. 24.

"My dear Mrs. T. "I write to say that I hope to be with you in the course of the first week of the new year. It is, however, doubtful whether I shall not be detained till the 9th or 1 0th of January. I shall at all events write before I set off.

"What detains me is the wish to complete the four Gospels before I leave this place, lest I should never return. 'For what is our life?' sakh St. James, ' It is even a vapour, that appeareth for a little time, and then vanisheth away.'

"I have had another visit from Mr. S. and Mr. L. W. on the subject of the Jewish Society. Iproposed that the institution, in whatsoever degree supported by Church members, should be exclusively a Church of England Society. I declined, however, pledging myself for its support, further than by offering my best advice. I desired them to communicate their plans and wishes to all good and eminent ministers in the kingdom, to request useful hints and affectionate support, and to do nothing of themselves-.—not to call their Society, ' for conversion of the Jews:' but a Society for the education of Jewish children; for diffusing the New Testament among the Jews; for corresponding with them concerning the Messiah in all lands; and for the diffusion of Jewish literature. Lastly, to connect the Institution with the Church Missionary Society, the end being the same.

"I have just received letters from India. Sabat, who had left his Christian society, and it-was feared would never return, has returned to Calcutta, and is again translating the Scriptures. He confessed to Mr. Thomason, that he could find no rest for the soles of his feet.

"Mr. T. sends me the third annual Report of the Calcutta Auxiliary Bible Society, which I shall take down with me, if I remember it. My love to all till I see you.
Your very affectionate Son,
C. Buchanan."

Dr. Buchanan's visit to the north was but of short duration. On the.19th of January 1815, he returned to Broxbourne; from whence he wrote to Mrs. Thompson as follows.

"My dear Mrs. T.

"I could have reaehed this place yesterday, but I reserved seventeen miles for this morning. I slept on Monday night at Carleton Hall. I travelled about a hundred miles next day in post chaises; and though it snowed, I was warm and comfortable all the way. My only mishap was losing my diamond pin somewhere, which I have had for ten years. I now use one of those Augusta gave me. Thus we cease to sparkle.

"I found all at home well. One of the letters on my table was from Mr. John Thornton, nephew to Mr. Henry Thornton, informing me of the illness of his uncle, and requesting letters of introduction for his brother going to India.

"Another letter was from Mr. Macaulay, mentioning the increasing illness of Mr. Thornton, and comparing him, after twenty-two years acquaintance, rather to the character of the saints in the next life, than in this; 'The just man made perfect.'

"I request you will alter any thing in my written or oral instructions to Charlotte and Augusta, according to your discretion. If the verse in the morning appear to be an unfruitful task, it may be discontinued by both.

"My love to them; and believe me to be, "My dear Mrs. T..
Your very affectionate Son,
C. Buchanan."

"Thus I have been enabled to accomplish a journey of four hundred miles with health and strength. Bless the Lord, O my soul, for all his goodness. May I only live to his glory!"

A letter to Mr. Macaulay on the same day on which the preceding was dated, briefly but emphatically notices the fatal termination of Mr. Henry Thornton's illness, and the anxiety of Dr. Buchanan to pay the only tribute of respect which remained to his memory.

"Broxbourne, Thursday, 19th Jan. "My dear Friend, "On my return from Yorkshire this morning, where I have been for a fortnight on a visit to my family, I found your letter of the 11th inst. lying on my table.

"The first intimation I had of Mr. Thornton's illness was on Monday last at Garleton Hall, Worksop. On ray arrival here, I found your letter, and one from Mr. John Thornton confirming the painful intelligence. I was just going to sit down to request that he would communicate to his uncle my feelings on the occasion, and my request to go to town to visit him if he had strength to see me, when casually looking into the paper, I found that he had died on the Tuesday. All I can now do is to attend the funeral of this good man, my earliest and most particular friend and benefactor. I have requested Mr. John Thornton to let me know on what day the funeral takes place. In case of mistake, will you have the goodness to mention to me the time and place, and I shall go out early in the morning, and return in the evening, as my present work will not permit me conveniently to be absent a night.

"I desire to thank you most unfeignedly for your kindness to the two Cochin Jews.

"With kindest regards to Mrs. M.

"I am very affectionately yours,

C. Buchanan."

On the 22d Dr. Buchanan wrote again to Mr. Macaulay as follows. "My dear Friend,

"I have just received your note, and I propose to go on Tuesday morning, so as to be at your house by twelve o'clock, if I should not have joined the procession before that time. I shall be happy to dine with you, and to take a bed at your house, and return next morning after breakfast.

"Yours ever affectionately,

C. Buchanan."

It was upon the solemn and affecting occasion thus referred to, that the Author of these Memoirs met Dr. Buchanan for the last time. A crowd of other friends, distinguished by their talents, rank, and piety, united in lamenting the loss of the eminent person around whose tomb they were assembled. Amidst that mourning throng, it will readily be believed by those who recollect his obligations to Mr. Thornton, as well as his just appreciation of the various excellencies of his revered friend, that no one shed more sincere tears over his grave than Dr. Buchanan. Doubtless he then felt, as he seemed to feel, in common with a multitude of other persons, that another of those ties by which he had been linked to this world was destroyed. The writer of these pages remembers, with sensations of melancholy yet pleasing regret, the peculiarly holy and heavenly strain of conversation with which Dr. Buchanan cheered and edified his friends on the evening of that mournful day, and on the morning of his return into Hertfordshire; little thinking that it would be the last opportunity of their enjoying that privilege.

Of this short and affecting visit to Clapham, the following interesting anecdote has been communicated by the friend at whose house Dr. Buchanan took up his abode.

"He was relating to me," observes this gentleman, " as we walked together from the churchyard "where we had deposited the mortal remains of "Henry Thornton, the course he was pursuing with "respect to the printing of the Syriac Testament. "He stated, that his solicitude to render it correct "had led him to adopt a plan of revision, which "required him to read each sheet five times over be"fore it went finally to the printer. The particulars "of the plan I do not very distinctly remember. It "was, however, something of this kind. He first pre"pared the sheets for the press. When the proof "was sent, he read it over attentively, instituting a "comparison with the original, and looking into the "various readings, &c. A revise was sent him, "which he carefully examined, making corrections. "This was submitted to Mr. Yeates. When it "came from him, he read it again, adopting such of "his suggestions as he thought right. When the "printer had made the requisite corrections, he sent "a fresh revise, after being read, to Mr. Lee, and re."perused it when it came from him. A third revise "was then procured, which he again examined be"fore it was finally committed to the press. I do "not know that I am precisely accurate in this "statement, but it was something of the above de"scription.

"While giving me this detail, he stopped sud"denly, and burst into tears. I was somewhat "alarmed. When he had recovered himself, he "said, ' Do not be alarmed. I am not ill; but I "was completely overcome with the recollection of "the delight which I had enjoyed in this exercise. "At first I was disposed to shrink from the task as "irksome, and apprehended that I should find even "the Scriptures pall by the frequency of this critical "examination. But so far from it, every fresh "perusal seemed to throw fresh light on the word of "God, and to convey additional joy and consolation "to my mind.'"

How delightful is the contemplation of a servant of Christ thus devoutly engaged in his heavenly Master's work, almost to the very moment of his transition to the divine source of light and truth itself!

The pious and elevated frame of Dr. Buchanan's mind is evident from another incident which occurred at this time.

In passing through London on his return to Broxbourne, he spent a few hours with a friend whom he had met upon the solemn occasion of the preceding day. In the course of their conversation, his friend observed how affecting was the consideration of the removal of so many great and good men, whom they had lately had occasion to lament, in the prime of life, and in the midst of their usefulness. To this observation, Dr. Buchanan replied— So long as they "were still on earth, and the Divine will was not "known, it was our duty fervently to pray for their "recovery and lengthened life; but when once that "will has been discovered by the event, we should "rejoice, and praise God, that he has received them "to himself, and hasten to follow them to his "heavenly kingdom." It was not long before he himself afforded another illustration of this remark; which, though not unfrequently made, was peculiarly characteristic of that spirit of calm and habitual submission to the will of God, and of lively faith in the realities of an eternal world, by which he was distinguished.

The extreme severity of the weather had excited some apprehensions in the minds of many as to the probable effect of Dr. Buchanan's exposure to it during some hours of the preceding day. He did not, however, appear at the time to have suffered by it, and reached Broxbourne on the 25th of January in safety.

On the first of February he wrote to Mrs. Thompson, informing her of the solemn scene at which he had lately been present, describing the numerous and respectful attendance at the funeral of Mr. Thornton, and expressing his earnest desire to be a partaker with him of the same blessed inheritance.

This was the last communication of Dr. Buchanan to his distant friends. The time of his departure was now fast approaching. He continued, however, his Christian undertaking to the last. On his return from Yorkshire, he had proceeded with the preparation of the Syriac version of the Acts of the Apostles, and had advanced, on the day preceding his death, to the twentieth chapter; in which the zealous and affectionate Apostle, in his address to the elders of Ephesus, expresses his conviction of his final separation from his friends in these remarkable words. "And now, behold, "I know that ye all, among whom I have gone "preaching the kingdom of God, shall see my face "no more." The chapter which thus closed the labours of Dr. Buchanan, and in which he seemed to bid farewell to eveiy earthly association, was but too prophetic of the event which was about so shortly to take place. Of his few remaining days, and of his sudden removal to that higher world, for which he had long been ripening, the following letter to the Rev. Mr. Kempthorne, from his confidential servant, who was his only attendant in Hertfordshire, though unavoidably inadequate to the anxious wishes of his friends, affords a minute and faithful account.

"Broxbourne, 12th Feb. 1815.
"Rev. Sir,

"In case of your not having been made acquainted, through the public papers, of the decease of my dear master, Dr. Buchanan, I feel it my duty to write to you on the subject.

"The Doctor's state of health, as you may have understood, had improved, during his residence here, up to the time of his late visit to Yorkshire: but the fatigue of that journey, probably, added to an attendance, in a week after his return, in bad weather, at the funeral of Mr. Henry Thornton, brought on an apparently slight indisposition, which the Doctor himself, I believe, considered merely a cold. On Thursday last, however, while making a morning's call on some of the neighbours, he was taken with something of a fainting fit, which passed off, without his considering it of consequence enough to require medical assistance. As the sickness came on again towards evening, I took the liberty to disobey my master's orders, and to send for the medical gentleman, whose skill had so much appeared in the improvement of the Doctor's health in the preceding months. This gentleman was with him about nine o'clock in the evening, and did not express any apprehension of danger. Dr. Buchanan retired a little past ten, saying he was better; and as he expected to get a little sleep, wished me not to disturb him, to take the second medicine, till he rung the bellAbout half past eleven, sitting on the watch for the summons, I fancied I heard something of an hiccough; which induced me, contrary to orders, to enter the chamber, and to enquire if he was worse. He signified he *was* worse. On which I instantly alarmed the family, and sent for assistance; and then returned to the bedside, where my master appeared labouring under a spasm in the breast. He intimated a wish for me to hold his head; and in this posture, without struggle or convulsion, his breath appeared to leave him; so that before twelve, by which time Mr. Watts the printer, Mr. Yeates, and a few other neighbours, were with me, we were obliged to conclude, that our excellent friend's spirit had joined the glorified saints above. I should have mentioned, that on returning home in the morning after the fit, Dr. Buchanan seemed lame on the left side; but, as it went off, he did not think it of any consequence. I have reason to think it might be a third attack of paralysis. The medical man, on his corning after my master's dissolution, said it did not surprise him. A letter was immediately forwarded, by express, to communicate the melancholy intelligence to my master's family in Yorkshire; from whence some one is hourly expected. Mr. Macaulay was also written to; and Mr. Simeon, at Cambridge. On Saturday Mr. Babington, the member for Leicester, came down, and approved of the precaution and arrangements taken immediately after the departure of my master; both as to putting seals on the drawers, study, &c. &c.
"With the greatest respect,
I beg to subscribe myself,
Rev. Sir,
Your most obedient, faithful servant,
T. Vaux."

Such was the sudden summons by which, on the 9th of February 1815, in the 49th year of his age, this eminent servant of God was called to his heavenly rest. To himself it could scarcely be said to have been unexpected. The debilitated constitution which he brought with him from India, and the repeated shocks it had subsequently sustained, led him habitually to regard his continuance in life as extremely uncertain and precarious; while his various afflictions, personal and domestic, had tended to withdraw his thoughts and affections from the world, and to fix them on spiritual and eternal objects. We have seen, that in fulfilling the important engagement which terminated his earthly course, he evidently appeared to be working while it was called "to-day," and to be constantly anticipating the near approach of " the night," in which he could no longer work. Of his habitual preparation for the hour of his departure, no one can entertain a doubt, who has marked the scriptural foundation of his faith, and the unquestionable evidences of its sincerity, in the long and uniform tenor of his truly Christian career. It might, perhaps, have been desirable, both for himself and for others, that some interval, however short, had been vouchsafed; in which this " good and faithful ser"vant" of his Lord might have had an opportunity of renewing his repentance, of testifying his faith, of perfecting his patience, of purifying and exalting his charity, of bidding a more solemn and VOL. II. B b express farewell to " things seen and temporal," of preparing more deliberately and devoutly for an immediate entrance upon " things unseen and eter"nal." Such an interval, however, so precious to the generality of mankind, and usually so important, the Divine Wisdom did not see fit to grant to the subject of these Memoirs. Neither, indeed, can it be said to have been necessary. The readers of the preceding narrative have already observed Dr. Buchanan in India, upon what he strongly, though erroneously, believed would prove his death-bed; and they have witnessed the deeply penitent, yet resigned and peaceful frame of mind, which he then exhibited. Such, as we are evidently authorized to conclude, only of a more mature and heavenly nature, would have been his testimony and his feelings, had he been allowed again to express them. In the absence of any such opportunity, we must be contented to recur to that scene; and, together with the recollection of his subsequent "work of faith, and labour of love, and patience "of hope," endeavour to enter into the full meaning of the following brief sentence, which occurs amidst a few other "private thoughts," and in which its author appears plainly to have anticipated the probability of some final stroke, which should impede the exercise of his faculties, and See the exquisite defence, by the pious and learned Hooker, of the petition in the Litany against " sudden death." Ecclesiastical Polity, vol. ii. p. 175.

prove the prelude to his departure. "If," said he, "my mind and memory should be affected by ill "ness of body, I shall look to my head, Christ. "I am but a member." From any painful infliction of this kind, Dr. Buchanan was mercifully spared; and, after having paid the last sad tribute of affection to the friend and benefactor of his early years, was removed almost contemporaneously, and reunited to him, and to other kindred spirits of the "just made perfect," in regions where sickness and sorrow, change and separation, are for ever unknown.

In consequence of a wish he had expressed to Mrs. Thompson, not long before his death, the remains of Dr. Buchanan were removed from Broxbourne to Little Ouseburn, in Yorkshire, and deposited near those of his second lamented wife. A monumental inscription, written by the Rev. W. Richardson, of York, records in plain but expressive language the leading particulars of his life and character

It may, perhaps, be expected, that a more definite and comprehensive review should be given of both, at the close of these Memoirs. The length, however, to which they have been already extended, and the distinctness with which the events of Dr. Buchanan's life, and the features of his character, have been marked, will only require such a general See the end of the volume.

recapitulation as may assist the reader in forming a correct judgment of the whole.

In reviewing the history of Dr. Buchanan, our attention must be first directed to his religious character. It was this which originally introduced him to our notice, and by this he was principally distinguished throughout his benevolent and useful career. The deep and solemn impression of religion, which, through the grace of God, was made upon his mind in his twenty-fourth year, formed the commencement of a life devoted to the service of Christ. We have traced the effects of this great spiritual change in the course of his studies at the University of Cambridge, during his various labours in India, and his continued exertion's after his return to this country. Amidst these diversified scenes and engagements, an energetic conviction of the infinite importance and value of the Gospel, and a lively sense of his own obligations to that grace which had made him effectually acquainted with its blessings, were the commanding principles which actuated his conduct.

Those who know little of real Christianity may, perhaps, attribute his earnestness and activity in religion, as they would that of the great Apostle himself, to enthusiasm, zeal for proselytism, or the love of fame. But the whole tenor of this narrative sufficiently proves, that no corrupt, weak, or worldly motives swayed his mind. The great object, to which he devoted his life, engaged him in an unceasing contest with the principles and the prejudices of those whom a regard to his worldly interest would have led him carefully to conciliate; and though his benevolent exertions undoubtedly procured him many valuable friends, few men of such sober and practical views, and of such genuine philanthropy, have gone through a greater variety of " evil" as well as of " good report." With still less justice can the activity of Dr. Buchanan in the great labour of his life be ascribed to a controversial or innovating spirit. He was, on the contrary, disposed, both by constitution and principle, to avoid rather than to court opposition; while, during several years, the languor of declining health was continually urging him to self-indulgence and repose.

Amidst such powerful inducements to a very different line of conduct, it is scarcely possible not to perceive that Dr. Buchanan could only have been actuated by pure and disinterested motives. The love of Christ and of the souls of men, and a fervent desire to be the instrument of imparting to others that unspeakable blessing which he had himself received, were in reality the springs both of his public and private exertions. These were the principles by which he was animated, and which supported hiin with equanimity and patience amidst labour and reproach, infirmity and sorrow, and even rendered him joyful in tribulation.

Combined with these motives, Dr. Buchanan possessed a spirit of lively and vigorous faith, which substantiated "things not seen," and led him to think and act under a strong impression of their truth and reality. He was therefore eminently a practical man. Though inclined by natural taste, and the habits of a learned and scientific education, to indulge in speculative pursuits and pleasures, the strength of his faith, and the ardour of his love towards objects of spiritual and eternal concern, rescued him from their fascination, and taught him to account all knowledge, and all occupation, vain and unimportant, compared with that which tended to render himself and others "wise unto salvation." Hence, from the period at which the religious necessities of his own countrymen in India, and the moral state of its benighted native inhabitants, first impressed his mind, the life of Dr. Buchanan exhibits a continued series of strenuous, self-denying, and disinterested efforts to supply the deficiencies, and to ameliorate the condition, which he lamented.

For the accomplishment of this great purpose, he was admirably qualified both by natural and acquired advantages. Sagacious and observant, calm and persevering, resolute, yet mild and courteous, he took a penetrating and extensive survey of the various objects around him; and, omitting points of inferior consideration and importance, fixed his attention on the grand and prominent features by which they were distinguished. The temper also and habits of Dr. Buchanan were peculiarly calculated to soften the asperities, and to remove the prejudices, of opponents, to treat with men of every rank upon their own grounds, and to engage them in promoting the great objects which he himself had in view; while the comprehensiveness of his mind, and the munificence of his disposition, enabled him both to conceive and execute designs of no ordinary difficulty and magnitude.

We have accordingly seen in the course of these Memoirs, that, by the publication of authentic documents and convincing statements, by the proposal of magnificent prizes, by the active exercise of his influence with those who respected and esteemed him, and by personal exertions, which included a journey of several thousand miles, amidst many difficulties and dangers, he endeavoured to extend and perpetuate among the European population of India the national faith and worship; and, unmoved by the obloquy of opponents, and by the want of cordial assistance on the part of some who might have been expected to support and cheer him, laboured unceasingly to diffuse among millions, immersed in the thickest darkness, "the light that leads to "heaven."

Nor did he labour in vain. Whoever has attended to the state of public opinion, and to the course of public events, in this country and in India during the last twenty years, must perceive the revolution of sentiment and feeling, which has taken place in that period, upon these important questions. The general acknowledgment, and the recognition in Parliament, of the solemn duty of attending to the religious interests of British India; the establishment of our Episcopal Church, and the facilities afforded to the efforts of Christian piety and zeal to promote the knowledge of the Gospel in that extensive empire; and the progress which has been actually made in this great work, demonstrate the truth of this assertion. It is equally certain, that to the able and persevering exertions of Dr. Buchanan must this happy change of opinion and these salutary measures be principally attributed. Of his claim to the merit of having successfully pleaded the cause of an Ecclesiastical Establishment for British India, and thus of having prepared the way for the most effectual civilization and moral improvement of the natives, there can be no doubt; and of his zealous participation in the great plan of oriental translation, his original proposal of the Malayalim version, and of a new edition of the Syriac Testament, and his generous and self-denying exertions to promote both those important works, are proofs which neither can nor will be forgotten. Millions yet unborn will, doubtless, on account of these and many other great and truly Christian services of this eminent man, have reason to rejoice, and will hereafter " rise up and call him blessed."

The qualifications of Dr. Buchanan as a writer were peculiarly suited to the task which he had undertaken. Bold, perspicuous, and decisive, he is distinguished in all his works by the accumulation and display of new and striking facts, connected, for the most part, by brief, pointed, and sententious observations. Even in his writings which are more strictly theological, he adopted a similar plan; seldom pursuing a long train of reasoning, but laying down certain undoubted facts, truths, or principles, and arguing from them directly and practically to the conclusions which he had in view. The style, however, of Dr. Buchanan, though in general simple and unambitious, was, as we have more than once had occasion to notice, frequently dignified and eloquent. But upon this point we may refer with advantage to two most competent and respectable authorities. The first is that of Dean Milner; who, in speaking of Dr. Buchanan, observes as follows.

"I perfectly well remember that the circumstance "which very soon marked his character, even in the "early part of his residence, as an undergraduate, "was plain, sober, good sense, with a perspicuity "and brevity of expression in all his English com"positions on religious and moral subjects. He had no pretensions to elegance; but he was alto"gether free from that vicious, flowery style, into "which young students are apt to fall. Buchanan "had always too much matter to allow him to be "very wordy."

The other testimony to which a reference has been made is from the review of one of his works in the Christian Observer.

"Dr. Buchanan is characterized, as a writer, by "ease, and by a colouring of the picturesque, with "which he contrives to invest his subject. Some great writers have laboured to clothe fiction in the "garb of truth; Dr. Buchanan's peculiarity is, that "he gives to truth many of the charms and orna"ments usually appropriated to fiction. In con"sequence of this, he has, we think, eminently the "power of touching some of the best feelings of the "mind, and of winning over those whom dry rea"soning might not convince."

The subjects to which Dr. Buchanan devoted his attention did not require or even admit the display of learning, strictly so called. It has, however, sufficiently appeared, that without affecting the character of a consummate scholar, from which he was precluded by the duties of an active and laborious profession, his attainments in European literature and science were of no ordinary nature, and such as qualified him to sustain with credit the important offices to which he was appointed in India. His acquaintance with oriental learning, if not critical or profound, was extensive and considerable. After making some progress in the Persian language, he relinquished it, from a conviction of its compa rative inutility to himself, soon after his arrival in India; but with the Hindostanee he was familiar; and of the Hebrew, Syriac, and Arabic, he possessed a very competent knowledge. His grand object, however, being popular and practical, his chief excellence consisted in the collection and exhibition of important and various information, and in bringing it, by convincing and luminous deductions, to bear upon some weighty and interesting question. In this talent he stands nearly unrivalled; and to this must be in a great measure ascribed the success of his appeals to the understanding and the heart upon the great subjects discussed in his writings.

The sentiments of Dr. Buchanan as a divine have been for the most part fully developed in these Memoirs. They have appeared to be truly scriptural, and in perfect unison with the doctrines of the Church of England. With respect to one disputed point, which, for the very reason that it is now for the first time noticed, evidently formed no prominent part of his creed, he was what, for the sake of distinction, may be called moderately Calvinistic. The avowal of his belief in the doctrine of personal election does not occur in any of his publications, and was in very few instances introduced into his discourses from the pulpit. It appears, however, somewhat remarkably in the preamble to his last will; which is expressed in the following words.

"I Claudius Buchanan, of Little Ouseburn, make "this my last will and testament. I commit my "soul and body to Jesus Christ, the Saviour of lost "sinners, of which sinners I am one, the chief of "sinners; but I trust I have obtained mercy; and "I look for eternal salvation through the obedience ' of Christ unto death, even the death of the cross. "I account the origin of my salvation to be the love of God the Father, who loved my soul in Christ its head before the foundation of the world. I "renounce all works as a claim of merit. All my "works have been mixed and sullied with sin and "imperfection. Whatever has been acceptable to "God is his own, even the work of his Holy Spirit; "it is not mine. Glory be to God the Father, Son, "and Holy Ghost, for ever and ever. Amen."

Such is the emphatic declaration of his faith, with which the eminently pious subject of these Memoirs bade adieu to every earthly concern, and anticipated an eternal world. While the grand truths of which it consists accord with the sentiments and feelings of every real Christian, and can scarcely be read without a deep impression of their importance, it certainly recognizes a position with which some will not agree. Though Dr. Buchanan was thus reserved upon this mysterious subject, it was, however, one on which he had thought and read much. He left behind him an unfinished work, entitled, " a Testimony to the true "faith," in which it was fully but cautiously discussed.

It is easy to dispose of this great controverted question in a summary way, and to deny that there is any scriptural foundation for what is commonly termed the Calvinistic view of it: but those who are aware of the difficulties in which the whole subject is involved, whatever may be their own sentiments respecting it, will be neither surprised nor offended at those of Dr. Buchanan. That he was far from being the retailer of other men's opinions, or from blindly and indiscriminately adhering to the tenets of any earthly " master," is evident, not only from the general tenor of his character, but from his express declaration in a note to one of his published sermons"; in which, referring to the general propensity to render the religion of Christ a human system, and to enlist under the banner of some celebrated leader, he observes, that the enlightened Christian acknowledges no name but that of Christ; and exclaims with indignant surprise, "Calvin and Arminius! Is it not an insult to men "of intelligence and learning, humbly receiving the "revelation of God, to suppose, that, instead of "drawing pure water from the fountain-head, they "should drink from such shallow and turbid, " streams!"

Of human guides to the knowledge of divine truth, Dr. Buchanan was undoubtedly disposed to follow the decisions of the Church of which he was a member; and upon no other point more readily than upon the doctrine of the divine predestination,

The Healing Waters of Bcthesda.

as contained in the seventeenth article. He considered that admirable composition as expressing nearly in the language of Scripture the mysterious truth, of which it has been seen that he declared his own solemn belief; and as doing this in so guarded a manner, as to preclude all objection and abuse, except such as is corrupt and wilful. Whether right or wrong in this interpretation of Scripture and of our Church, may be a matter of discussion; but if he erred in his view of the doctrine in question, let it not be forgotten, that he erred with many of the greatest divines and brightest ornaments of the Church; with Whitgift and Hooker, with Davenant and Hall, with Usher and Leighton. And where, it may be safely added, so far as mere human authority is concerned, are more illustrious names to be found? Or who will venture to throw contempt upon opinions thus accredited and adorned?

Dr. Buchanan's view of this profound subject, like every other sentiment which he entertained, was far from being merely speculative. Whenever he thought it right to inculcate it, which, as it has been observed, was but seldom, it was not crudely or exclusively; but with reference to certain specific marks of the Christian character, in connection with other scriptural truths, especially such as declare the obligations and responsibility of man, as an intelligent and accountable being, and in harmony with the general promises of the Gospel.

But more than enough has, perhaps, been said upon a point thus incidentally introduced, and upon which nothing but the wish faithfully to exhibit what appeared to the Author to form a part of Dr. Buchanan's doctrinal sentiments would have induced him to offer a single remark. It is more congenial with the spirit of the extract which occasioned this digression to recal the attention of the reader to the genuine and elevated piety which pervades the whole; and which formed so consistent and satisfactory a close to a life devoted to the service of that Saviour, in the faith of whose Gospel he thus calmly resigned his spirit.

The observations which have been already made, as well as the specimens which have been given of his discourses, render more than a few remarks upon Dr. Buchanan as a preacher unnecessary. His delivery was slow, but impressive, and though far from being studied, was yet pleasing and persuasive. His sermons were often doctrinal, but more frequently practical and experimental; and generally interesting, either from the historical or parabolical form, or from the simple yet energetic and affecting style in which they were composed. So far as mere popularity of manner is concerned, he may not be considered as entitled to much distinction. But if success be admitted as any test of merit, he must be allowed to rank high as a Preacher. Both in India and in this country he was honoured as the instrument of converting many from " the error of their "way," and of instructing and edifying others in the faith of the Gospel.

Preaching was not, however, that by which Dr. Buchanan was chiefly distinguished. His peculiar excellencies as a public character are to be discerned in his enlarged and truly Christian philanthropy, in the extent and acknowledged importance, utility, and disinterestedness of his plans, and in the boldness, generosity, and ability with which he laboured to accomplish them.

Of his fidelity, diligence, and activity, in the fulfilment of his official duties, the conduct of Dr. Buchanan, as Vice-Provost of the college of Fort William, is a striking and satisfactory instance; and it is no slight proof of the value of his services, that the year in which they were superseded by the abolition of this office is distinctly marked, by a very competent witness, as the period of the declining usefulness of that important institution. During his residence in India, independently of his acknowledged value as a faithful minister of the Gospel, and as a public servant, he was, according to the memorialist of his excellent colleague, " beloved and "admired by many of every rank for his fine abilities, "and for the estimable qualities of his heartand, See Mr. Fraser Tytler's " Considerations on the State of "India." after his return to this country, his uninterrupted labours in the cause of Christianity, amidst accumulated infirmities and sorrows, equally secured him the respect and esteem of all who are capable of appreciating pure and undefiled religion, and exalted virtue.

Dr. Buchanan, however, sought not " honour "from men/' His faith enabled him to " over come the world," and rendered him comparatively indifferent to its applauses and its frowns. He lived, "As ever in his great Task-master's eye;" and appeared on all occasions supremely anxious to fulfil his appointed duties, and to hasten towards the heavenly prize. "He parried about with him," observed one of his intimate friends, " a deep sense of the reality of religion, as a principle of action; and "from various conversations which I recollect with "him, I could strongly infer how much he laboured "to attain purity of heart." His last commonplace book contains various proofs of his simple, devoted, and progressive piety. Observations occur, chiefly founded upon passages of Scripture, on the great doctrines of the Gospel, particularly on faith in the atonement, on divine grace, on holiness, on the love of God and of our neighbour, on humility, on communion with God, and on the world of spirits.

One brief extract, entitled, " A general topic of "Prayer," may serve to shew the practical piety, VOL. II. C C and the humble and subdued disposition of its author.

"Let us," says this excellent man, " endeavour "to seek happiness and contentment in our own "place and condition, not looking abroad for it. "Let us seek and expect it in existing cir"cum"stances; contented with little domains, little "possessions, a little dwelling; that we may pre"pare for a less house, a smaller tenement under "ground."

If we descend to the more private features of his character, the reader of his Memoirs must be struck by his patience under protracted weakness and suffering, and his submission to the will of Cod under frequent and severe privations of domestic and personal happiness, and by his extraordinary liberality and diffusive charity. Of the more remarkable instances of these virtues, sufficient notice has been already taken; but Dr. Buchanan was cordially and habitually generous; and, independently of those munificent acts which were unavoidably public, the writer of this narrative has met with many others scarcely less noble, of which the world never heard; while, in addition to his liberal support of various Christian institutions which adorn our country, there were, no doubt, numerous exertions of private benevolence, which were utterly unknown.

It may seem scarcely necessary to add, that Dr. Buchanan was, from deliberate conviction and choice, warmly and steadily attached to the estaWished constitution of his country, both in Church and State. Of his exertions to extend the one throughout the British empire, the reader needs not to be reminded; while his loyal and zealous support of the other is abundantly testified by his Jubilee Sermons, and by various excellent discourses both in India and in England.

His social virtues require only to be mentioned. His invariable kindness and candour, his forbearance and readiness to fcrgive, together with all the charities of domestic life, are excellencies which, though happily too common to be much dwelt upon, were conspicuous in him, and will long live in the recollection and regret of his family and friends. To him, indeed, in these, and in some other points which have been noticed, may not improperly be applied the tribute of a Roman historian to a man of eminent merit in degenerate times; "Civis, ma"ritus, gener, amicus, cunctis vitae officiis sequa"bilis, opum contemptor, recti pervicax, constans "adversus metusV

An enemy, however, for such it seems he had, or even a less partial friend, might here be disposed to say, with a celebrated French annalist, when describing a man of extraordinary qualities, "Tour"nez la medaille." To such a proposal there can in this case be no objection. It is by no means Tac. Hist. lib. iv. c. 7- The Due de Sully.
necessary to the just appreciation of Dr. Buchanan, to represent him as a faultless character; and if it were possible for him to interfere with so unwise and unchristian an attempt on the part of any of his friends he would be the first to deprecate and to resist it. His defects were such as are incident to the talents and dispositions by which he was distinguished. Naturally bold and ardent in his conceptions, feelings, and jexpectations, he unavoidably communicated his own impressions in his delineations of human good and evil. Hence he has been accused of severity in his strictures on the ecclesiastical negligences and deficiencies of our eastern administration, of a dictatorial tone in his suggestions, and of exaggeration in his representations of the religious state of India, and of the probable results of the measures which he recommended.

"II y a dans cela," to adopt an expression of a celebrated personage, " un fond de verite." Let us, however, define the nature and extent of the admission. If it be meant by such animadversions to insinuate that Dr. Buchanan either intentionally, grossly, or even materially misrepresented or overstated any facts or incidents which he has undertaken to relate, his friends would have no hesitation in denying the charge, until some specific proof of such allegations be adduced; and in the mean time they would express their calm and undoubting acquiescence in the result of a full and impartial examination. It may be added, that a man of so much integrity and ingenuousness as Dr. Buchanan, when, at the close of life, he was urging upon the attention of the missionary" the importance of a strict and cautious adherence to simplicity and truth in his periodical reports, could scarcely be conscious of any personal failure in the performance of a similar duty.

If the objections in question refer merely to the warmth of colouring which pervades his descriptions, the reply has been anticipated in the sanguine nature, complexion, and character of his mind; which would as necessarily produce such a style, as the opposite temperament of another writer would naturally lead to colder and less vivid representations. If this consideration should be deemed unsatisfactory, it can only be lamented, that what in writers, who have but little else to recommend them, is freely forgiven, and even admired, is severely visited upon one whose claims to general credibility and regard are of no ordinary magnitude. But it is remarkable, that while the world will readily approve the coldest and most inadequate statements upon religious subjects, the man who treats them with any degree of fervour proportioned to their importance, will be discredited and condemned. That Dr. Buchanan should have been resisted and misrepresented by those who consider his zeal for the conversion and salvation of men excessive and en See page 339 of this volume.
thusiastic, and his plans and expectations visionary and extravagant, not to say rash and dangerous, ought not to excite our surprise. Time, however, and that which it will doubtless bring with it, additional information and experience, will, it is confidently presumed, gradually dissipate these illusions, and prove to the satisfaction of all, who are not under the influence of inveterate prejudice, the substantial correctness as well as importance of his statements; though, as it will ever be more easy to cavil than to disprove, to criticise the productions of others than to add to the general stock of knowledge and happiness, it is vain to expect that minute and pertinacious objectors will either be satisfied or silenced.

"I ever considered," observes a friend , whose testimony is peculiarly valuable, (in speaking of the efforts which have been made to depreciate the authority of Dr. Buchanan,) "such attempts as "the effect of dislike to the plans in which he was engaged. I apprehend no one will ever be "able to invalidate any of the facts recorded by "Dr. Buchanan, though some, who possess not "his spirit, will not view the circumstances as he viewed them, and therefore will not speak of them "as he did." This latter remark forms, in fact, the key to the greater part of the insinuations which have been circulated respecting the subject of these The Rev. D. Corrie.

Memoirs, and at the same time furnishes an antidote to their poison. Let but the same spirit of faith in the Gospel, and of love to the souls of men, animate those who are now inclined to treat with negligence or contempt the statements and reasonings of Dr. Buchanan; and it may be asserted, without incurring the charge of uncharitableness, that they will not be long in acknowledging the truth and correctness of the one, and the force and value of the other. Let men, in short, only be convinced, that ignorance of the true God is the grand cause of all the moral evil in the world; that to "know Him, and Jesus Christ whom he "hath sent, is *life eternal*;" and that multitudes are every where " perishing for lack of" that " know"ledge;" and they will at once be disposed to admit, that there can scarcely be any exaggeration in describing the wretchedness of those who are destitute of it, or any excess in their zeal who labour to make known to every creature under heaven that Gospel, which has " the promise of the life that now "is, and of that which is to come."

If the imperfections of Dr. Buchanan

as a private Christian have not been studiously exhibited, it is because, from his remarkable simplicity, and, if the expression may be allowed, his careless confidence of integrity, the defects as well as the excellencies of his character can scarcely fail of being sufficiently noticed by an attentive reader of these Memoirs. The assistance too of a biographer is seldom required to point out the errors of men who have acted a prominent part in the world % while the benefit of such representations, in works not sanctioned by infallible authority, is very doubtful; mankind in general standing much more in need of being animated by the exhibition of eminent merit, than consoled or gratified by the disclosure and delineation of defects inseparable from the condition even of the most advanced Christian. Of those which were incident to his own character, no one could be more humbly sensible than Dr. Buchanan, more watchful for the discovery of unknown faults, more anxious for their correction, or more diligent in endeavouring, under the influence of divine grace, " to perfect holiness in the fear of "God."

After all the deductions, therefore, which may be due to the paramount claims of truth, or urged by the severer demands of a less friendly scrutiny, there remains to the subject of these Memoirs a residue of solid, and undoubted, and indefeasible excellence, of which the conviction and estimate will, it is firmly believed, be gradually and certainly augmenting. He may be slighted by some, and misrepresented or misunderstood by others; but among those who can justly appreciate distinguished worth, genuine piety, and enlarged and active philanthropy, there can surely be but one opinion—that Dr. Buchanan was " a burning and a shining light," and a signal blessing to the nations of the East. We may, indeed, safely leave his eulogy to be pronounced by future generations in Great Britain and Hindostan, who will vie with each other in doing honour to his memory, and unite in venerating him as one of the best benefactors of mankind; as having laboured to impart to those who in a spiritual sense are " poor indeed," a treasure,

——— " Transcending in its worth
"The gems of India."

But if it were possible that men should forget or be insensible to their obligations to this excellent person, he is now far removed from human censure and applause; his judgment and his work are with God; his record is on high, and his witness in heaven. He has " entered into peace," and will doubtless stand in no unenvied lot "at the end of the "days;" when "they that are wise shall shine as "the brightness of the firmament, and they that "turn many to righteousness as the stars for ever "and ever."

Lightning Source UK Ltd.
Milton Keynes UK
UKOW012155260912

199708UK00004B/38/P